PARIS

FROM

THE

GROUND

UP

PARIS

FROM

THE

GROUND

UP

JAMES H. S. McGREGOR

THE BELKNAP PRESS OF

HARVARD UNIVERSITY PRESS

Cambridge, Massachusetts

London, England

First Harvard University Press paperback edition, 2010

Library of Congress Cataloging-in-Publication Data

McGregor, James H. S.

Paris from the ground up / James H. S. McGregor.

   p. cm.

Includes bibliographical references and index.

ISBN 978-0-674-03316-0 (cloth)

ISBN 978-0-674-05738-8 (pbk.)

1. Paris (France)—Description and travel.

2. Paris (France)—History.

I. Title.

DC707.M443   2009

914.4'3610484—dc22   2008043696

CONTENTS

PARIS

FROM

THE

GROUND

UP

INTRODUCTION

Paris for many is the city of enlightenment where
high culture, grand literature, and precise expression
have reigned for centuries. Their city sets an absolute
standard for correctness in art and life. For others,
Paris is the capital of Modernism—the place where all
the significant revolutions in taste and practice first took hold and where the
great movements in anti-academic art began their worldwide careers. They
honor the paintings of Gris and Picasso, along with the writings of Gertrude
Stein, James Joyce, the young Hemingway, and other expatriates. The city
that these people hold dear rejects all boundaries and rules.

But in the minds of many others, the so-called Modernists are as outmoded as the academic painters of the nineteenth century—who, ironically,
have enjoyed a great upsurge in reputation over recent decades. Postwar
Paris, where Sartre and Camus set the intellectual agenda, is the emotional
capital for a large segment of the city's admirers. But there is also a Paris for
medievalists, another for Catholics or Protestants, yet another for revolutionaries both historical and modern. There is a Paris of cinema, of experimental
theater, of world music, of high fashion, of Afro-pop.

Through all its changes of identity, Paris has persistently ranked as the
unofficial capital of the world. Yet even during its most influential years,

the city has experienced more than its share of disaster. Sacked by the
Vikings, occupied in the Middle Ages by the English, invaded by the
armies of nineteenth-century Europe allied against Napoleon, and overrun
by the German *Wehrmacht* in World War II, Paris has also endured famine,
flood, and plague. But nothing the city has achieved or suffered has left
a more indelible mark than the actions of its own inhabitants during the
French Revolution.

That epochal event subjected all of the city's past to a trial by fire.
The revolutionary aim was absolute: to become the founding event of a
people with a millennial tradition. In its efforts to wipe the slate clean, the
Revolution forced every artifact, term, and idea from the French past to
undergo a process of review, revision, and potential excision. In the end,
the Revolution failed to reset the historical clock, but the attempt was so
thorough and so far-reaching that the revolutionary decade colored not
only the future of the city but the history of every institution and object
that lived through it.

The long strand of the city's history that eventually threaded the
needle's eye of Revolution began during the early years of Roman coloni-
zation, in a Gallic fortress sheltered by marshland at a bend of the River
Seine. A trans-European trade path that crossed the river near this settlement distinguished it from the many similar towns upriver and down. In a
vain effort to starve out Caesar's legions, the local Gauls—the Parisii—set
their own town on fire and in a single night destroyed it so completely
that no physical trace has ever been found. The victorious Romans built
a colony on the sloping southern bank of the river well uphill from the
lowlands the Gauls preferred, and the old trade path became a major road
through its center. Lutetia—primitive Paris—was a Roman town, but its

inhabitants were ethnically not all that different from the tribesmen who had resisted Caesar's assault.

In the second and third centuries AD, the increasingly muddled policies of the empire's distant rulers began to affect frontier colonies like Lutetia. Foreign invaders surged into territories that the center was too weak or too preoccupied to defend. To save themselves, the Parisii moved downhill to the most easily defensible part of their city. This was an island— now called the Ile de la Cité—located a bit off-center in the main channel of the Seine. Dressed stones that had once been seats in Lutetia's theater or retaining walls beneath its forum became raw material for a defensive perimeter. When Roman imperial armies wintered in the city during the fourth century, their command post was a modest palace on that protected island. When Christian missionaries brought their new religion to Paris, it too was headquartered on the Ile de la Cité.

The name Lutetia died with the Roman hillside colony, and for centuries Parisians remained confined within the narrow limits of their island sanctuary. Many kingdoms that embraced but largely ignored Paris rose and fell in the half millennium between 300 and 800 AD. For a brief period during the reign of Charlemagne, the city was absorbed within a realm that insulated and protected it. But shortly after its founder's death in 814, Charlemagne's dynasty began to collapse under the weight of its own rules of inheritance.

Late in the ninth century, a new foreign enemy took advantage of the endless dynastic struggles among successive rulers. For the next two centuries, Norse raiders threatened the entire European coastline, and Paris, with its navigable river emptying into the English Channel, was as vulnerable as coastal cities. Without effective royal leadership, defense of the city fell to the bishops and the highest ranking civilian leaders, the counts of Paris. Together, they resisted the wave of invaders, and from one generation to the next their influence grew. In July 987 one of the counts—Hugh Capet—became king of France. Though his territory was small, his status was grand. Over time the king and his successors came to understand the city as a reflection of royal power and authority.

Under a steady succession of kings whose abilities ranged from outstanding to mediocre, the people of Paris multiplied. The countryside was fertile, and the Seine brought the goods of the region to the doorsteps of the rich and powerful. Business began to concentrate around the Place de Grève on the northern bank, just opposite the upstream end of the Ile de la Cité. As this commercial quarter grew inland street by street, the Left Bank, to the south, teemed with students, drawn by the growing reputation of Paris's schools. Throughout the city, the towers of Gothic churches expressed the taste for architectural novelty as well as the religious aspirations of Parisians.

From the twelfth through the fifteenth century, France was plagued not by Norsemen but by their heirs, the Norman kings of England. The Hundred Years War, which lasted from 1337 to 1453, was only the culminating episode in this centuries-long conflict. With Paris's population overflowing an early ring of earthen walls, the resourceful King Philippe Auguste built a wider circuit. Downriver, where the English were likely to begin their assault on the capital, he anchored the city's defenses in a fortress called the Louvre. The rapid growth of Paris in the next two centuries, combined with the ongoing threat of invasion, led King Charles V to stretch the defensive perimeter even further, embracing three times as much territory on the right bank as before. The Louvre, once the city's frontline defense, was suddenly marooned behind these new fortifications and deprived of any strategic purpose.

At the end of the Hundred Years War, with the English threat receding, the French kings themselves became aggressors. Their invasion of the Italian peninsula in the mid-1490s led to thirty years of destructive warfare. The French reaped the benefits not so much of conquest as of exposure to the most advanced European civilization of the time. French kings suddenly became devotees of Italian achievements in painting, sculpture, and architecture, and in the more elusive arts of amenity and grace.

Among the most devoted was King François I, who enticed Leonardo da Vinci to spend the last years of his life in France. The Renaissance king made Paris his primary residence, and that decision was ratified by his successors, some of the most powerful and effective rulers in the kingdom's history. With a remodeled Louvre as their center of government, these kings and queens, along with their ingenious advisers, created a city that served not only as the capital of a country but as its brilliant model. The life of the city and the court merged, making Paris the place to be, the place to succeed in every undertaking. Parisian culture, language, architecture, literature, and art shone throughout Europe as the epitome of civilized life. The dominant position of Paris at the center of national thought was not informal or accidental: by institutionalizing Parisian culture, the absolutist monarchs gave political muscle to the city that showcased their qualities and achievements.

Louis XIV—the Sun King—disliked Paris, however, and in 1682 he left it for Versailles, where his architects and landscape designers had created a royal palace on an unprecedented scale. The nobility went with him. But abandonment by the court did not mean the eclipse of Paris.

Commerce, which had always been the city's economic mainstay, continued to flourish. Paris became an increasingly important manufacturing
center as the eighteenth century progressed, and Parisian design reached
a world market through the widespread sale of industrially produced luxury
goods. A century after the *ancien régime* took up residence in Versailles,
the Revolution reaffirmed that Paris was the center of French life and
the locus of power. For the first time, the red and blue colors of the city
united with the white of the Bourbon kings to become the emblem of a
nation.

In time the Revolution that aimed to preempt history became historical itself. But though its innovations became traditions, the fault lines
that the Revolution exposed and in many cases deepened did not disap-
pear from the scene. Since 1789 France has lived through five repub-
lics, two empires, and two constitutional monarchies, to say nothing of
directorships, provisional governments, and governments in exile. Each of
these systems of rule succeeded only as long as it could hold the multiple
threads of the revolutionary heritage and the equally strong cords of
counter-revolutionary reaction in some kind of constructive tension.

For the last three centuries, Paris has played the role not just of national but of European, then world, metropolis. During the last years of the
Revolution, the city was the capital of a militantly anti-monarchical Terror
that threatened to sweep throughout the continent. Under Napoleon,
Parisian ascendancy over its neighbors was secured by unmatched military
strength. But for the most part, Paris has led the world by the force of
example. In the eighteenth century, it combined elegance with intellectual and artistic brilliance. Enriched by poets and shepherded by the
Académie Française, its language became preeminent throughout Europe.

Colonial adventurers spread Enlightenment ideals to the New World and transplanted French language and culture to Africa and Asia.

Then, in the nineteenth century, Paris became the bourgeois capital of the world. Noble birth retained its cachet; but stripped of its former monopoly on wealth, the nobility was socially and politically impotent. As the general population soared to new heights, the capital—now a commercial powerhouse securely linked to the rest of the nation by a webwork of railways—once again expanded its city limits. Hygienic reforms and a sweeping urban redesign in the 1860s under the direction of Baron Haussmann made Paris infinitely healthier, safer, and more livable than London, Rome, or New York. Paris's stately neo-Baroque buildings, with their steep roofs and elaborate pavilions, were imitated on every continent under the name Second Empire. This architectural style was quickly followed by Beaux Arts neoclassicism, an ornate and eclectic variation on Greek and Roman themes that influenced such American landmarks as Grand Central Terminal and the New York Public Library.

Just as French neoclassicism was reaching its peak of popularity in painting, sculpture, and architecture, the city that had given birth to academic art transformed itself into a mecca for artistic experimentation. Painters and sculptors, along with collectors, critics, novelists, poets, dancers, singers, and musicians, flocked to the city, where breaking the rules in every genre was suddenly the norm. The creative artists who passed through Paris in the late nineteenth century ushered in the Modern period, and by the Second World War the city had once again reconfigured the history of Western art.

Yet at mid-century, as Paris struggled to recover from the dislocations of war, the city looked on as New York and Los Angeles came to embody urban modernism. The automobile and the skyscraper—then transforming American cities—seemed to be the most progressive forces in the postwar era. But the global conflict that had brought Hitler's troops to the streets of Paris had longer-ranging effects in France than an eclipse of its prestige on the world stage. The humiliation of occupation was followed by equally soul-wrenching losses of power in Africa and Asia. In the wake of these political setbacks, Paris experienced demographic changes unparalleled in European history. A city that had always regarded itself as culturally and ethnically homogeneous suddenly had to face pressures imposed by diversity.

In recent times, Paris has taken on a new task with international implications. Like many other Western countries, France is struggling to apply the ideals of its Revolution—liberty, equality, and brotherhood, along with a resolute secularism and a tradition of democratic debate—to an increasingly diverse population that does not always share these values.

Chapter One

OUTPOST OF EMPIRE

The human history of the place that became Paris
is exceedingly long. Neanderthals may have hunted
the marshes along the Seine hundreds of thousands
of years ago, though they left no evidence of their
passing. Some forty thousand years ago anatomically
modern humans colonized Europe. The two species coexisted for another ten
thousand years before the Neanderthals finally disappeared. So far genetic
research has failed to find any echo of Neanderthal DNA in the European
genotype, but the search is ongoing. Agriculture and, according to some
theories, Indo-European language spread from the Near East westward in a
slow rippling advance that reached the Seine about six thousand years ago.
Agricultural villages began to replace hunter-gatherer collectives. Both these
ways of life have left archaeological traces in the alluvial soils of Paris.

Technological revolutions increased the advantages of farmers over hunter-
gatherers. Carts and plows pulled by animals boosted agricultural productivity.
Ceramics created new forms of storage and new trade goods. Metals replaced
flint implements, making tilling and harvesting more effective. Working with
bronze and iron axes, farmers cleared the great forests that once covered
central France and opened incredibly rich new soils for cultivation.

While they adopted the crops and technologies of the Near East, the
societies of Northern Europe remained less complex and less organized than

the great urban civilizations of the Mediterranean. The wide-ranging trading peoples, the Phoenicians and the Greeks, were the first to report on
their contact with the inhabitants of what we now call France. Because
these Mediterranean civilizations had a written language, they were able
to record their impressions of men and women the Greeks called Celts.
Later when the Romans replaced the Phoenicians and Greeks as the major
Mediterranean power, they added their views of a people they called Gauls.

By and large these reports were favorable if more than a little patron-
izing. In the case of the Romans, the reporting was more equivocal, since
their first encounters with the Gauls came at a period in their own history
when Mediterranean domination was well beyond their reach. Around
the year 387 BC, Gallic invaders defeated the disciplined, heavily armed
Romans and raided their capital city. The Roman picture of these warriors
remained fixed in imagination and art. Gallic warriors were tall and fairer
skinned than the Romans; they confounded the Romans' disciplined co-
horts with their habit of fighting naked. The wounded or dying Gaul, naked
and semirecumbent, became a favorite motif of Roman sculpture.

Despite their respect for the fighting power of the Gauls, the Romans
invaded their territories and gradually incorporated them as a province
in their empire. Julius Caesar, who carried out the most widespread and
brutally effective campaign, wrote a narrative of his conquest that was for
generations known to every Latin student. Though *De Bello Gallico* is no
longer standard reading, it remains a unique if biased source of information on the character and political organization of the Gallic territories
before their complete assimilation into the Roman empire.

Caesar thought of the Gauls as a large ethnic group that was subdivided into multiple, frequently warring tribes. He believed that each tribe

had a loose but hierarchical political organization and a regional capital. Since all of these notions reflect Roman practices, it is hard to know how closely they mirror the lifeways of Caesar's enemy. Archaeology does confirm the existence of numerous Gallic towns, though it cannot corroborate his views of regional politics. One of these Gallic tribes, called the Parisii, held territory on both sides of the River Seine, according to Caesar. They established their capital on firm ground surrounded by marshland at a bend in the river where an island created a shallow crossing.

Long before the Parisii settled near the river, a trade path that began in Spain and ended on the shores of the North Sea had crossed the Seine at this point near the site of their settlement. Amber from the Baltic passed along it southward for thousands of years. By about 600 BC, products from a Greek colony in what is now Marseille had entered the web of river routes and trade paths that would eventually form the infrastructure of Gaul. In the late second century BC the Gauls began striking gold and silver coins of great beauty that were based on Greek originals of about a century earlier. Phoenician colonists in Carthage and Spain traded with the Gauls as well.

Like every other Gallic tribe, the Parisii were divided into three social classes of unequal size and status. Most Gauls lived on farms near scattered villages and tended their fields. Once opened by forest clearance, the rich loess soils of the Seine valley—a product of repeated glaciation—attracted settlers and supported growing populations. The political rulers among the Parisii—overlords of the farmers—made up a second social class. They were members of a hereditary nobility whose traditional talent and training were in warfare. During peacetime, this warrior elite was active in trade. Trade goods included agricultural products, ceramics, and the work of a highly skilled group of native craftsmen who created weapons, plows, and armor but also designed jewelry, carved dies, and stamped coins.

Responsibility for the conduct of religion belonged to a select but nonhereditary class called druids. Intensively trained from an early age, these priests learned the will of the gods by carrying out sacrifices to them and reading natural signs. Since they were also well versed in the social laws, they passed judgment on misconduct and mediated disputes. In battle they might throw themselves between the opposing sides and try to prevent bloodshed, or they might stand apart and deliver rhythmical, terrible curses against one side or the other. The Gauls transcribed their language in Greek characters and later in Latin ones, but the druids—for whatever strategic or philosophical reason—did not commit their learning and tradition to writing. The Romans, who usually tried to assimilate the gods and goddesses of conquered peoples to their own pantheon, worked instead to undermine Gallic religion. As a result, we know little about the Gauls' actual beliefs.

The Greek colonists had stayed close to the sea, their source of trade and contact with their homeland. The Romans, by contrast, were a mainland people who preferred roads to ships. At first they exerted their political influence over Gaul indirectly by forming alliances and by setting rival tribes against one another. They also used trade as a source of influence and power. Among the goods they monopolized were Mediterranean wines shipped in Roman amphoras to favored Gallic noblemen. Both the divide-and-conquer strategy of the Romans and their selective distribution of alcohol would be repeated by Europeans in their nineteenth-century conquest of native Americans.

In 52 BC Vercingetorix, a Gallic prince from the town of Gergovia (near Puy de Dôme and Clermont Ferrand), overcame the resistance of pro-Roman nobles in his own tribe and began to mobilize others to stop the Roman incursion. Julius Caesar, governor of southern Gaul, and his chief lieutenant, Titus Labienus, matched their legions against the forces under Vercingetorix. When Caesar attacked Gergovia his army was defeated, but in the later battle of Alesia he was successful. Vercingetorix surrendered and was taken captive to Rome, where he was imprisoned for five years. In 46 BC, during Caesar's first triumphal procession through Rome, Vercingetorix was forced to march in front of Caesar's chariot. At the end of the victory celebration (which the Romans called simply a "triumph"), the prisoner king was strangled, along with the rest of the celebrity captives, and his body was exposed on the road leading from the Forum to the Capitoline hill.

During this campaign, Titus Labienus led a small force of Romans against outlying tribes, including the Parisii. In 56 BC, while Labienus and his Roman legions marched along the Seine, Gallic warriors under the command of the veteran Camulogenus assessed their chances. Though their fortress was well protected by marshy ground along the river, the Gauls were clearly outnumbered, and they chose to burn their supplies and their town rather than have them fall into Roman hands. This scorched-earth strategy was one that Vercingetorix had used successfully in other places.

For many generations every Parisian knew where the Gallic fort had stood. The island called Ile de la Cité, where the ancient trade path crossed the Seine, had been so long at the center of the city's history that any other site for the Parisii town was unimaginable. The fact that no pre-Roman remains were discovered in the numerous casual excavations for basements and foundations, streets and sewers, was confusing but not disturbing. That no trace of a burnt-over layer was dug up anywhere on the island was a bit more puzzling. Today, archaeologists and historians generally believe that the ruins of embryonic Paris still lie undiscovered somewhere in the broad floodplain of the Seine, but not on the Ile de la Cité.

Whatever the site of the Gallic town that burned in a night over two thousand years ago, the site of the Roman town that followed—called Lutetia—is a matter of firm record. On the south side of the Seine, which Parisians call the Rive Gauche (Left Bank), a hill rises from the waterside. (Map 1) The surviving structures of the Roman town that grew on that hillside come in all shapes and sizes, but almost all of them are completely submerged in the modern city. Roman settlements sometimes incorporated elements of earlier villages, but more often the Romans laid out their towns according to a standard plan. The core feature of every colony was an intersection of two major roads called the cardo and the decuman. All other streets in the town, with rare exceptions, paralleled one of these two major roads. Roman towns expanded from this central intersection in orderly rectangular blocks.

At or near the intersection was the town's forum and capitolium. The forum was the center of commerce and administration, while the capitolium was a temple consecrated to the three primary deities of the Roman state: Jupiter, Juno, and Minerva. Above ground, Lutetia's forum was fairly simple, but it had complex underpinnings. To create a level space on its hilly site, engineers constructed vaulted underground galleries. A level platform a little smaller than a football field was laid out above them. The platform was closed in on all four sides by single-story porticoes. These shedlike structures with their exterior colonnades were a provincial reflection of the arcaded and vaulted porticoes that flanked public buildings in Rome. Spaces between columns were used for shops or municipal offices.

The open area of the forum served commercial or administrative needs as well as hosting shows and exhibits of various sorts. The temple of the state gods that stood near one end of the open area was small and undistinguished. Images of the gods inside the temple looked out over the forum and over a public altar where sacrifices were performed in their honor. As a Roman town developed and grew, the repertoire of buildings expanded. Public baths were a significant part of imperial life, and every Roman town of any size included buildings where citizens could bathe at little cost, exercise, and even read in a setting that in the largest cities was enriched with sumptuous materials and decorated with frescos, mosaics, and sculpture.

Baths required massive amounts of water, much more than could be provided by wells or rivers. Roman engineers solved the problem by collecting clear water from distant sources and channeling it through aqueducts, either underground or suspended on arched supports. The result was a water system of enormous reach and complexity. Bringing water from distances of twenty or thirty kilometers required the assembly and finishing of tons of raw material and the organization of hordes of workers over long periods of time. The greatest challenge was to maintain the gentle downward slope of the aqueduct over the entire length of the system. From the mountain source to the town, the height of land might decrease by only a few hundred feet. The slope of the conduit at any point in the system was only a fraction of a degree away from horizontal.

1

The instruments with which Roman surveyors consistently achieved this stunning degree of accuracy are unimaginably crude by today's standards.

The Paris aqueduct followed a steep ridge that led from the collection basin near the town of Rungis. For most of its course the aqueduct was a buried channel constructed of concrete. Water flowed in a trench formed by molds set in the concrete bed before it hardened. To prevent leaking and contamination, the trench was lined with plaster and tiles were cemented over the top. Then the structure was buried.

The largest surviving pieces of Roman Lutetia are remnants of three bath complexes and two theaters—one of them quite unusual. The more conventional theater was a modestly sized structure near the corner of Rue Racine and Boulevard Saint Michel. Diagonally across from it stood one of the bath complexes; another was a few blocks away. The other theater sat a little outside town on a hillside overlooking the River Bièvre, which was buried in the nineteenth century. This structure was a curious hybrid, common in Gaul but rare elsewhere in the Roman empire, that merged amphitheater and stage in one building. From their seats, spectators were able to watch battles of various kinds on the arena floor or dramatic presentations on the stage. The foundations of the stage set, the outline of the arena, and two small banks of seats from the curved end of the theater survive and are still visible near the intersection of Rue Monge and Rue de Navarre. (1)

The most visible trace of the Roman town is buried in plain sight in the layout of streets on the Left Bank. Rue Saint Jacques comes in from the southwest along the crest of a narrow ridge. Just before it reaches the old limits, it takes a slight jog left, then cuts across the ridge before it heads downhill toward the Ile de la Cité. It crosses to the island on a bridge (Petit Pont) that is in the same place as one the Romans built; it runs through the island as the Rue de la Cité and continues on the right bank as Rue Saint Martin. This route was the cardo of the Roman town. It is paralleled by the main avenue of the Rive Gauche, the Boulevard Saint Michel. That, too, was a Roman street, though not a major one. And between the two, near their intersection with Rue Soufflot, stood the Roman forum. The aqueduct that supplied the two baths followed Rue Saint Jacques toward the forum. Outside the city limits, tombs flanked the roadway, as they did in every Roman town.

Houses and shops lined the streets around the forum, and a few of them followed the road downhill to a cluster of buildings on the island and a second small settlement on the right bank. In time, two administrative offices moved downhill as well. One of these was a basilica and the other was a palace. A basilica was a multipurpose structure often used by the Romans for law courts or administrative offices. At one end of the typical basilica the wall bulged out to form an apse, where figures of author-ity sat on elevated thrones while they addressed an audience or passed judgment. Porticoes around the perimeter of the building provided shelter in bad weather. Areas marked off by columns in the porticoes and in the interior could be closed with curtains or set off in other ways to create small offices, hearing rooms, or specialized courts.

The building that has been identified as a basilica in Paris occupied an entire city block. Incomplete traces of its outer walls and interior colonnade have been found to the west of the Rue de la Cité near what was then the water's edge on the north side of the island. Putting this building along the river rather than in the forum suggests that the officers it housed were responsible for commerce and the regulation of the port.

Excavations under the cathedral of Notre Dame and the open square in front of it have uncovered a few Roman structures, and this archaeological site (open to the public) offers a narrow window into the life and fate of the Roman town. A trench dug in 1845 gave the first hints of what lay beneath. Systematic excavations began at the west end of the cathedral in 1847 when a confusing overlay of buildings from various periods was uncovered. Further campaigns in the late twentieth century have expanded well beyond the limits of these earlier digs and have uncovered structures that sketch the history of this core area of the city from the Roman era to the medieval period and beyond.

The most striking characteristic of the site is one that is easily lost on the modern visitor. The Seine, which now flows at a distance inside its walled channels, was, at the time the structures uncovered here were built, flowing right alongside them. Quite by accident, the 1847 excavators uncovered a small portion of the original shore of the island. The excavators also exposed the Roman engineering that transformed the Ile de la Cité from a midriver mudflat of uncertain form into a permanent and well-consolidated mass. Sometime in the first century AD, workers began stiffening the edges of the island with wood pilings. In trenches above these pilings they dumped masses of soil, rock, and rubble to create a solid foundation. Atop and beside this rubble core, walls were built to hold the river back. Stairsteps here and there in the river walls gave access to boats anchored along the quays. A roadway immediately behind the walls was left open so that ships could be loaded and unloaded.

In the middle of the third century AD, the quayside was disrupted by a public work of great cost and extent. On top of the open roadway a massive rampart was hastily thrown up. Building materials reflect the urgency that drove this project. Blocks of limestone were scavenged from public buildings, primarily the theater and amphitheater, and transported to the site. Once there, they were piled up efficiently but without regard to the finished or rough surfaces of the block. The completed stone wall, which ringed an island much smaller than the one we see today, was still only about six feet high. Probably too low for adequate defense, it may have been topped with a wooden palisade. The city on the Left Bank had never been walled, and the island became a fortress in which the citizens of Lutetia found refuge.

The emergency that led to the creation of this island fortress was a series of raids by non-Romanized tribes. Northeastern Gaul, where Paris was located, stood near the frontier between the empire and these invaders, and every Roman city in the region experienced the same transformation from unprotected urban center to armed camp. The emperor Valentinian lived in Gaul for long periods of his reign, while he attended to these major threats to his empire. Between 356 and 360 the future emperor Julian led a large contingent of Roman troops in campaigns along this frontier. Julian was the son of the emperor Constantine's half brother. Constantine is best known for his conversion to Christianity and his transfer of the imperial capital from Rome to Constantinople.

Moving the capital to Constantinople not only deprived Rome of its historic mission as capital of the empire but severely complicated the business of protecting the borders, especially those in the now quite distant west. In response to attacks on the frontiers of Gaul, Constantine's successor, Constantius, appointed Julian as associate emperor in 355 and granted him the title of caesar, while he kept for himself the more distinguished title of augustus. Constantius assigned his junior partner responsibility for stabilizing Gaul and protecting its frontiers. Though Julian lacked military training, he proved to be a successful commander who won the respect of his troops. For three years he led his men against the massed tribes of Franks and Germans who had settled the area east of the Rhine River and south of the North Sea. At various times the Franks, who spoke a Germanic language, and the Alamanni, members of the German confederation, were allies and opponents of the Romans, mounting frequent raids into imperial territory. In the winter, when warfare was impossible, Julian rested his army in Lutetia.

Julian's successes inspired jealousy rather than appreciation. The senior emperor ordered many of the divisions of Julian's army to be transferred to the eastern frontier, where troops under his command were battling the Persians. A contingent of Julian's troops called the Petulantes refused to move, and in the early spring of 360, while the army was still camped at Lutetia, they proclaimed Julian as augustus. Though he had resisted their acclamation once before, this time he accepted. He wrote to Constantius to proclaim himself a full partner in imperial rule. Unwilling to share power, Constantius prepared to lead his troops against his rival, but before their armies could engage Constantius became fatally ill. On his deathbed, he named Julian sole emperor.

During his Paris winters, Julian lived in a palace on the Ile de la Cité.
Not as grand as it sounds, the palace was a building designed to house a
senior administrator or provincial governor. Often its most distinctive feature
was a two-story colonnade, an exterior courtyard, and a set of imposing
steps. The physical remains of Julian's palace have vanished completely,
though its general site along the northeast shore of the fourth-century island
is known because the building was melded into the palaces of later rulers.

Paris is cold and rainy in the winter; it snows regularly. On the winter
solstice there is only a bit more than eight hours of daylight. Soldiers in
tents or other temporary shelters set in neat rows along muddy, rutted
streets likely found the city boring as well as cold and dark. Their leader
probably had a better time of it. Although the furniture of the palace cannot be guessed at, remains of private houses offer some clues. When the
island became a fortress, the wealthiest families appear to have moved
there. The warehouse remains of the first centuries were replaced by
houses with different ground plans and interconnecting rooms.

The most striking feature of these houses is their inclusion of what
are called hypocaust floors. These floors are distinguished from others by

piles of bricks or tiles in
a regular pattern every
few feet all across the
surface of the floors. (2)
Originally these pillars
supported a pavement.
Fires sent hot air into the
space beneath the pave-
ment to heat the house.

2

If private houses on the island had central heating, we can be certain that the imperial palace was kept warm in the same way. Scattered finds of precious objects and fragments of mosaics, marble columns, and capitals suggest that the standard of living of the well-to-do was very high.

Creation of a comfortable, fortified enclave on the Ile de la Cité did not eradicate the hillside city on the Left Bank, though it largely replaced it. Romans always buried their dead outside the limits of their towns and cities. In the decades after the ramparts went up on the Ile de la Cité, graves begin to appear in areas within the street grid of the old city. This reuse of the hillside site to bury the dead reveals the shrinking of the settlement not only in fact but in the minds of its inhabitants.

Julian, known to history as the Apostate, was the last Roman emperor to encourage the worship of the Roman state gods. Before the end of the fourth century, the emperor Theodosius I proclaimed Christianity the official religion of the empire. In support of his choice, he banned the sacrifices and cults that had been the cornerstone of Roman devotion. The consequences of this conversion were soon felt in the creation of a religious hierarchy that mimicked the secular bureaucracy governing the Roman empire. Gaul was divided into a series of episcopal dioceses with a bishop in charge of each. These bishoprics, laid out in the fifth century, persisted more or less unchanged until the French Revolution. When the Roman Empire dissolved and its remains were parceled among Germanic invaders, the dioceses and their leadership remained intact. In many parts of the empire, the church, cloned on the imperial administration, took over the day-to-day rule of provinces that had no other political organization. In this first partition Paris was made a diocese subordinate to the archbishop of Soissons. It was only in 1622 that the city became an archdiocese.

Paris already had a Christian population at the time of the empire's official conversion. According to Catholic tradition, in 250 AD Pope Fabianus sent six carefully chosen bishops into Gaul to found new churches and to give organizational help to the Christian communities scattered throughout the region. A religious leader somewhat improbably named Dionysius, after the Greco-Roman god of wine, was sent to Paris, along with two companions, Eleutherius and Rusticus. Nothing definite is known about the work the three did in the city. All that their legend records is a bizarre and dramatic martyrdom.

When certain pagans revealed the trio's identity to the authorities, the men were arrested and tortured. After enduring extremes of cruelty, they were beheaded. Some accounts place their martyrdom on the Ile de la Cité. The more commonly accepted story makes Montmartre—its name means the Mount of Martyrs—the scene. Wherever the martyrdom took place, its most noteworthy feature occurred after the head of Dionysius, who in French is called Saint Denis, had been struck off. With a fountain of blood surging up from his neck, the martyr bent down and picked up his own head. Cradling it in his arms, face foremost, the saint began to walk. And as he walked to his chosen place of burial, the head delivered a lengthy sermon. Over time a great shrine and church dedicated to Saint Denis rose on the site where the martyr finally came to rest, on the north side of the city.

Sometime after the conversion of the empire in the fourth century, the city and its bishop were provided with an official Christian worship center. The 1847 excavations under the pavement directly in front of Notre Dame cathedral uncovered foundations of the kind of building that was typically created in the Roman empire to house Christian worship. While there may have been earlier worship centers in private homes or nearby warehouses, no evidence of them has been found. In fact, there is little evidence of any sort of religious practice in the city during the antique and late antique periods. And with the exception of the temple of the Capitoline trio in the open space of the forum, no other place of worship, either pagan or Christian, has ever come to light.

The foundations of the Christian building discovered in 1847 suggest that it was of substantial size. The portion excavated (none of which is visible to the public at the archaeological site, sadly) is more than a hundred feet long and nearly as wide. Apparently it was a five-aisled basilica with a narrow porch or narthex on its front. The central aisle—the nave—was about thirty feet wide. A colonnade at each of its long sides would have supported a high wall with windows that lit the interior. Between each nave colonnade and the outside wall were two aisles separated by a second row of columns. The roof of these aisles would have been lower than the windows that lit the nave. The two aisles would have been lit by windows in the low outside wall. On the south side of the basilica, this outer wall was built over or into the rampart. Some archaeologists have guessed that the basilica incorporated fortifications of its own.

The two basilicas that have been excavated on the island—this one for Christian worship and the earlier one for administration—are a wonderful representation of the rough-and-ready adaptations the empire made as official worship shifted from the ancient Roman gods to the God of Christianity. The small temple isolated in the open plaza of the forum suited the worship of the old gods. Christian worship, by contrast, required that the congregation participate in a ritualized meal—the Eucharist—that exemplified the central mystery of the religion. Christians needed room to assemble, and they needed to hear the words of the mass that sanctified the sacrifice. Roman temples were not suited to this task, and even if they had been, the political situation during the early years of Christian toleration put these venerable structures off limits for the new religion. Among the Roman repertoire of building types, the one best suited for Christian worship was the basilica. It carried no religious connotation for the Romans, so its adaptation was not unsettling to either side. It provided shelter for large numbers of people, and its apse was designed to amplify the voice. The celebrant of the mass and the choir used the apse to make themselves heard, just as Roman secular authorities had done.

The effort of Roman soldiers to hold the frontier met with greater success in the fourth century than it had in the third, but both the victory and the means of achieving it represented by Julian's campaign were short-lived. Julian directed a mixed force of assimilated troops from Italy and Gaul and auxiliary regiments made up of men newly converted to the Roman cause. The Petulantes who had mutinied when they were ordered to the East were not Italians or even Gauls but Franks. In the last decades of the fourth century the makeup of the army and especially of its officer corps experienced sudden and dramatic change. Despite repeated efforts to recruit troops from long-term residents of the empire, Rome was forced to bring a large number of recent immigrants and allied peoples into its regular army. In return for enlisting, these new recruits demanded the same inducements and opportunities for advancement that Roman veterans typically enjoyed.

Generals of great ability emerged from this diverse officer corps, including the Vandal Stilichon, the virtual ruler of Rome in the early fifth century, and the German or Scythian Aetius, one of its most successful midcentury generals. Despite their ability, indeed because of it, both men fell victim to jealous emperors. Honorius had Stilichon arrested and killed in 408. In 454 the emperor Valentinian III himself stabbed and killed Aetius, whose successes, like those of Stilichon before him, had made him too powerful. These actions, and the attitudes that drove them, fractured the army. Ethnic Romans kept their traditions and their officers, while the non-Romans maintained their regional and tribal allegiances. In 408 Roman troops mutinied and murdered large numbers of German-born officers. But despite such isolated rebellions and the occasional removal of high-ranking officers, the Roman army gradually became ethnically Germanic, and the provinces and ultimately the Italian peninsula fell under their control. In 476 German commanders ousted the last Roman emperor and placed their own leader, Odoacer, on the throne.

Throughout the fifth century, the empire, under both Latin and Germanic rule, tried to hold on to the territory that had been won centuries before, but without success. Tribes whose homes were far beyond the imperial borders made their way through the homelands of Rome's long-term enemies, to strike at the heartlands of the empire. Among the most aggressive and successful of these invaders were the Huns led by the "Scourge of God," Attila. In the late winter of 451, fresh from successful raids into Byzantine territory, he led his troops and allies across the Danube River and west toward Gaul. The Huns attacked and burned cities east of the Rhine, then headed northwest toward Lutetia. Here their advance was turned aside by the woman who would become Saint Geneviève, the patron saint of Paris.

"Hearing that King Attila of the Huns was laying waste to Gaul, the citizens of Paris were wild with fear. They thought that it would be best for them to leave the city and take all their merchandise and belongings to the security of safer places. Geneviève called together the women of the city and persuaded them to begin vigils, prayers and fasts in hopes that they could avert the impending catastrophe. The women agreed to her plan and for several days they remained in the baptistery of the church in prayer, fasting and wakefulness. As Geneviève urged, they continually called on God. She also persuaded the men not to ship their goods out of the city. Now those cities that the Parisians would have chosen as their refuge were ravaged by the furious Huns. Paris itself was saved and through the protection of Christ remained inviolate" (*Acta Sanctorum,* vol. 1, p. 139).

Geneviève is a Gallic name with etymological links to others like Guinevere, Gwynith, and Jennifer. The child who would become Saint Geneviève may have been born in the town of Nanterre, a short distance west of Paris. Nothing reliable is known about her family or early life. In 429 AD two prominent clerics, Germain of Auxerre and Loup of Troyes (both later declared saints), passed through her village on their way to a Church council in Britain. Among the crowd that greeted the two men and listened to their sermons was a young girl whose unusual attentiveness and evident piety caught their eye. The traveling clerics urged her to embrace a life of religious devotion, and after they left she began living a regime of self-denial and austerity that seemed to annoy a great many of her neighbors. At the death of her parents, she moved from Nanterre to Paris, where she lived with her godmother.

When the Huns turned away from Paris—if indeed they had ever approached it—they headed toward Orléans in southeastern France. There they were met by a large force under the command of General Aetius, then at the height of his power. His army included Roman regular soldiers along with contingents made up of Alamans, Franks, and other Germanic tribes. In an unusual moment of solidarity with a group who had themselves invaded Roman territory, Aetius' men were joined by Visigoths under the command of Theodoric. In their first encounter with the Huns, Aetius' mixed force was overcome, but fifteen days later when the two armies met in the battle of the Champs Catalauniques near Troyes, the imperial armies were victorious.

This battle did not put an end to the devastation of Gaul. The ultimate effect of the victory was not very different from Geneviève's success in Paris. It did not overwhelm the enemy but simply nudged him into a different trajectory. Attila took his forces into northern Italy, where they devastated the Po Valley. Attila's attempt to sack Rome was halted by Pope Leo the Great. The pope bought the city's safety with a large gift of treasure. In hagiography, however, Leo joins Geneviève as a saint who turned aside the murderous Huns through divine favor. The Huns were finally overcome not by Roman forces but by a rebellion among the Germanic tribes beyond the imperial borders that they had long dominated.

While control of the Italian peninsula was passing from Italians to ethnic Germans, a similar transformation was taking place in Gaul. During the second half of the fifth century, Franks established a dynasty of rulers called Merovingians, descendants of a perhaps legendary king named Merowig. According to much later accounts, Merowig was the leader of the Frankish warriors who fought against the Huns. Some sources make him an adopted son of Aetius. His kingdom of Salian Franks lay beyond the borders of fifth-century Roman Gaul in the area of modern Belgium. Childeric, reputedly the son of Merowig, is the first Frankish ruler known to history. The northern kingdom over which he ruled was one of a handful of loosely bounded, mutually antagonistic realms that held de facto control over the former Roman province.

The lands directly south of those he controlled—with Paris at their center—remained in the hands of Romanized Gauls. Synargius, who had served as a general in the Roman army, proclaimed himself king of the Romans sometime after 464 and ruled this last vestige of Gaul from the city of Soissons. Saxons invading from across the channel to the north menaced the coastline of Childeric's territory, while the autonomous Breton people raided it from the west. On the southeastern frontier, the Burgundians held power, and to the southwest the Visigoths, who ruled in Spain and North Africa, posed a recurrent threat.

Childeric's son and heir was Clovis. This name is a Romanized version of a Germanic word that might better be transcribed with an H at its beginning rather than the C the Romans used to represent an unfamiliar diphthong. The final S is also an approximation. Romans pronounced V as we pronounce W. If the name is restored to something like its original sound, it becomes Hlowis or Hlowig. As Hlowis it morphed into Louis, the traditional name for the kings of France. As Hlowig it became Ludwig, the traditional name of German rulers.

When Clovis I began a series of military campaigns to expand Frankish territory, his goal was to capture the Roman province to the south and reunite it under a single ruler. In his 486 campaign against Synargius at his capital in Soissons, the Franks won the battle—according to the historian Gregory of Tours, writing about a century later—and began sacking the city and dividing up its treasures. Since Clovis was a devotee of the traditional gods of his people, the churches of the old Roman territory were stripped of their treasures, as were the secular buildings. Allying himself with the Ostrogoths, Clovis next began a succession of campaigns that extended his control over much of modern-day France.

In 493 he married a Burgundian princess named Clotilde, who was a Christian, and in 496 after defeating the Alamans, Clovis converted to Roman Catholicism. He was baptized by Saint Rémi d'Auxerre. After his conversion, Clovis shared the orthodox religion of the areas he had conquered, and this alienated him from the majority of Germanic princes, who had accepted Arian Christianity, later declared heretical. Clovis fought against the Burgundians at Dijon in 500, but the effort added little to his domain. Then, at the battle of Vouillé in 507, he defeated an army of Visigoths—a conquest that effectively limited Visigothic territory in Europe to the areas of modern Spain and Portugal. After this final campaign, Clovis established his capital in Paris. Having overcome his enemies, he tightened his control over the conquered territories by eliminating rivals among the princes of the Franks.

According to the legend of Saint Geneviève, when Clovis arrived in his new capital, the holy woman was there to greet him. Whenever she interceded on behalf on someone he had sentenced to death, Clovis was willing to forgive. Geneviève died early in the sixth century; the exact year is unknown, though her death is traditionally commemorated on January 3. At her passing, Clovis ordered a basilica to be built in her honor in or near the cemetery where she was buried on the Left Bank. Construction had barely begun at the time of his own death in 511. His queen, Clotilde, carried on the project. The building they created was similar in form to the worship center excavated at Notre Dame, but its purpose was different. This was not a church but a shrine dedicated to the saint, and its main role was to host funeral and commemorative masses and to provide burial spaces near the saints.

At its founding, the basilica was dedicated to Saint Peter and the Holy Apostles, just as the Apostoleion in Constantinople, where the emperor Constantine and many of his family members were buried, had been. In imitating the dedication and perhaps in planning his own burial in the church, Clovis may have revealed the extent of his imperial and dynastic ambitions. In any case, the apostles were dropped from the title of the church in the seventh or eighth century, and the basilica was referred to informally as Saint Geneviève. After a number of miracles were attributed to her intervention, the name was officially changed in the eleventh century. The basilica was supplanted in the eighteenth century by the Pantheon and dismantled in the early years of the nineteenth century.

The hilltop on which the Romans had planted their colony of Lutetia eventually took its new name from the enormous abbey that began to grow up around the tomb and basilica of Saint Geneviève. The character of Paris had changed entirely by then. The Ile de la Cité was its center, and the Roman ruins on the Left Bank had either disappeared or been engulfed by other structures. The Roman aqueduct had long ceased to carry water. Even the grid of roads that the Romans had so carefully laid out had all but disappeared into a web of streets that met for the most part at odd angles and ran obliquely through old intersections. The great exception was the road now known as the Rue Saint Jacques. Originally a pre-Gallic highway, the road still ran into Paris and straight across the Ile de la Cité. Its Christian name, however, indicated a new purpose in traveling the old road. International trade was no longer its major burden.

Instead, it carried pilgrims along the great road to Compostela and the shrine of Saint Jacques, who is called Santiago in Spanish.

Following the custom of the Franks, Clovis's will divided his kingdom among his sons. Childibert, who reigned for nearly fifty years, inherited Paris and the rich country that surrounded it. Shortly after his death, the kingdom was briefly reunited under the kingship of Clovis's last surviving son, Clotaire, but within a few years it was again divided among Clotaire's sons. For the next two hundred years, the history of Paris is buried in the expansion and contraction of kingdoms, the multiplication of heirs, and the vigorous, often brutal reconquest of a repeatedly fragmented heritage.

Throughout this long period, the Rhine served as a convenient fault line in the Frankish domain. When the kingdom was integrated under a powerful ruler, the Rhine was an internal river. In the more typical situation when the kingdom was divided, it tended to fracture along this line. Preoccupied with their dynastic struggles, the Merovingian kings failed to notice that real power in the territory was gradually falling into the hands of functionaries responsible for the royal palace east of the Rhine. These men, often referred to as "mayors of the palace," were hereditary stewards of the heart of the royal domain. Pippin the Elder held that office in the early seventh century. By the middle of the next century his heir and namesake, Pippin the Younger, was crowned king of a reunited Frankish realm.

Pippin's son Charlemagne added to his father's domain and by the year 800 ruled a territory that included all of the ancient Roman province of Gaul, the northern half of Italy, and the home territories of the neighboring German tribes that Rome had never been able to conquer. Charlemagne made Aachen in the Rhineland his imperial capital. But like earlier Frankish kings, he divided his holdings among his heirs, and in

843, by formal treaty, his empire passed to his three grandsons. Charles the Bald inherited Gaul, Lothair received an unsustainable middle kingdom that stretched from the North Sea to Rome, and the third grandson, Ludwig, inherited the Germanic territories. Ludwig's successors eventually absorbed the middle kingdom, and by the late ninth century proto-France and proto-Germany faced each other across the Rhine.

The descendants of Charlemagne squared off in the same protracted dynastic warfare that had engulfed the Merovingians. But by the ninth century, institutionalized fratricide had become considerably more costly. A new and powerful force from the north was entering the region, ready and able to take full advantage of its political instability. Like the barbarian tribes that came before them, Norse raiders appeared suddenly and inexplicably along the fringes of Europe. Their first recorded raid took place in 787, but the beginning of two centuries of Viking invasions is usually dated to June 8, 793, when dragon-prowed ships suddenly beached at the abbey of Lindisfarne on the northeast coast of England. From that year onward the pillagers returned every summer to coastal villages and towns along the North Sea and Atlantic. In time their ships entered the Mediterranean and traveled as far as the Black Sea. Eventually the raiders turned colonizers, and Viking or Norse kingdoms were established in Sicily, northern France, England, Kiev, and Novgorod and on islands throughout the North Atlantic. From their colonies in Iceland and Greenland, they made a precocious and unsuccessful bid to colonize North America.

Paris should have been far enough from the coast to be safe from these sea-faring raiders, but the Seine, the city's great thoroughfare and the source of its prosperity, became a dangerous asset in the Viking era. The raiders began to attack towns along the lower Seine valley in 820.

In May 841 a larger force looted and took captives upriver. Sixty-eight of their prisoners were ransomed by the monks of the abbey of Saint Denis on the northern outskirts of Paris. Four years later a fleet estimated at 120 Viking ships reached the city. From the river they laid siege to its island garrison. Unable to drive the invaders away by force, King Charles the Bald paid an enormous ransom.

In the mid-850s, Charles abandoned his policy of appeasement, and his soldiers defeated the Norsemen. But the tide turned again in the Vikings' favor in 858, when their combined forces led retaliatory raids against towns surrounding Paris that Charles's soldiers could no longer protect. Vikings plundered the city of Chartres and executed its entire population. When they again threatened Paris, Charles bought them off as before. But when the king became entangled in a dynastic war with his brother, the Vikings took advantage of his distraction and raided more freely. From well-established safe harbors in the lower Seine valley, they began to ravage the countryside frequently and in greater numbers.

In 885 a force of Norsemen left their bases near the modern city of Le Havre and marched ahead of their fleet through the countryside, pillaging and burning. They took Reims in late July and in November overwhelmed a Frankish garrison blocking the river below Paris. At the end of the year they attacked the city from both the land and the river. After the raids of the 850s, Charles the Bald had built a bridge between the Ile de la Cité and the right bank more or less where the Pont Neuf is today. The bridge had limited use as a connector; its main task was control of the river.

Military engineers had designed two towers at its ends, but when the Viking raiders appeared, the tower on the right bank was still incomplete and came under immediate attack. Citizens and soldiers reinforced the tower with a wooden rampart, which, surprisingly, held for months. Unfortunately for the defenders of the city, a flood in early February washed away the bridge. Facing no impediment, dragon ships quickly filled the channel between the Ile de la Cité and the right bank. The right bank tower was overwhelmed and its defenders slaughtered. The fortified island remained the only sanctuary for the terrified Parisians. The Vikings ramped up their attacks.

The legend of Saint Geneviève records a number of rather meager miracles during these Viking incursions. In the two periods of greatest threat, the late 850s and the winter of 886, the saint's relics were removed from the unprotected Left Bank basilica and carried to castles outside Paris. Despite Geneviève's success against the Huns, no one seemed to expect her relics to withstand or divert the Vikings. Nevertheless, an abundance of miracles did occur both while the relics were being taken away for safe keeping and more commonly during the joyous processionals that brought the relics back to the basilica. The importance of these miracles was not so much their scale but their role in the creation of a local saint who shared with the people of Paris the ongoing history of the city. Her continuing legend made her the focus of a kind of devotion that blended religious veneration and local pride. Saints of this kind were especially important in the Middle Ages as cities established their identity both locally and in the minds of their competitors. A city with an illustrious saint gained preeminence.

Though Paris was an important and wealthy city in the Carolingian era and was frequently visited by rulers like Charles the Bald, it was not a royal capital. The defense of the city fell to a Frankish nobleman, Odo, who held the hereditary title of count of Paris. Like his predecessors, the count saw to the fortifications and food supplies, and in this emergency

sent messengers secretly out from the city and through the Viking lines
to plead for relief from neighboring nobles and the royal army. At some
point during the prolonged siege, Odo himself slipped out of town to beg
for help from Charles, who had recently vanquished his brothers and proclaimed himself emperor.

During Odo's long absence, leadership of the island's defenders fell
on Gozelin, the bishop of Paris. Throughout the struggle the bishop had
been busy encouraging, feeding, and ministering to the people, while in
his spare time he supervised repairs to the island's walls. Now he was the
embattled town's sole leader. With no immediate prospect of relief, Gozelin opened negotiations with the Norsemen, but he fell ill and died before
a truce could be reached. The Vikings themselves proclaimed his death to
the people of Paris in an effort to win through psychological warfare what
they still had not achieved through siege.

Finally, at the beginning of August, eight months after the attack
began, Charles the Bald and his troops arrived in Paris. Instead of driving
the Vikings away, the king signed another treaty and paid yet another
ransom. In a gesture typical of what passed among Frankish rulers for
political wisdom, he offered the Vikings safe passage through his kingdom
in exchange for their promise to attack the Burgundians to the southeast.
In 911 another Carolingian king, Charles the Simple, signed a treaty with
the Norse leader Rollo that ceded the entire lower Seine valley to him
and his successors. This act recognized a Scandinavian enclave within
the Frankish realm that still has the name Normandy—the territory of the
Norsemen. A century and a half later, in 1066, Norman troops under the
direction of William, duke of Normandy, invaded and conquered England.
After King Harold died in the battle of Hastings, William ascended to the

English throne. The Norman dynasty has endured in Great Britain, with numerous genealogical twists and turns, to the present day.

The inconclusive and self-destructive dynastic warfare of the Carolingian monarchs continued through the tenth century. In 987 the nobles of the western half of the once-again divided empire met in the cathedral at Reims and elected Hugh Capet as their king. Though Hugh was not the heir of the former king, Lothair, he had multiple, overlapping genealogical links to the Carolingian rulers, and he had been a powerful political figure in the fragmented kingdom during the last years of Lothair's inept rule. Most significantly for Paris, and for the subsequent history of France, Hugh was the hereditary ruler of towns and cities in the region known as the Ile de France. And like Odo, who withstood the Vikings a century before him, he held the hereditary title count of Paris.

Not that Hugh Capet ruled much of the kingdom that had passed to Charles the Bald in the division of Charlemagne's empire: Hugh's territories were tightly grouped around Paris, and his real power beyond his own boundaries was practically nil. Elsewhere, counts and dukes held similar territories in their own right and by their own strength and cunning. The dynastic warfare of the Carolingian rulers that had left its territories unprotected from Viking raiders had also enabled nobles of the second rank, like Odo and Hugh, to achieve absolute sovereignty over small sections of the country. In time the intricate system of obligations among rulers of different ranks that is commonly known as feudalism (a term in eclipse among specialists) would gradually overcome this fractionalization, at least in theory, by exalting the authority of monarchs.

Hugh Capet may have been nothing more than a count in pragmatic terms, but by title he was a king. Anointed at the time of his coronation with a sacred chrism and reputedly endowed by God with the power to cure through his touch the so-called "king's evil" or scrofula (a form of tuberculosis affecting the lymph nodes of the neck), the new ruler was no mere count. There was something ineffable, magical, and—in the contemporary view—sacred about his office. He continually cultivated this distinction, and so did his heirs. Once Hugh returned to his city as a king rather than a count, Paris could claim both royal sponsorship and divine support.

Hugh Capet at his death passed along his title and holdings to his son, Robert II. And unlike the Carolingian kings, whose sons immediately began killing one another in an effort to gain control over everything their fathers had possessed, Robert II passed along his title and holdings exclusively to his eldest surviving son, Henri I. This novel pattern of inheritance strengthened the Capetian dynasty and contributed to its remarkable longevity. Every French monarch except Napoleon Bonaparte was a descendant of Hugh Capet—a fact that would help to keep Paris at the center of French political and religious life for the next millennium.

Chapter Two

THE CATHEDRAL OF NOTRE DAME

The Capetian kings ruled from their base on the Ile
de la Cité, an island that had proved its value against
enemies of every sort since the fourth century. But
the strategic advantages of the site were matched by
other important characteristics: its links to—indeed,
its potential strangle-hold on—the city's commercial life, and its tradition of
imperial and royal government. The island also housed the city's bishop, the
religious anchor and support of Capetian kings. If the ninth-century siege of
Paris underscored the fragility of the Carolingian rulers, it also revealed the
power that had accrued to Christian bishops since the fourth century. The
Romans' transfer of authority from civil to religious leaders that began while
Gaul was still part of the empire persisted virtually unchanged through the
Merovingian and Carolingian periods. While bishops were sometimes caught
up in dynastic struggles, their day-to-day focus was on the health and spiri-
tual well-being of their own people.

Almost nothing is known about Hugh Capet's palace beyond its location
and its link to earlier palaces on the site. It may have been built into the
rampart wall, its fortifications merged with those of the island itself. Though
the shape and exact location of successive royal palaces remain a mystery,
the buildings that made up the bishop's domain are well documented. His
residence stood along the south side of the island and overlooked the Left

Bank. The bishop of Paris, who became an archbishop in 1622, continued to live next to his church until 1830, when his palace was invaded and sacked during one of the aftershocks of the Revolution. A year later the palace was vandalized again. Despite the bishop's insistence, the palace was never rebuilt, and the area where it stood—between the south wall of the cathedral and the river—is now a public park and promenade.

Next to the cathedral and palace was a complex of hospices, churches, monasteries, and hospitals that served the diseased and disadvantaged. Hospices also sheltered men and women setting out on the spiritual journey to Santiago de Compostela in northern Spain. Over time these charitable institutions swarmed across the bridges to the Left Bank, where they continued to proliferate. Three fires in the eighteenth century devastated the sprawling island complex, and what remained was almost completely obliterated by the mid-nineteenth-century reorganization of the island.

At first the bishop's throne sat in the apse of the early Christian basilica that is now partially covered by the cathedral of Notre Dame. Though only the scantiest archaeological evidence has come to light over the years, most scholars believe that there was once another church further to the west. The partially excavated basilica was dedicated to Saint Stephen, while in all probability the submerged church was dedicated, like its successor, to Notre Dame, Our Lady the Virgin Mary. In the early ninth century, Saint Stephen was probably the more important of the two churches, but in the decades that followed the Viking invasions, it was replaced in importance by Notre Dame. By 1160 when work on a new, larger cathedral began, Saint Stephen may already have been in ruins.

The reversal of fortune that raised the church of Our Lady to preeminence was probably the work of an order of canons founded in the eighth century. Canons were ordained priests who lived together like a community of monks and shared responsibility for a major ecclesiastical building. The canons of Notre Dame lived in a collection of houses on the north side of the island. As their influence grew, they gained control of the election of the bishop of Paris. One of the first signs of their emerging power was a remodeling of their church in the early twelfth century. A stained glass window was donated to that project by the celebrated abbot of Saint Denis, Suger, and a richly decorated doorway was created at about the same time. Before the end of the century, the remodeled church again proved too small, and the canons conceived an even grander project that required the demolition of both the church of Our Lady and the church of Saint Stephen. Under the leadership of a former canon, Maurice de Sully, who became bishop of Paris in 1160, a radical new building was imagined.

Though construction of the cathedral of Notre Dame began decades after Suger's death, the abbot celebrated for his architectural adventurousness may have inspired its construction. In 1140 he had urged the razing of the venerable basilica to the north of Paris that had been built over the grave of Saint Denis and its replacement with a vast new cathedral in a distinctly modern style. This was the same delicate task the popes of the Italian Renaissance would face when they argued for the destruction of Constantine's basilica built on the tomb of Saint Peter and its replacement with an entirely new building. Suger based his case on the insufficiency of the old structure to decently house the crowds that thronged to visit the saint's tomb. The new church would be longer, wider, and higher than the original, but, more importantly, it would be built in a new architectural style.

The style Suger advocated, and the one that Bishop Sully inaugurated in Paris, has, since the Renaissance, been called Gothic. Art historians have described the Gothic as an architecture of the sky rather than the earth. While it created enclosed spaces of unparalleled extent, its distinctive features are its steep arches, vertical towers, and soaring walls. Its heavenly aspirations are reflected in the beaked pinnacles that top every vertical and extend the building's reach as high as possible into the sky. The sky itself entered the structure through enormous windows. Filtered by richly colored glass that changed intensity as the day passed, light became the most absorbing and lively spectacle within these vast spaces.

These characteristics are most apparent when Gothic cathedrals are compared to churches of the Romanesque period that came immediately before. Yet despite the obvious differences between the two, the new architecture, like its Romanesque predecessors, was firmly rooted in the early Christian basilica. The ground plan of Saint Stephen was a scaled-down version of the ground plan of the Gothic church that supplanted it. And when viewed in section, the low side aisles and higher central nave of Saint Stephen were preserved in the cathedral of Notre Dame. Though fixed by tradition and by liturgical needs, these architectural forms also represented a response to the pragmatic demands of the building itself. A basilica was designed to provide as much open floor space as possible and to allow light to reach every part of the interior. Windows in the side wall lit the aisles, but the central nave was too far from the side walls to receive much light from windows there. Skylights would have been an ideal solution, but they were a technological impossibility before the nineteenth century. The next best thing was to build the walls of the central section higher than the roofs that covered the aisles and to put windows in those walls. Gothic churches are higher than most early Christian churches, but they are lit in the same way.

The walls of early Christian basilicas were made from nearly uniform masses of brick or stone. Their strength depended on their thickness, and cutting holes into them made them weaker. Because of the need to maximize visibility at floor level, the high central walls of early Christian basilicas rested on colonnades (rows of evenly spaced columns) or arcades (rows of evenly spaced arches supported by columns or piers). The openings between the columns or piers made it possible for people in the side aisles to see what was going on around the altar of the church. But slender supports meant that nave walls could not be very heavy or thick, and this limitation restricted their height. And because of the walls' uniform construction, the windows cut into them could not be very large. Yet glazing even small windows was a difficult problem throughout the late antique and early medieval period. Glass was extremely expensive and hard to come by, and windows in many early Christian basilicas were left unglazed.

A new approach to building nave walls was the first of two striking innovations that transformed the lighting of church interiors in the Gothic era. No longer envisaging the walls of a building as a continuous protective and supporting structure like the exoskeleton of a beetle, Gothic designers imagined walls as a system of supports and protective membranes. Instead of using short columns to support a heavy wall, tall columns were extended from floor to ceiling, where their tops were joined with ribs to create vaults and roofs. These massive columns, which could take many forms, bore the weight of the structure. The stonework between columns provided cross-bracing and kept out the elements (much like plywood sheathing nailed to studs in a modern house wall), but it bore little weight. Even when the wall was pierced through with enormous openings for windows, the building remained strong.

The creation of Gothic architecture coincided with a revolution in the production of glass. For reasons that remain unclear, techniques that Byzantine artisans had understood for centuries suddenly came into widespread use. The glass they made was of a particular type, not for the most part clear but richly colored in a limited range of very strong but still harmonious shades. Sometime in the late tenth or early eleventh century, builders began to glaze the small slit-like windows of Romanesque churches with mosaic patterns made from this colored glass. By the twelfth century in Paris and the surrounding towns in the Ile de France, glassmakers were joining the construction crews of the great cathedrals and creating masterpieces of stained glass.

A building on the scale that the canons projected demanded a site far larger than the old church of Our Lady and the basilica of Saint Stephen combined. Maurice de Sully's solution was ingenious. Rather than reach westward from these old sites into the thickly settled neighborhoods of the island where demand kept real estate prices high, he decided to expand in the other direction, toward the east. The canons owned a small island just upstream from the Ile de la Cité at what would be the apse end of the new church. By driving piles and adding rubble to fill in the channel between them, the two islands could be linked. The work progressed quickly, and the site was ready for the builders by 1160.

The bishop also had plans for the area in front of the new cathedral, and to carry them through he could not avoid buying and demolishing some houses. Just as he had anticipated, the few structures he was forced to purchase cost enormous amounts of money, and decades passed before their transfer was complete. Finally, these island properties were leveled to create a small open square in front of the church, the ancestor of the now much larger area—created in the nineteenth century by Baron Hauss-mann—called the parvis of Notre Dame. To join the church and its little square to the main road crossing the island, builders cut a narrow street westward. This street, which was on a direct line with the center door of the cathedral, has since been absorbed into the expanded parvis, but its trace is preserved in white marble in the pavement there. The roadway, though small, extended the vista from which the full height of the church could be seen and appreciated.

A building on such a grand scale required enormous amounts of raw material of suitable strength and durability. While the site was being pre-pared, workers set about quarrying stone. Some of it was probably pilfered from Roman ruins that had not been fully stripped of their materials when the island was fortified. But the bulk of the limestone was cut from outcrop-pings on a little hill opposite Mont Saint Geneviève. In an age when trans-portation of heavy cargoes was difficult and expensive, having convenient access was important. The blocks were brought down to the banks of the now-buried River Bièvre and then floated on barges to the Seine.

Work began at the eastern end of the church, the choir. This is where the altar stood and the canons heard mass. If we think of the construc-tion of Gothic cathedrals as the work of centuries, the building of Notre Dame seems remarkably fast. The first stones were laid in 1163, and by 1182 the choir and its double aisles were complete. The altar was conse-crated and services for the canons began. During the next twenty years, workers finished all but the two westernmost bays of the nave. Work on those bays was deliberately postponed so that the western façade could be constructed from both sides. When the façade was tall enough to clear the side aisles, the nave was completed and the two separately built sections were joined together.

Almost as soon as the building was enclosed, workers began to reconfigure what had already been put up. Chapels were built along both sides of the nave. The wide area between the choir and nave, called the crossing or transept, was extended so that its outer walls lined up with the new chapels. At the end of the thirteenth century, a forty-year project to surround the choir with chapels began. At about the same time, most of the windows in the nave were made even larger and reglazed.

Despite these improvements, by the eighteenth century the cathedral that had become so important in French national life was hopelessly out of touch with the refined neoclassical tastes of that era. Architects did their best to update it, but there was very little they could do. They managed to replace most of the—to their eyes—gaudy medieval stained glass with softly translucent white glass, and they cloaked the Gothic pillars of the choir with wooden structures that mimicked the arches and applied columns of the Romans. By the time the revolutionary mobs got to the church late in that century, there was little glass left. They expressed their resentment at centuries of clerical abuse by destroying sculpture, bas-reliefs, and paintings. They also looted the sacristy of the church, stealing gold and jewels and defiling relics that had been collected over centuries. Nineteenth-century restorers worked to undo both of these attacks. Their work was so skilled and their record-keeping so spotty that it is difficult for anyone but an expert to distinguish between medieval originals and nineteenth-century recreations.

The cathedral that is visible today is the product of at least five signifi-cant historical events: the first building campaign of the twelfth century, striking remodelings carried out in the thirteenth and fourteenth centuries, a devastating redirection of the building in the early eighteenth century, the French Revolution of 1789, and a major project of salvage, restoration, and new construction carried on in the mid-nineteenth century.

The glorious west façade of Notre Dame can be seen from the en-larged parvis in front of the church. Both physically and aesthetically, the façade is nearly independent of the structure behind it. Its wide rectilin-ear frame masks the church and gives little hint of its spindly support-ing buttresses or the great disparity between high nave and much lower side aisles. Suger thought of the façade he envisaged for Saint Denis as a much expanded version of a Roman triumphal arch—a free-standing structure through which a victorious general's procession passed during the celebration of foreign conquests. The designers of Notre Dame may have had a similar idea in mind. Though there is apparently little common ground between the Roman triumphal arch and the Gothic cathedral, the fusion works here, both architecturally and intellectually. (3)

The west façade is divided into three vertical sections and three or four horizontal zones. The three doorways at ground

3

level are each set into the thickness of the wall and surrounded by a series of bands decorated with sculptures that enlarge and frame the entries. The central doorway is the highest and widest. Above the doorways, an ornamental frieze spans the width of the building. There, in individual niches flanked by columns, stand images of the biblical kings of Israel. (4) Revolutionary leaders mistook these figures for the historical kings of France and ordered their removal. Those charged with this act of vandalism buried the heads. Many of them resurfaced in the late twentieth century and are now among the treasures of the Cluny Museum on the Left Bank.

4

Above the center door, the spokelike framing of the great rose window fills the wide bay. To each side a peaked frame similar to those enclosing the doorways below outlines two windows with arched tops surmounted by a rosette. The twin bell towers of the cathedral spring from the next level of the façade. Their bases and the open space between them are spanned by an extremely steep colonnade crowned by elaborately interlaced moldings, a cornice, and balustrade. The square towers with their narrow louvered openings shelter the cathedral's carillon. Between them through the openwork of the upper arcade, the peak of the nave roof and the spire above the crossing can just be seen.

If it is indeed accurate to think of the western end of Notre Dame as a triumphal arch, then it is also possible to talk about the entire façade as a uniform composition not only in its architecture but also in its themes. The triumphal arches through which Roman generals passed were symbolic gates that represented passage from one status to another. For the victor, the transformation was very positive. But as Vercingetorix discovered, the captives who were paraded through the streets in front of the general's chariot passed through the same gateway, usually on their way from life to death.

Great arches like those that survive in Rome, southern France, and a few other spots throughout the empire were enriched with sculpture that represented the twin themes of the triumph: glory, often represented as a wreath presented by angelic winged victories, and subjection, personified by the bound captives in foreign-looking clothes whose images abound on the archways. Other scenes, with hordes of small figures fighting on land, swarming off ships, or besieging an enemy city, filled in the historical details of victory and defeat. In similar fashion, the three doors on the west façade of Notre Dame represent singular triumphs and defeats and fill in the background narrative of the key figures given prominence above each of the doorways and in the ornamental frieze above. Though triumph is more evident than defeat, there is both a record of adversity and, in the central doorway, a memorial of failure and destruction.

The three doorways on the west façade as well as the two at the ends of the transept have similar shapes. At the center of each is a pair of wooden, iron-framed doors separated by a prop called a trumeau. Above the doorway are two horizontal lintels, and above the two lintels is an area shaped like half an almond, called a tympanum. Rippling out from the tympanum are successive decorative bands (archivolts). The verticals beneath each archivolt that parallel the door's edges are the jambs. Every door at Notre Dame has multiple decorations in each of these areas, and the accumulated weight of the many little figures that take their special place in the array is dizzying both to the eye and to the mind. Fitting the multitude of scenes and figures into a complete, unified, ideal program is not only daunting but probably inconceivable today, if indeed it ever could be done. The devastation of the cathedral and the thorough nineteenth-century restoration have made it unlikely that we will ever know exactly how every piece of the medieval puzzle fit together.

It is still possible, however, to understand the broad thrust of the decoration and to appreciate how bits and pieces of Bible lore, the lives of saints, and the providential history of Israel were arranged in a meaningful ensemble. The doors narrate in some detail a short span of years that medieval theologians understood as the key to the history of all times and places. The narrative begins in the south door dedicated to Saint Anne, the mother of the Virgin Mary. (5) Her story, based on apocryphal texts that enjoyed great

5

popularity in the Middle Ages, begins to the left on the lower of the door's two lintels, when she and her husband, Joachim, are turned away by the high priest because she is childless. After a miraculous visitation like the one her daughter will welcome, Anne becomes pregnant while remaining a virgin. Joachim learns the news of this immaculate conception in a dream and rushes to join Anne. The couple share a hug when they meet before the gates of Jerusalem. Their child Mary is born. At the age of three she is presented to a now-welcoming high priest; she leaves her family to live in the temple precinct until she reaches maturity.

The scenes represented in the second lintel, just above, are among the most familiar. Isaiah, who predicted Christ's birth to a virgin, is the first figure on the left. His image is followed by traditional episodes: the angel's annunciation to Mary of her impending conception, the visitation of Mary to her cousin Elizabeth, mother of John the Baptist, the nativity and the annunciation to the shepherds. The sequence ends with King Herod addressing the three magi.

In the tympanum, Mary sits with the baby Jesus in her lap on a throne that is set off by columns and topped by a dome and towers. This is not just a throne, but the image of the altar beneath the domes of a Romanesque church. Adoring angels stand to either side; a bishop, who may be Maurice de Sully or Saint Germain (there is no way to tell), stands at their side, while other figures kneel on the right and left. There are angels in the tapering space above the Virgin whose figures are remarkably like the winged victories on Roman arches. In the archivolts, angels, prophets, biblical rulers, and the old men described in the Book of Revelation surround the Virgin and adore her. The attenuated figure on the trumeau is Saint Marcel. The jamb figures are kings and prophets.

The doorway marks the beginning of the triumph of Christ. The figures in this first doorway have all overcome adversity through God's grace. Their attendant figures—the kings and prophets of Israel—were men of great merit who finally achieved entry into the heavenly Jerusalem through the intervention of Anne's grandchild, Jesus. The elders of the Apocalypse look forward to the end of time when all the people of earth will be summoned before the door of judgment and their eternal fate decided.

The northernmost door of the western façade, outlined by a triangle, is dedicated to the Virgin Mary. At the top of the tympanum, Mary is crowned and shares a throne with her son. Angels kneel beside them holding lighted candles. This scene is a version of the final episode in Mary's life, the

6

assumption, when she, to the amazement of the mourning disciples, is suddenly taken up by God, body and soul, directly into heaven. The center band of the tympanum represents Mary on her deathbed, while Christ's disciples attend her. This episode is commonly called the dormition (sleep) of the Virgin. (6)

The much-restored trumeau of the north door represents the fall of man in three scenes: the creation of Eve from the side of a sleeping Adam, the couple disobeying God by eating the apple, and their expulsion from the Garden of Eden. The sin of Adam and Eve is the beginning of the history of human failure. These two figures, whose poor choices made them captives to sin, are redeemed through the sinless character of Mary and her son and through the self-sacrifice of Christ that overpowers sin and death. The figures in the surrounding archivolts represent the conflict between good and evil in the contemporary world, through symbols of the virtues and vices

7

juxtaposed with calendar figures representing the labors of the months. Labor is both the consequence of the fall of Adam and Eve and also one of the ways that its effects were repaired.

The central portal represents the triumph of Christ at the end of time. (7) Seated on a throne, the risen Christ opens his hands to show the holes made by the nails that held him to the Cross. Angels displaying the other instruments by which he was wounded stand beside him. Mary and Saint John kneel next to them. In the upper lintel beneath Christ's feet, Saint Michael and a monstrous Satan weigh the souls of all the risen dead. The blessed look upward toward heaven, while shaggy-legged demons haul the damned to hell. The lower lintel of the door represents the moment when the trumpet of the Last Judgment sounds and the dead rise from their graves. Angels and demons fill the archivolts.

The figures of the biblical kings that span the façade play a part in the same triumphal theme. These rulers of Israel represent God's work in history and the promise of redemption in the New Testament. The long sequence of kings is both completed and redeemed by the birth of Christ depicted in the doorways below. Even the rose window, seen from the outside where only its rim and spokes are visible, has a part to play. (8) The wheel was a typical medieval image of Fortune, the semi-divine force that, under God's covert control, governed the successes and failures of men and women. Its message was very much the same as that of the Last Judgment. Some will rise by grace while others fall prey to sin. The brooding grotesques that perch on the towers contribute to the symbolism. These figures, which have escaped their proper role as gargoyles, remind the faithful of the frivolous distractions that menace them even in the supposedly safe precinct of the church. (9)

8

9

The exterior side walls of the church are divided into repetitive bays by a file of massive stone towers. These towers, which are nearly as tall as the nave, originally stood outside the walls of the cathedral. By the time the fourteenth-century remodeling began, the space between each tower had been filled in with a chapel. Their ornamented gabled ends now form a series of peaks along the outer edge of the church. (10) Two delicate stone bridges stretch from each tower toward the center of the building. A lower arch leans across the chapels and the first side aisle to prop up the walls of the balcony that surrounds the nave. A longer and more graceful prop reaches from the top of each tower to shore up the clerestory wall. (11)

Arched beneath and flat on top, these angled buttresses serve two purposes. They resist the tendency of the interior columns to bow outward, and they channel rain water from the roofs of the nave and balcony toward the ground. The water travels down the bridges and through the towers, to be discharged at a distance from the stonework through the grotesque mouths of gargoyles. In French they are called *chimères* (chimeras), but their English name, which sounds like "gargle," gives a better sense of what they are meant to do.

The long line of towers and buttresses is broken on the north and south by transepts. At the end of the north transept is another monumental entryway similar to those on the west. Above a single door dedicated to the Virgin is a small gallery and two rose windows. The trumeau figure

of the Virgin and
Child is the only
large-scale Gothic
sculpture that
remains in its
original place on
the church. (12)

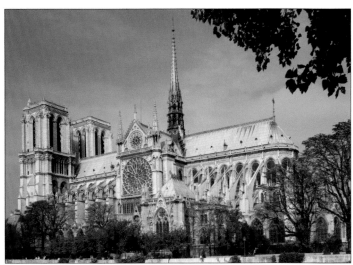

The tympanum
combines scenes
from the life of
Christ with others

10

illustrating the story of the legendary archdeacon Theophilus. This hero was
offered the office of bishop but refused it, because he felt himself to be
unworthy. The man who was then offered the position not only accepted it
but demoted Theophilus. In anger, Theophilus made a pact with the devil.
Sometime after writing and signing a contract and putting it in the devil's
hands, Theophilus had second thoughts and prayed to the Virgin for help.

When he woke up the following
morning, he found the contract
lying on his chest. This legend in
a much-modified form became
the foundation of the Faust story.
The tympanum scenes show
the signing of the contract, the
archdeacon's immediate rewards,
his prayer, and the figure of the
Virgin snatching him away from

11

12

a demon. The new bishop tells Theophilus's wonderful story to an amazed crowd while the archdeacon, seated beside him, holds out the contract with his name on it.

The external structure of the choir is similar to that of the nave, but its effect is much more striking. (13) The buttresses that circle the choir are widely spaced, and the monolithic towers that ground the nave arches are replaced here by stone plinths decorated with multiple pinnacles and decorative niches. Though the choir buttresses are now one of the most admired parts of the church, they were not part of the original structure of Notre Dame. What some architectural historians have pictured is an original choir built up of three stepped layers like an oblong wedding cake. There were no chapels; the first and widest layer contained the outermost aisle around the choir. The second taller layer sheltered the inner aisle and the balcony above it. The final layer was the clerestory. Angled roofs, of which traces were found in the nineteenth-century excavations, topped each successive story.

The master builder who oversaw the renovation of the choir that began in the 1330s transformed this earliest part of the building, which represented Gothic architecture as it emerged from the Romanesque, into a structure that reflected the taste and adventurous spirit of the fully matured Gothic style. To begin this transformation, he removed the angled roofs between stories and replaced them with flat roofs ringed by balustrades. Stretches of wall once hidden behind tiles and rafters were suddenly visible, and the architect took advantage of their exposure to lengthen the windows in the clerestory. Flat roofs collect water, which was drained along the tops of the long buttresses linked to the clerestory and the smaller ones supporting the second-floor gallery. Between the bases of the buttress towers, a ring of chapels filled in the spaces between supports.

Through iron gates on the south side of the church, it is possible to glimpse the south transept doorway dedicated to Saint Stephen, whose church was replaced by Notre Dame. Much of the sculpture was created in the mid-nineteenth century, but the tympanum and its decoration date from the mid-thirteenth century when the transept was completed. The feast of Saint Stephen is celebrated on December 26. Unlike Theophilus, whose legend is very circumstantial but poorly founded in either history or scripture, the martyrdom of Saint Stephen is recorded in the Acts of the Apostles.

In a series of scenes framed in four-lobed panels, the doorway captures something of the life of Paris in the thirteenth century. The labors of the months and images of the virtues and vices are the official way to incorporate daily life into the grand historical theology of the church. These scenes, like images in the margins

13

of Gothic manuscripts, have the same underlying purpose, but they are apparently more candid, humorous, and informal. Many of the scenes involve young men, apprentices perhaps or more likely students, who were beginning to crowd the colleges on the Left Bank. The youths make fun of a woman who is punished for some petty crime; there is a foot race. Dogs chase children in the street.

Little survives of all the extraordinary riches that once decorated the inside of Notre Dame cathedral. In 1845 two men were commissioned to restore the heavily damaged church in a way that would reflect its long life and its role in the history of the nation and the city. Five years later, with his partner dead, Viollet le Duc redefined the project. Instead of restoring the church as originally planned, he decided instead to recreate the cathedral as it had been left just after the medieval building campaigns were completed. Anything that was not Gothic he removed if he could. What he could not repair or restore of the Gothic church he replaced with new work in the Gothic style. The result must have come as a shock to those who commissioned the renovation. Expecting to see Notre Dame returned to them in a form they remembered, they saw instead the creation of a pure Gothic memorial stripped of any reference to its subsequent history. (14)

Like the soaring architecture of the Gothic style, stained glass has been described as a striking innovation without precedent in earlier churches, but this is inaccurate. Many styles of figural decoration can be found in both early Christian and Romanesque churches. Walls were frequently decorated with mosaics, and where mosaic techniques were unknown or impractical, churches were decorated with frescoed images or painted sculpture. The figures and scenes of Gothic stained glass windows were more or less the same ones that had been depicted in these other media.

All French Gothic cathedrals exhibit a great similarity in the colors, figures, and techniques of their glasswork. Experts are unsure whether these similarities reflect a uniform culture of glassmaking shared among many workshops or a small number of masters who moved from one construction site to another as needed. To make the glass, master workers mixed wood cinders or ash with river sand and sea salt and fired the mix in small ceramic pots. They added minerals to create color. Blue glass was made by mixing in cobalt oxides that came from distant mines in Germany and the Balkans. Red was produced by the addition of copper filings and rust (not gold, as many people believe). The best reds were so deep that the glass became opaque. Glassmakers had to sandwich clear glass between thin red layers to maintain translucence. Slight impurities in the blend turned red to purple. Copper dioxide produced green glass; an oxide of iron or manganese produced yellow.

The molten mixture was collected on a long hollow pipe, and the glassmaker blew it either into a cylinder or a flat bubble. The cylinders were slit and unrolled to form

14

flat sheets after the ends were cut away. The bubbles were detached from the end of the blow tube, creating an opening in the glass. By reattaching the opposite end of the bubble to the pipe and putting it back in the fire, the glassmaker could twirl the glass like pizza dough while it expanded and flattened. Crude versions of this technique produced the round, distorting window panes called bull's-eyes. Both techniques produced glass with minute air bubbles, veins, and ridges that varied the shade and luminosity of the glass in an interesting way.

Almost all early stained glass windows were rectilinear, and their proportions, like those of the buildings they decorated, were many times higher than wide. In the tradition of the mosaics, paintings, and sculptural reliefs they replaced, these windows represented sacred figures or biblical scenes. With a drawing of the scene to be represented laid out in front of him, the windowmaker used nippers to cut cold glass of the appropriate color to fit his pattern. Facial features, drapery folds, and other details were painted onto the colored glass with a gray slurry of metal filings suspended in vinegar or gum. The same material was used to heighten or lessen the transparency of the glass and create dimensional effects. Then the glass was reheated to fix the painted details. The glass pieces were bound together with lead strips like those still in use today. Solder bound the strips together, and lead filaments like baggy ties bound the finished window to an iron armature that was then fitted into the stone moldings of a window opening.

The oldest surviving window in Notre Dame is the great rose window on the west end that was installed in 1220. It is obscured in part by the cathedral's organ. Though restored in the eighteenth century and again in the mid-nineteenth, it still gives the impression of a thirteenth-century original. The Virgin sits at its center, with the kings of Israel surrounding her. The outer medallions contain depictions of the virtues and vices and the labors of the months. The window sums up the scheme of theological history that is crucial to the western façade. The Virgin is the central figure who mediates between the biblical past and the day-to-day present.

The rose window in the north transept is the second oldest in the church and the one that is best preserved and most authentic. (15) It was finished and put in place in 1260; the restorers of the nineteenth century had little need to work on it. In its center, the Virgin sits with Christ on her knee. Three concentric bands of scenes radiate out from her. The first band is filled with the figures of Old Testament prophets, who foretold the coming of Christ. These men are encircled by the ancestors of Christ and the patriarchs and high priests of Israel. The smaller window above is modern.

The southern rose, the youngest of the three, suffered the most damage during the centuries. Cracks in the window's masonry support required a complete rebuilding in the middle of the eighteenth century, and a second one a hundred years later. The eighteenth-century restorer had no way to duplicate the painted panels of the original window, so he substituted panels from other windows in the cathedral. In this

15

way he introduced a series of scenes on the life of Saint Matthew that had nothing to do with the main theme of the window, but his clumsy restoration at least had the virtue of preserving precious early glass that would otherwise have been lost. The nineteenth-century restorers, who were certainly capable of duplicating the appearance of medieval glass, wisely chose to respect the earlier restoration. Christ in majesty sits at the center of the window; he is surrounded by the apostles and martyrs. The scenes from the life of Saint Matthew are included in the outermost band.

The long chain of carved and painted reliefs on the outside of the walls that enclose the choir are the most complete and best preserved of the surviving medieval sculptures in the church. Created in the thirteenth and fourteenth centuries, they were only slightly damaged during the Revolution, and the nineteenth-century restorers did little more than replace missing hands and feet and add a bit of paint. The scenes on the north side of the choir illustrate the infancy, ministry, and passion of Christ. Those on the south wall recount episodes after the Resurrection. These include the appearance to Mary Magdalene and the scene of Doubting Thomas. (16)

The eighteenth-century reworking of the cathedral glass and choir pillars shows how completely the intellectual and spiritual world of the Middle Ages had passed away by that time. Even the nineteenth-century restorers, who were more aware of medieval history, more respectful of its technologies, and more attuned to the beauties of its style, understood the art they were working on in ways that were quite different from those who created it. Viollet le Duc, the greatest restorer of medieval architecture, had a profound emotional connection to the cathedral, but it is not one that his ancestors would have shared or perhaps even understood. In his *Essays on Architecture,* Viollet le Duc described a childhood experience that shaped his attitude toward medieval stained glass throughout his life: "The cathedral was almost dark, my eyes were drawn to the south window where the rays of the setting sun shone through, tinted with the most brilliant tones. I can still see the exact spot where we were stopped by the press of the crowd. All of a sudden the great organ began to sound. In my mind, it was the rose window I was staring at that had begun to sing. This impression grew stronger and stronger, and I began to sense in my imagination that particular panes of glass produced the deep tones and that others produced the high notes. I was seized by such a violent terror that I had to be taken outside."

The child's impressions stayed with the mature architect and drove him to resurrect the lost world that had produced these intense and terrible impressions. Though history always played a leading part in his restorations, it was always history attuned to the soul of a romantic.

During the decades that Notre Dame was being built, France —like much of the rest of Europe—was gripped by crusading zeal. During the Seventh Crusade the sainted king, Louis IX, acquired a relic of singular importance. For reasons that are

16

not clear, he decided not to present the relic to Notre Dame or to Saint Denis, though both churches were closely connected with the Capetian dynasty. Instead, he commissioned a separate chapel for it in a courtyard within the walls of the palace complex, just west of Notre Dame. Built with incredible speed between 1243 and 1248, the Sainte Chapelle stands, today, within the precincts of the great judicial complex known as the Conciergerie. (17)

The superbly restored Gothic chapel is simple in plan and clear in its exterior design. Two superimposed porches with large arched openings provide an entryway to the building's two levels. Rectangular buttresses support its side walls. Between each buttress is a wide and high stained glass window divided by slim stone ribs and intricate lobed ornaments into multiple panels. These huge windows light the upper chapel. The lower chapel is lit by small demilune windows. A great rose window opens above the upper porch, and a smaller rose is centered in the gable above it. Pinnacles crown the towers that flank the rose and complete each but-

tress. An openwork spire reaches high above the steeply pitched roof.

The lower chapel is often compared to the crypt beneath the choir of a medieval church. Its dominant features are the ribs that frame the arcades and ray across

17

the ceiling to support the floor
of the upper church. (18) The
painted decoration, designed
by Viollet le Duc, highlights
the architectural members and
increases their presence. The
upper church is richly painted,
too, but the painting and the
architecture are overwhelmed
by the extent and the intense
luminosity of the multiple
windows. Slender columns
bearing statues of the twelve
apostles stand between them.
Aligned with the main external
buttresses, these sculptures
suggest that the symbolic
weight of the building rests
on those who spread Christ's

18

message rather than on any tangible support. Indeed, the preponderance
of glass over stone is so obvious that the building appears to be held up in
some magical or miraculous way.

The glass of Sainte Chapelle suffered extensively over the centuries.
The original panes of the rose window have completely disappeared. The
windows of the lower chapel were destroyed in a flood at the end of the
seventeenth century. As early as the fifteenth century, damage to windows

19

in the upper chapel was evident, and it was extended by a fire in the early seventeenth century. Restorers set to work on the windows in the eighteenth century, but early in the nineteenth century the chapel fell prey to the demands of the law courts of the Conciergerie. To make the chapel more serviceable as an archive for legal documents, the stained glass was removed from the bottom of each window to a height of nearly ten feet and the openings were blocked. Much of the glass removed from the chapel was destroyed, but some of it was preserved and sold to collectors. It can now be found in museums in France and London. These attacks on the integrity of the glass made the task of nineteenth-century restorers exceptionally difficult. What they restored, created, and rearranged at that time is what the modern visitor sees. (19)

The eight windows in the main hall of the chapel—four on each side of the nave—are nearly fifty feet high and fifteen feet wide; the seven in the rounded apse are somewhat smaller. The enormous surface area of the glass is divided into narratives broken down into individual panels, more or less in the manner of a comic book. The panels are set within ornamental frames.

Each window contains scenes from books of the Bible. A visitor who stands under the rose window and looks toward the rounded apse has scenes from the book of Genesis in the first window on her left. Events from the book of Exodus are narrated in the next window. These include scenes from the life of Joseph, but the main focus is Moses. His life and leadership of the Israelites are displayed in a sequence of scenes that range from his discovery by Pharaoh's daughter to his consecration of Aaron. The third window, based on the books of Numbers and Deuter-onomy, includes more than seventy original scenes that continue the story of the Israelites under the leadership of Moses and Aaron. The fourth nave window on the left records the story of Joshua, the conqueror of Jericho, and is especially rich in military action. In the small lobed windows at the top of the panel are scenes from the life of Ruth, Joshua's wife.

Scenes from the book of Judges fill the first of the narrow apse windows. David, Solomon, and other ancestors of Jesus are celebrated in a genealogical figure called the Tree of Jesse in the second window of the apse. The life of Saint John the Evangelist and the infant Christ are the themes of the third. The window that stands in the center of the apse directly on axis with the altar of the chapel narrates the story of Christ's passion. The three narrow windows on the right side of the apse show the Old Testament prophets Daniel and Ezekiel, along with John the Baptist, the forerunner of Christ. Together, the apse windows present a picture of the origin of Christ through his genealogical links to the kings of Israel on the one hand and his prophetic links to the underlying spiritual movement that Christianity discerned in Old Testament prophecy.

The nave windows on the right, which return to Old Testament scenes, frame Christ's story within a parenthesis of prefigurations. Judith, who seduced and killed the tyrant Holofernes, and Job, who was tested by God, are the subjects of the first full-size window. The story of Esther, Ahasuerus, and the tyrant Haman follows. The second to last window narrates episodes from the book of Kings.

The last window on the right is one of the most controversial. As restored in the nineteenth century, it represents events in the recovery of the central relic of the chapel, the crown of thorns. This extraordinary object was enshrined in the chapel's altar, which now stands, much restored, under a Gothic baldachin in the apse. The crown of thorns revered in Sainte Chapelle was first heard of in the twelfth century as a possession of Baldwin, Latin king of Byzantium. Baldwin pawned it to a Venetian financier, who sold it to Louis IX when Baldwin defaulted. While Louis (who would later become Saint Louis) probably acted from pious motives, the relic had a peculiarly important meaning for a member of the Capetian dynasty. The crown of thorns, along with the *titulus* or notice board proclaiming Jesus of Nazareth King of Judea, had been created by Pontius Pilate in ironic recognition of Jesus' status. At Christ's resurrection, the essential truth proclaimed by these two objects became clear, and they were recognized as true symbols of Christ's universal sovereignty.

For a Capetian King like Louis IX, the crown of thorns was both a relic of divinity and also the ultimate charter of political legitimacy. Its possession underwrote the dynasty's claim to divinely sanctioned rule. Through its acquisition and prominent enshrinement, the sainted king realized the exalted ambitions of Hugh Capet, the onetime count of Paris.

Chapter Three

GOTHIC ASCENDANCY

After the Viking raids subsided near the end of the
ninth century and the Capetian kings came to power
near the end of the tenth, the hills and valleys on both
sides of the River Seine were reclaimed as cropland
and vineyards. These new settlements were at first
protected by an earth wall. More like a dike than a fortification, and more
like a Gallic defense work than a Roman one, the wall was built by digging a
ditch and piling the dirt on the inner side. Though the existence of this wall
on both sides of the river has long been known to historians, its location has
not been pinpointed.

Under King Philippe Auguste (Philip II), who ruled from 1180 to 1223,
a more ambitious and wider circuit wall was created to defend the sprawling city. (Map 2) Like the cathedral of Notre Dame that was being built at the
same time in the heart of Paris, the wall required building materials of many
kinds, both local and imported ones, and a host of skilled and unskilled
laborers. The speed with which these two enormous projects were carried
out shows that the city had fully recovered from the Viking depredations and
Carolingian dynastic struggles.

Work on the new wall began in 1190. Six feet thick and thirty feet tall, it
was built of dressed stones and studded with round towers every two hundred
feet. By 1208 it completely enclosed the right bank. The longest surviving

20

section stretches along the western edge of a narrow park near the Pont Marie called the Jardin Saint Paul. (20) A partial turret survives at the corner of Rue Charlemagne, and a second one juts from the wall near the center of the park. (Map 3)

The new perimeter's most important and long-lasting defensive innovation was a fortress created just at the point where the wall met the river on the downstream side. The Vikings had exposed an obvious vulnerability—that the key to attacking Paris was to head upriver straight to the city's heart, the Ile de la Cité. Parisians had banked everything on controlling this gateway, but with mixed results. As the city expanded in the twelfth century, Philippe Auguste chose a new cinch point on the river, downstream from the old barrier at the Ile de la Cité. On that remote site, his engineers created an enormous square block of masonry with projecting round towers at each of its corners. In its center they built a free-standing circular tower that served as the last refuge of its garrison. A purely utilitarian military stronghold, the building was the beginning of what would eventually become the royal palace, the Louvre.

Although the right bank was already the commercial center of the city, the new circuit of walls there enfolded territory that was still garden, pasture, or vineyard. Development of the commercial district before the wall was built had been heaviest along the major roadways that rayed out from the riverside and the two island bridgeheads. Once the walls were built, however, the spaces between and beyond these roadways began to fill in, and over the next century the city on the right bank grew to the limits of the walls.

For the complete defense of the city, it was necessary to protect the Left Bank as well. Though this hillside had been the center of the Roman town, it had lost both commercial and political power long before the Vikings attacked. In the aftermath of the Viking raids, monastic foundations with their fields and dependent communities occupied most of the land. More out of necessity than generosity, the king took on the expense of walling this part of the city. The work was completed by 1220. Built in the same style as the fortifications across the river, the Left Bank wall started from the river's edge opposite the Louvre, ran uphill to encircle the church and abbey of Saint Geneviève, then cut down into the valley of the River Bièvre on its way back to the Seine.

Throughout the twelfth century, Paris had become an increasingly popular center for advanced study. At first scholars were drawn to the cathedral, and students lived and studied on the crowded island. The chancellor of the school at Notre Dame controlled the distribution of the one professional qualification that a medieval professor had to have, a *licentia docendi,* a license to teach. As student demand rose, licenses were granted to increasing numbers of instructors, who set up shop along the Petit Pont, the short bridge connecting the Ile de la Cité with the Left Bank. Still, students and potential faculty continued to complain that licensing was too restrictive and the cost prohibitive.

Dissident students and faculty began to evade the chancellor's monopoly by moving to the under-populated Left Bank. The most powerful clerical figure there, the abbot of Saint Geneviève, supported their revolution by issuing teaching licenses on his own authority. The result was a confrontation between the chancellor and the abbot that endured until 1222, when Pope Honorius III finally decided the issue. He supported the abbot and gave official approval to the migration. The cathedral school eventually disappeared altogether, and since the thirteenth century the Left Bank has been the center of Parisian student life.

The medieval college curriculum was based on the seven liberal arts that had been codified in the schools of the Roman empire. Students entering a college began with the preliminary group of subjects called the trivium. These included grammar, primarily the study of Latin; rhetoric, which meant writing persuasively in Latin; and logic, the methods of argument and proof. The quadrivium embraced arithmetic, geometry, astronomy, and music. At first the curriculum in Paris was limited to these broad categories, but early in the thirteenth century another tier of studies was introduced. Students beyond the age of twenty who had completed their core courses could specialize in medicine or law and earn a doctorate in six years. Theology—the nuclear physics of the Middle Ages—was the most prestigious and the most challenging subject. A doctorate required fifteen years of preparation.

At first, academic life on the Left Bank was informal, with instructors and their students meeting where and when they could. The majority came from outside Paris and had to find their own shelter, food, and supplies. Students lived together in whatever space they could afford to rent and took their meals in the inns, taverns, and restaurants that soon peppered the area. School books were nonexistent in the era before printing, and on the Rue de la Parchemenerie students bought bound quires of carefully prepared sheepskin and the materials for transforming them into textbooks. The words to put in the book had to be copied from other texts, and students generally did their own copying. But getting their hands on a text to copy could be a challenge. The most important books were eventually made available to students in libraries, where they were chained to the walls. Students could read or copy them, but even the most ingenious or unscrupulous could not remove them.

During the thirteenth and fourteenth centuries, a college was basically a dormitory where students were fed and housed, not an institution of learning. Most colleges were run by small charitable organizations and were reserved for students from a particular country or region. In the mid-thirteenth century the king's chaplain, Robert de Sorbon, bought a building near the top of Mont Saint Geneviève that was big enough to house sixteen students. Sorbon restricted the dormitory to the upper echelon of students, those in theology. Evidently the success of the first generation of graduates was impressive enough to inspire other donations, and the hilltop college quickly expanded. (21) Now the centerpiece of the French university system, the Sorbonne's multiple departments offer training in language, literature, and culture—a curriculum somewhat akin to the medieval trivium.

Academic life on the Left Bank attracted thousands of students and masters. All of them were male, and the majority were young. Most were

21

members of colleges, where they had some adult supervision, and were destined for a life in the Church, so they probably had some inkling of decent behavior. Outside the cloister and the classroom, however, they were typically portrayed as rowdy, drunken, ribald, and riot-prone. As clerics, they were under the judicial authority of the abbot of Saint Geneviève and beyond any secular jurisdiction, but in most cases he failed to discipline his charges.

King Philippe Auguste's circuit of defensive walls left some important institutions unprotected. These were for the most part wealthy, walled foundations with the ability to defend themselves in the normal course of events and with the right to transfer their people inside the city walls in times of distress. The Knight's Templar—a heavily armed crusading order—was one such foundation on the north rim of the city. They were probably able to fend for themselves in any situation.

On the Left Bank, the Benedictine abbey of Saint Germain des Prés was in a similarly vulnerable position, with few but still formidable resources for self-defense. Indeed, for many centuries after its creation, the church looked more like a fortification than a place of worship. The monastic complex was completely surrounded by a high wall, and from its shelter three massive towers surveyed the landscape. One of these structures, combining the roles of a belfry and a castle keep, still stands at the west entrance of the church. The base of a second tower is visible on the southern face just east of the transept doors. Prominent flying buttresses —a prosaic version of those surrounding the choir of Notre Dame—were added in the thirteenth century, though the apse with its small windows was perfectly stable without them.

The monastery served a church that was originally dedicated to the Holy Cross and Saint Vincent. In 542 Childibert, the son of Clovis, endowed the church with funds and a relic of the Spanish saint. The Viking occupiers left the church and monastery in ruins. When new construction was begun in the eleventh century, workmen replacing the church floor discovered the tomb of Saint Germain, the sixth-century bishop of Paris who was made a saint by acclamation, along with tombs of King Childibert and his descendants. These Merovingian rulers had been buried near the saint in the Romanesque chapel of Saint Symphorien at the west end of the church. The Merovingian tombs were left where they had been found, but the relics of the saint were removed to the central altar. The church was renamed for Germain, and the addition of the words *des prés* to the dedication reflected the location of the church and monastery "in the meadows."

In 1790 the monastery was suppressed by the Revolution. The church was allowed to remain open to serve the parish, but in 1793 it too was closed. The monastery buildings were sold and the church was converted to a factory where potassium nitrate, used in gunpowder manufacture, was refined. In 1803 the factory moved out, but damage from abuse and from the corrosive chemical was so severe that the building was nearly demolished. A series of campaigns rescued and restored it, and Saint Germain des Prés became a church again.

The building that survives today shows characteristics of both the Gothic and the Romanesque, though elements from both periods were significantly changed by seventeenth- and nineteenth-century restorers. The nave is the oldest part. Its five bays were built in the early eleventh century when the Romanesque style, with its rounded arches, thick walls,

22

and small windows, was still current. (22) The groined arches of the ceiling were added in the seventeenth century; the columns and capitals of the nave were replaced in the nineteenth-century rebuilding. The U-shaped choir is ringed by a vaulted walkway (an ambula-tory) and surrounded by radiating chapels absent in the nave. Round columns with carved Romanesque capitals support rounded arches along the flat sides of the choir. The smaller openings at the end of the apse have pointed arches between them. The nearly round chapel at the very end of the apse is a nineteenth-century addition.

In the twentieth century the renown of the church was overshadowed by the reputation of the bistro across the street. Les Deux Magots was the meeting place of Paris intellectuals, especially those close to the existentialist Jean-Paul Sartre. For many, this remains the true spiritual center of the neighborhood.

The story of the church of Saint Germain des Prés was repeated in Gothic churches throughout Paris. The church of Saint Severin just off Rue Saint Jacques was also of Merovingian origin. It began as an oratory—a site for prayer—built at or near the grave of a sixth-century hermit named Severinus. The hermit was credited with converting Saint Cloud, who belonged to the Merovingian dynasty. During the seventh and eighth centuries, many others were buried nearby. Like the rulers who chose to be buried near Saint Germain, the men and women who were buried near

Severinus expected to benefit from the saint's holiness at the moment of resurrection. In the eleventh century, King Henri I gave what little of the original church the Vikings had spared to the canons of Notre Dame for conversion to a parish church. As the student population increased, the parish grew with it, and the church expanded in the thirteenth, fourteenth, and fifteenth centuries. In the eighteenth century, the round end of the choir was reconfigured to replace Gothic groined arches and bundled columns with Roman arches and square piers inset with porphyry.

The Revolution closed the church in 1793. Gunpowder was stored there, and later the building was converted to a hay barn. In 1802 it was reconsecrated. The church was refurbished in the nineteenth century, and the façade of Saint Pierre aux Boeufs, demolished in 1837, was tacked onto its western end. Above its doorway, flanked by pinnacled towers and topped by an elaborate gable, is an enclosed gallery, a balustrade, and an elongated demilune window. This window with its remarkable flamelike tracery was part of the last great remodeling of the church at the end of the fifteenth century.

The glorious interior of Saint Severin is filled with light that streams through two tiers of windows surrounding the nave and choir. (23) Above Gothic arches that separate the nave and side aisles, paired windows in each bay are topped by a clerestory window

23

that reaches the height of the ceiling vaults. The multi-lighted rose window at the west end of the church is partially hidden by the pipes of an
enormous organ. The most extraordinary and beautiful part of the church
is the ambulatory that surrounds the choir, which was built at the very end
of the Gothic period. The many piers supporting its roof are crowned by
multiple rays of stone. The French writer Joris Karl Huysmans compared
these columns to a grove of palm trees.

On the main axis of the nave, in a brilliant transformation of archi-

tecture into sculpture, a single column
gathers the many ribs of the roof into
a spiraling bundle in its twisted shaft.
(24) This serpentine column belongs to
a venerable tradition. Constantine donated columns with contorted shafts to
Saint Peter's basilica in Rome, and Gian
Lorenzo Bernini crafted gigantic bronze
versions of these imperial gifts to hold
up the baldachin over that basilica's
high altar. The most elegant column in
Saint Severin tries to reconcile itself
to a suite of abstract stained glass
windows that perfectly illustrate the
shortcomings of modern liturgical art.

Eighteenth-century taste and revolutionary zeal combined to destroy all
but the most durable pieces of Parisian

24

Gothic. Those objects that survived this
cultural pincer movement from elites on the
one hand and the oppressed on the other
are displayed in the Musée National du
Moyen Age Thermes de Cluny, the national
medieval museum located in the former
Roman baths of Cluny. There they are
joined by objects from the Roman era in a
building whose architecture reflects both
periods. The Roman baths that form part
of the museum structure were built in the
first century and continued in use until the
Germanic invasions. During the long period
when Mont Saint Geneviève was abandoned
or occupied by raiders, the baths fell into

25

ruins. Today, only the frigidarium—the room devoted to a cold water
pool—and a few rooms next to it, along with portions of the substructure, survive. As the university quarter grew in power and influence in the
fourteenth century, monks from the influential abbey of Cluny in Burgundy
built a college for their novices and began to acquire some houses next
to the baths for important visitors. In the late fifteenth century, Jacques
d'Amboise, a prominent member of the nobility and the abbot of Cluny,
razed the buildings on the property and built a private palace (called in
French a *hôtel particulier*) in the Gothic style. (25)

The revolutionary government seized the house and sold it. In 1843
the French government bought it back. When the city of Paris donated the

26

baths next door to the national government, along with a collection of Roman and medieval sculpture that was exhibited there, the two properties were combined. Around the same time, the collection of Alexandre du Sommerard, which was already exhibited in the Cluny palace, came into the government's possession. Du Sommerard was one of a handful of Parisian collectors who had recovered objects scattered and scorned by the revolutionary generation.

Crenellated walls guard the entrance to the restored Gothic house. With wings that embrace a small courtyard, the building has two main stories and an attic under a high roof that is lit by richly ornamented projecting gables. An octagonal tower in the main block and two smaller towers at its corners enclose spiral stairways that link the floors. Rectangular window frames and doorways, and wall openings generally set one above the other, give the exterior more the look of a Renaissance house than a medieval one. Inside the palace, however, especially in the chapel, the characteristics of the mature Gothic are magnificently represented.

Among the treasures from the Roman period displayed in the frigidarium (26) is a commemorative column dedicated to Roman and Gallic gods. The Sailors' Pillar (Pilier des nautes) was a surprise discovery made during excavations under Notre Dame at the beginning of the eighteenth century. Five carved stone blocks intended to be piled one on top of the other form what remains of a stone monument that may have originally been twenty feet high. During the Germanic invasions, the monument was taken down, and these blocks were built into the defensive wall around the Ile de la Cité.

Commissioned in the early first century AD, the pillar advertised the piety and wealth of the corporation of merchants and sailors that controlled commerce on the Seine. Though other monuments of this kind have been discovered, the Sailors' Pillar is the earliest and in many ways the most interesting, since its pantheon of gods includes both Roman and Gallic deities. (27) While the Romans generally favored the assimilation of their gods with those of the people they conquered, the case of Gaul was unusual. After encouraging syncretism in the earliest period of occupation, as this monument attests, the Romans eventually changed course, forbidding the representation of Gallic deities and persecuting the druids who worshipped them.

Among the Roman gods on the pillar are Jupiter, Mars, Mercury, Fortuna, and the warrior twins Castor and Pollux. This ensemble represents both the chief Roman god, a sort of chairman of the board, and others more closely associated with commercial enterprises that required luck as well as skill. The names of the Gallic gods are known from inscriptions on the blocks, but since the Romans were so effective in wiping out the druids' religion, we know little about the gods' stories or their functions.

The bulk of the Cluny collection focuses on the nation created by the Romans' successors, but objects from Paris are among its greatest treasures. Twelve Romanesque capitals taken from the church of Saint Germain des Prés during the nineteenth-century renovation

27

are displayed in Room 10. Rather than reproduce the standard forms of capitals with their Ionic curls or Corinthian acanthus leaves, Romanesque artists decorated capitals with devotional images. The Romanesque capitals on display in the Cluny cannot compare with the masterpieces of Romanesque art found in remote towns like Vezelay or Poitiers, but they do show the routine practices of the period and establish the historical background out of which Gothic architectural sculpture developed.

While church illustration usually focused on biblical events or the lives of saints, the capitals from Saint Germain were dedicated to the mystery of transubstantiation: the moment in the mass when a cup of wine and a wafer of bread become the body and blood of Christ. The host, which to us is a vehicle of the Communion ritual, took on a literary life of its own in the medieval period, and glorifications of its sacred character, as here, vied with popular stories of miracles performed by

28

or on behalf of Communion wafers. In the final capital of the sequence displayed in the center of the group, Christ surrounded by a mandorla—an almond-shaped full-body halo—sits enthroned with an open book in his left hand. In his right hand, which is disproportionately large, he holds a coin-like representation of the Com-

munion wafer. (28) The elaborate drapery of the figure and the fluidity of the work tie the sculpture to Byzantine images that the artist would have known either through book illustrations or metalwork. The figure is a two-dimensional representation written on the stone, rather than a figure cut out of it.

29

Across the room, three heads from jamb figures on the west portal of the basilica of Saint Denis reflect some of these same characteristics. Removed from the church in a pre-revolutionary updating and severed from their columnar bodies, three of the six surviving heads have been regrouped at Cluny. Those on display represent Moses, the Queen of Sheba, and an unknown prophet. All the figures share the same approach to the stone. It is treated more or less as a graphic medium on which facial features are inscribed. The work, which can be very meticulous, as it is in the headband and beard of the prophet, records surface detail, not bone structure. (29)

The private chapel of the palace is a masterwork of Gothic sculptural architecture. The ceiling is overwhelmed by stone ribs that spray out of the tops of the slim central column to completely cover the surface with intricate interlocking rays. A second web of spiderlike tracery fills the spaces between the larger ribs. The effect is more like a forest floor covered with a tangle of roots than the canopy of palm fronds that Huysmans saw in the nearly contemporary ambulatory of Saint Severin.

Among the great prizes of the Cluny's collection are the wonderful Gothic heads of the kings of Judea that were removed from the front of Notre Dame by order of the revolutionary council. Though much abused before they were unexpectedly recovered in 1977, these heads reflect the ability of anonymous Gothic sculptors to represent faces with proper proportions and evident mass, and to present regal dignity in a variety of psychologically compelling figure types. The much-mutilated figure of Saint Marcel from the trumeau of the door of Saint Anne shows the Gothic sculptor's success in reconciling the contradictory demands of sculpture and architecture. The postlike form of the figure accommodates it to its role as a personified column. But the parabolic flow of the deeply incised drapery gives the figure a sense of movement that preserves its independence as the portrait of a human being.

The original statues of the twelve apostles that stood between the windows of Sainte Chapelle are some of the finest and most successfully restored Gothic sculptures on display in the Cluny Museum. Carved during the early years of the 1240s and set against the columns of the upper chapel, the figures are fully formed yet subservient to their architectural role. The heads of the apostles, like those of the kings of Judea, are convincing if somewhat generic portraits of individuals whose features suggest a mild-mannered beneficence. The sculptor's greatest and most visible accomplishment is in the masterly handling of the loosely gathered and deeply pleated robes that each figure wears. The diagonal hems and puckered gatherings of the cloth contrast with the subtle verticals created by the long parallel folds. Even if the human figure under the cloth is flat and virtually lifeless, the cloth itself is three-dimensional and full of movement.

Completely removed from its original setting in a niche on the south transept wall, the figure of Adam exhibited in Room 14 can almost hold its own as a free-standing sculpture. The fig tree that screens his groin also serves as an additional prop to support the weight of the stone. There

is no torsion in the figure; the hip-shot posture, accentuated by the movement of the arms, and the feet, which are more or less next to each other,
create a kind of sway from side to side in the body that is limited to two
dimensions. Framed by its rectilinear niche, this sinuous motion would
have created a visual counterpoint between rigidity and flow that the
figure by itself cannot sustain. The statue once held an apple in his hand
and was realistically painted. The nineteenth-century restorers ignored
these features and chose to emphasize instead its remote connection to
free-standing Roman sculptures.

   One of the great treasures of the Cluny Museum is a set of six wall-sized
tapestries that tell the enigmatic story of the Lady and the Unicorn. The
six works were discovered in the 1880s in a chateau in the south of France
and bought for the museum by the son of the collection's founder. The
sequence was commissioned by a member of the Le Viste family at the end
of the fifteenth century. The Le Vistes, who were active in government and
lived in Paris, had recently been ennobled, and their crest—three crescents
on a blue diagonal band—is repeated in every scene. The tapestries are
superb representations of a variety known as *millefeuilles* because of the
background, where masses of cut flowers are strewn across a single-colored
ground. Where exactly the tapestries were woven remains a mystery.

   The composition of each panel is very similar. Against the floral
background, which is interspersed with active and lifelike images of small
animals, a central scene is set on a floating blue medallion. The medallion
represents a garden enclosed by a tiny fence. Readily identifiable flowers
and herbs grow all over its surface, and dogs, rabbits, even monkeys sit
or walk on it. Trees, covered with ripe oranges, acorns, or holly berries,

30

grow from it. On this floating stage a great lady dressed in the most remarkable brocades and her occasional smaller and less stylish assistant carry out a series of simple acts. In every scene they are flanked by a lion and a unicorn which hold up Le Viste heraldic banners on standards and lances painted blue and covered with golden crescents.

A scholar early in the 1920s proposed that the lady and her assistant were acting out representations of the five senses. This solution to the riddle of the sequence has been so generally accepted that the tapestries are now called by the names of the senses they represent. Hearing is represented when the lady plays an organ (as her assistant works the bellows). (30) Showing the unicorn its reflection in a mirror represents sight, and grasping its horn symbolizes touch. The sense of smell is exemplified when the lady weaves a crown of flowers.

Still, in recent years scholars have begun to show some impatience with this reading. For one thing, illustrations of the five senses are usually more explicit than this set, where in most cases the unicorn and the monkey rather than the lady play out the exemplary scenes. This sequence

is also the first one known in which a woman rather than a man personifies the senses. The words for abstractions like justice, liberty, and truth
are all feminine in Latin, and so they have feminine personifications. But
sensus, which is a masculine noun, is usually represented by a male figure.
The purpose of the sequence has also been questioned. Why would the Le
Viste family, who have certainly written their name all over these expensive
tapestries, be interested in representing senses that everyone possesses?

More troublesome still is the identification of the sixth panel, which
is one too many from the point of view of the five senses. (31) In this
tapestry, an assistant holds an open jewel box toward the lady, who either
deposits a jeweled object in it or withdraws one from it. Behind the lady
and her maid stands a
glorious pavilion of dark
blue cloth worked with
golden tear- or flame-
shaped emblems. A
band around the top of
the tent walls reads *A
mon seul désir*—to my
one desire.

The most common
way to integrate this
scene with the five

31

senses is to make it into an allegory of renunciation. In the Middle Ages,
the senses were often described as the five doors by which sin entered
the unprotected heart. Having conquered the temptations that assail her
through her senses in five scenes, the lady receives a crowning jewel from

the box in the sixth. Or, alternatively, she shows her will power once again by refusing the jewel. One recent analyst has seen the five senses not as paths to sin but gateways to knowledge, as Aristotle described them. The five senses alone are insufficient without understanding, which Aristotle labeled as the sixth sense.

Other interpreters have tried to personalize the sequence and relate it to particular events in Le Viste family history. Among recurring events, the most suitable for this kind of presentation would be a marriage. And one interpreter has read the enigmatic sign at the end of the sixth tapestry inscription—an I or J—as the first letter in the name of a Le Viste bride. The subject of the series, in this reading, becomes an idealized preparation for marriage through an appropriate disciplining of the senses. The final scene represents the lady's choice of a jeweled belt, symbol of marital chastity, from the box.

These multiple possibilities are interesting to contemplate because they suggest the range of things that medieval men and women may have thought about when they looked at a complex, enigmatic, and beautiful series of images like these. The sources range from preacher's manuals, in which the senses and their particular temptations are addressed, to the text of Aristotle, the most important Greek philosopher, to medieval scholars. There is also room for popular unicorn lore. While the lion and the unicorn are typical standard-bearers for the arms of noble families, it was also believed that the unicorn could be captured only by a virgin. That seems to be what has happened to the unicorn in the tapestry representing sight. In that scene he has given up his ensign and rests his front legs on the lady's lap.

Not far from the Cluny Museum, the church of Saint Julien le Pauvre (also called Saint Julian the Hospitaller) may be the oldest church on the Left Bank. This eleventh-century structure replaced a sixth-century church dedicated to an obscure martyr by the same name which the Vikings had destroyed. According to legend, Julien le Pauvre surprised and killed a couple in his bed whom he took to be his wife and another man. In reality, the two were his parents, who had arrived unexpectedly for a visit. For his penance, Julien devoted his life to feeding and sheltering pilgrims and the poor. After many years, the penitent offered the fateful bed to a leprous beggar, and in the morning the guest revealed himself as an angel in disguise.

The Paris that the Vikings had sacked was just a way-station on the long pilgrimage path that followed the Roman road from the North Sea coast to Santiago de Compostela in Spain. But by the thirteenth century, the city was the northern starting point for the pilgrimage, which began at the Tour Saint Jacques on the right bank just across from Saint Julien le Pauvre. Unfortunately, during this time the church dedicated to the friend of pilgrims had remained as poor as its patron. Nearly a hundred years went by before its diminutive sanctuary was completed. No sooner was that work done than the changing character of the area created an entirely unanticipated role for the building that brought it brief prosperity. The church became the official site of meetings of the university community. It continued to serve in this way until 1524, when a student riot of major proportions damaged the building and offended the monastic community that maintained it. From then on, student meetings were held elsewhere. This was good for the neighborhood but bad for a church that was suddenly deprived of its main source of income.

In the early seventeenth century, the roofer's guild made the building
their headquarters. By this time the façade was badly damaged and falling
away from the main structure. To preserve what was left of the building,
the first two bays of the nave and the south aisle were taken down, and
a new façade was created a third of the way up the old nave. The north

32

aisle bays, which
were still solid,
were preserved
and turned into
a sacristy. During
the Revolution,
the building
shared the fate of
Saint Severin and
became a barn. In
1889 the church,
which had been extensively restored, became the Paris home of the
Melkite Greek Catholic Community. The church follows Byzantine ritual
but recognizes the authority of the pope. Arabic is its liturgical language,
though services are conducted in other languages as well.

The modern entrance of the church is overshadowed by the northern
section of the old west wall with its broken corner, Gothic pilaster, and
walled-up arcades. (32) In keeping with the makeshift repairs to its façade,
the interior is a combination of Romanesque and Gothic styles. Rounded
arches divide the nave from its side aisles; small arched windows provide
little light. The ceiling of the nave is vaulted. The transept and apse are

Gothic in style, with pointed arches, bundled columns, ribbed ceilings, and multiple windows.

Near the top of Mont Saint Geneviève, the church of Saint Etienne du Mont has shared the typical ebb and flow of the area's history. Founded by Clovis in the sixth century, it served as a parish church for the families of lay workers employed by the nearby abbey of Saint Geneviève. Enlarged in the early thirteenth century, it was rededicated to honor Saint Stephen when his basilica was absorbed by Notre Dame. By the end of the fifteenth century, the parish had again outgrown its church, and an entirely new fabric was proposed. Construction began at the choir end and moved along briskly for a decade or so before everything began to fall apart. Either the money ran out or there were problems acquiring property. Probably both, since the ground plan of the church as it was finally built has a kink in the middle that puts the choir and nave off axis and causes the north wall to bend in toward the south. The rebuilding finally ended in the early seventeenth century, more than 130 years after renovations began.

Despite these difficulties, the magnificent church represents the high point of Parisian Gothic architecture. Two rows of large columns with simplified capitals and rounded arches between them enclose the nave. A catwalk of sorts partway up these columns creates a precarious balcony. Each arcade terminates at the transept in a single gigantic column that stretches from floor to ceiling. Around these stolid elements wreathes some of the most spectacular stonework of what is called the flamboyant Gothic style. The window tracery, especially in the choir, is among the most intricate and beautiful anywhere in Paris. Its ribbing, shaped

33

like twisted tears, is meant to represent flames, from which the style (flamboyant means "flaming") takes its name.

In the center of the crossing, where a Renaissance or Romanesque architect would put a dome, the builders of Saint Etienne created a uniquely Gothic ornament. A star-shaped pattern of intersecting ornamental ribs comes to a point that hangs from the ceiling like a frozen droplet of liquefied stone. Imitating the pattern of ceiling support, this ornament rests on empty air and suggests a miraculous suspension of gravity. (33)

A bolder and even more adventurous Gothic feature of the church is an ornamental stone bridge between the central pillars of the transept. (34) Twisting around each column, spiraling staircases lead up to the bridge in one turn and then take a second turn above to link with the balcony over the choir. The balustrades of the bridge and the staircases are constructed of stone panels bent to shape and cut through with elaborate geometrical tracery. The handling of the stone is so assured that these functional pieces appear as light and flexible as cut paper. Mastered by an extraordinary art, the stonework expresses the same defiance of material limitations that is evident in the hanging stone ornament above. It is a statement about the superiority of spirit over matter.

Above a shallow arc, which rests on two pillars that merge into the verticals of the choir, triangular spaces enclose winged victories borrowed from the figural repertoire of Roman sarcophagi. Solid supports on the railing of the bridge are marked with leaf patterns, which were also favorite ornaments on late classical tombs. The dating of the bridge—its proper name is a jubé or altar screen—is uncertain. It was probably completed in the early sixteenth century when stoneworkers trained in the most refined and demanding techniques of flamboyant Gothic were still at work.

The jubé distinguished and protected the holiest part of the church. Altar screens of this type were universal in Western Christian churches until the Council of Trent in the late sixteenth century ordered their removal. The bishops meeting in that historic council were doing everything in their power to revitalize Catholic worship, which was threatened by the Protestant Reformation. This meant that the

34

altar screen, which had made it difficult for the congregation to see the action of the priest during the service of the mass, should be taken down. But in a few instances, as in Saint Etienne du Mont, there were compelling reasons for allowing the screen to remain.

An altar screen typically carried an image of the crucified Christ at its center. The bronze Christ by Pierre Biard the elder, completed and put in place in 1600, upheld this tradition in a most extraordinary and powerful way. Marble angels in the broken cornices of the side doors are also by Biard.

35

Through its association with the monastery of Saint Geneviève, the church of Saint Etienne du Mont came to be the shrine of the patron saint of Paris. The French Revolution, which did so much damage to churches lower down the hillside, spared Saint Etienne. In 1803 a portion of the saint's remains that had escaped damage during the Revolution were brought to the church, and in the late nineteenth century they were enclosed in a free-standing gilded tabernacle of Gothic Revival style in one of the choir chapels.

Rare sixteenth-century stained glass from the apse also survived the Revolution. In the cloister of the monastery annexed to the church, panels from these windows are exhibited at eye level. Among the most remarkable is a representation of the dead Christ. He lies flat on what appears to be a blood-covered slab, though in reality he is lying in a

tomb-shaped grape press. From a
spout in its side a stream of wine
pours out that is collected in bar-
rels by popes and cardinals. (35) In
the surrounding scenes, peasants
harvest the vineyards and store
the wine. Like the art of the earlier
medieval period devoted to the host,
this panel personifies the wine of

36

the Eucharist. Created in the early part of the seventeenth century, the window carries on a medieval tradition of representation but uses the devices
of Renaissance perspective to give apparent depth to the image.

When the builders of Saint Etienne at last reached the western end of
the nave, the Gothic was in swift retreat. Its influence is still visible in the
façade, but the dominant elements are neoclassical and reflect traditions
that had been in full flower in Italy for more than a century. By the time
the Renaissance neoclassical movement reached Paris, it had matured far
beyond its starting point. The builders of Saint Etienne du Mont joined
the movement where they found it, in the High Baroque. Set on the front
of the Gothic church, the façade is extraordinarily dissonant and not
unlike the clash between nineteenth-century buildings and postmodern
additions. (36)

In the last third of the fourteenth century, the bishop of Beauvais
established a college in the shadow of the abbey of Saint Geneviève. The
college buildings have all been destroyed, and only the chapel remains at
9 Rue Jean de Beauvais. Now a Romanian Orthodox Church, it sits behind
a restored façade that is decorated by a modern mosaic in the Byzantine

style. The church, which is similar in plan to Sainte Chapelle, is a unique survival of the many similar college and university chapels that once filled the Left Bank and reinforced the fusion of religion and higher education that the region and the era took for granted.

Bullet-shaped in plan with no internal divisions, the chapel is lit by five tall arched windows in its nave and another five in its rounded apse. During mid-nineteenth-century restorations, traces of paint found on the walls suggested that the chapel was decorated either with an overall pattern like that in the lower chapel of Sainte Chapelle or with portraits of saints or scenes from the Bible. Sculptures representing members of the founding family were removed at that time and placed in the Louvre. The remaining decorations of the chapel are a restored altar screen and wooden stalls along both nave walls for the clerical faculty of the college.

Some extraordinarily celebrated men served on the faculty during its nearly five-hundred-year history. From 1528 to 1530 Saint Francis Xavier, one of the founders of the Jesuit Order, was lecturer in Aristotelian philosophy at the college. The voice of tradition and the moving spirit of the Catholic Counter-Reformation were a little out of place in a college that later gained a reputation for unorthodoxy. Peter Ramus, an anti-Aristotelian whose theology supported the Protestant Reformation, taught at the college during the sixteenth century. Throughout the seventeenth century, the college supported the Catholic reaction against the influence of Aristotle that is commonly called Jansenism. Alumni of the college, many of whom were prominent in the Jansenist movement, were equally illustrious. The historical Cyrano de Bergerac, a seventeenth-century Parisian wit, playwright, and duelist on whom Rostand based his fanciful character, attended the college.

The playwright Jean Racine sent his children to school there, and the neo-classical literary theoretician Nicolas Boileau also attended.

While the Left Bank was growing as a center of education during the Middle Ages, the right bank opposite Notre Dame became the focal point of the city's river trade. Located upstream from the bridges connecting the island with the north side of the Seine, it was both protected from raiders and also under the watchful eye of customs tax collectors. The port of Paris was hardly more than a sandy shoreline near the Place de Grève (now Place de l'Hôtel de Ville), but anchorages differentiated by product type stretched downriver. Boats from the upper reaches of the Seine and its major tributaries—the Marne, the Yonne, and the Oise—brought the diverse products of the French countryside to this area. Their cargoes included wines from Burgundy, wheat and other grains from Picardy, along with paving stones, salt, and coal. Fish caught in the river were kept alive in tanks until they were sold.

By the middle of the twelfth century, merchants were organized into a tax-paying corporation, and their leader or provost was the de facto mayor of the city. The merchants were no doubt pleased when King Philippe Auguste paved the streets of the business district, though he taxed them to do it. And since the protection offered by his new wall would also benefit commerce, the king assessed the merchants to pay for its construction as well. On land purchased from the bishop of Paris, Philippe Auguste organized a large public market and established a system of regulations for it. A market endured on the site into the twentieth century.

Next to the public market, the city's butchers put up not just stalls but slaughter houses as well. The abbatoirs attracted other businesses

37

that relied on animal by-products like skin and hair. Tanners, whose work required animal skins and a steady water supply, set up shop between the butchers and the Place de Grève. The merchants of the city had their warehouses, storefronts, and homes between the river and the roughly parallel Rue de la Tissanderie. A tissanderie is a weaving shed, and the weavers, whose industry was one of the most important in Paris before the mid-fourteenth century, were concentrated along it. Basketmakers—whose products were essential for transporting grain—gave their name to a street in the area, as did the glassmakers, tanners, potters, and others.

Lombard Street was home to the Italian merchant bankers who maintained their trade partnerships with transferable credits. The Italians also introduced Arabic numerals and double-entry bookkeeping. Roman numerals can be added and subtracted without much difficulty, but they are nearly impossible to divide or multiply. A more fundamental problem in Roman notation is posed by the absence of a concept or symbol for zero. Roman numerals also lack the orderly repetition of a decimal system. So-called Arabic numerals, which were actually invented in India, have both a zero and a decimal base.

Leonardo of Pisa, more commonly called Fibonacci, described their advantages in his *Liber Abaci* in the early thirteenth century. Though an Italian from Pisa, Fibonacci grew up in a trading town in North Africa, where he learned the mathematics of Arab merchants and theorists. Through his book and their own contacts with the Arab world, Italian merchants began using these numbers to great advantage. Curiously, though Arabic numerals were used for calculations, they were not commonly used in contracts or account books. A tiny penstroke squeezed to the left of an Arabic number can multiply a debt or the value of a contract by a factor of ten. Like the numbers spelled out in words on a modern check, Roman numerals were harder for the unscrupulous to alter.

As long as the Normans in Britain remained a hostile power, there was little trade between Paris and the mouth of the Seine. But in the mid-fourteenth century, when hostilities temporarily abated, trade on the lower Seine opened up. Wine, grain, and firewood from this region were added to supplies from the interior. Apples and cider, still important regional products from Normandy and Brittany, came with them, along with fish from the English Channel and Atlantic coast. Cod, mackerel, and especially herring, which were salted and preserved, added variety to the Parisian diet.

As the commercial center of the city, Place de Grève became the home of local government. A town hall was built there in the fourteenth century, and the gallows and stocks stood outside it. (37) Destroyed by the Communards in the nineteenth century, the medieval town hall was replaced by the modern Hôtel de Ville, and the Place de Grève changed its name. The new building, designed by Théodore Ballu and Edouard Deperthes, sits in the place occupied by the earlier structure, but it is much larger. (38) Built between 1874 and 1878, its structure reflects the ideals of Second Empire architecture. Central pavilions on each side frame monumental

38

39

doorways. Pavilions at each corner anchor two- or three-story corridors lit by arched windows in the lower stories and smaller windows in the dormers that jut out from the steep roofs.

Two buildings typical of the houses that Paris merchants lived in during the late Middle Ages stand nearby, at the corner of the Rue François Miron and the Rue de la Cloche Percé. (39) Dating from the sixteenth century, the half-timbered houses were built on very narrow lots. Though they are of unequal height, they both include five stories of living space. The timbers that show on the façade are not ornaments but building supports. The wall is formed by filling the spaces between them with plaster, often supported by a matrix of interwoven branches. Their ground floors held shops, while the upper stories may have been home to an extended family or a multitude of renters. High, volatile, and crowded close together, the houses caught fire easily and were hard to escape.

At 1 Rue du Figuier, just a few streets away, stands one of only three private Gothic palaces that remain in Paris. The Hôtel de Sens was built in the late fifteenth century to house the archbishops whose see included the bishopric of Paris. Though much restored in the twentieth century, the castlelike building still has some of its original features. The arched doorway in its elongated surround is one of these, as are the two turrets at each end of the façade and the base of a square tower that was the archbishop's retreat in case of attack. The beautiful garden of the palace was also restored in the twentieth century. It is sunk below street level and laid out in a series of geometrical beds surrounded by clipped box hedges.

Throughout its long life, the church of Saint Gervais and Saint Protais (near the back of the Hôtel de Ville) was the parish church for most of the merchant community. Almost nothing is known about the twin dedicatees. According to legend, the pair, who may have been sons of a Christian martyr, were tortured and beheaded near Milan sometime during the reign of Nero or Diocletian. Their relics were moved to the cathedral of Milan in the fourth century, and until they were replaced by Saint Ambrose they were the dedicatees of that very important church. The prominence of the cathedral in what was for a time the main city of the Roman empire guaranteed that other churches would share the dedication.

Already in existence in the sixth century, Saint Gervais is the oldest church on the right bank. It was repaired after the Viking raids, and it may have been rebuilt in the thirteenth century. The present church is, like Saint Etienne du Mont, a very late example of Gothic building techniques and ornament. New construction began sometime in the 1490s, and the interior was completed in the first decade of the seventeenth century. Unlike the interior of Saint Etienne, where Renaissance details creep in like the early mammals that darted between the legs of dinosaurs, the Gothic in Saint Gervais remains in full command. The style, so long practiced and so thoroughly explored, is employed here with a unity of effect among different architectural members that is hard to match in any other genuine Gothic church. Its long vistas and soaring arcades work together to create a completely harmonious expression and powerful sensation of lightness and height.

40

The most complete, jewel-like part of the church is the Chapel of the Virgin set beyond the ambulatory in an extension of the apse. The chapel is on the main axis of the church but is divided from it like a tabernacle or holy of holies. (40) Nearest the church, the intersecting ribs of the chapel ceiling follow the same pattern as those in the rest of the ambulatory chapels, but in the innermost part they converge in the center of the ceiling and drop down, as in the transept of Saint Etienne. Here they form multiple extensions that hold a crown. The statue of the Virgin be- neath the crown is a nineteenth-century recreation of a medieval sculpture. The chapel windows with panels illus- trating the life of the Virgin retain much of their sixteenth-century glass.

The western end of the nave is dominated by an enormous organ with multiple arrays of pipes. Set in a balcony over the western doors, with its smallest range carried on the back of a sculpted angel, the organ is poised to flood the building with sound. In 1653 Louis Couperin, a keyboard player and composer from a small town a little distance from Paris, was appointed organist of the church. While he occupied this position and the nearby house that went with the job, he also played in the royal orchestra. Louis' compositional style influenced other Baroque composers. In a genealogical sense, his influence was even greater. A dynasty of Couperin composers succeeded him that reached its highpoint in Louis' grandson, François.

Like his grandfather and father before him, and his nephew, Nicolas, after him, François was appointed organist at Saint Gervais. In 1717 he became organist and composer to the royal court. The year before, he had published *L'art de toucher le clavecin,* a book on harpsichord fingering that Bach found helpful. François published four volumes of harpsichord music that continued to influence composers like Ravel and Richard Strauss long after the Baroque.

The façade of the church, like that of Saint Etienne, is an example of neoclassicism stuck on the front of a purely Gothic building. To fully experience the contrast, it is only necessary to walk from the eastern end of the church, with its rays of flying buttresses anchored between steeply roofed chapels, to the front, where in the blink of an eye times have changed. Stylistically, the façade makes no concessions to the church behind it. The designer's strategy is to create a screen that is sufficiently broad and high to transpose the Gothic triangle into a Renaissance rect-angle. The approach is to build a massive two-story wall divided into three vertical parts by four pairs of monumental columns, each topped by a broken entablature. Between the column pairs of the second level, where the Gothic windows of Saint Etienne peek out, the builder has created rounded openings that enclose statues or windows.

In the center of the first level, a portico juts out from the main façade. Topping the center bay of the second story is a similar portico with a broken entablature and a rounded cornice. The architectural orders of the three stories are different. The ground level is Doric, the middle

41

level Ionic, and the top Corinthian. This superposition of the Greek orders is found on Roman buildings like the Theater of Marcellus and the Colosseum. In overall effect, though, the façade of Saint Gervais is more like a Roman triumphal arch, with its niches and applied columns, than a Roman theater or amphitheater. (41)

Just a few blocks north of Saint Gervais and Saint Protais, the medieval cloister attached to the Protestant Temple des Billettes at 24 Rue des Archives recalls not only one of the most typical monastic structures of the Middle Ages but also one of the darkest faces of medieval Christianity. In 1182 Philippe Auguste expelled the Jews from Paris, probably at the merchants' instigation, though he might well have come up with that idea on his own. The Capetian kings, like the Spanish leaders of the Renaissance, defined themselves as defenders of orthodoxy. There were many crusaders among them, including King Philippe himself, and the idea of purifying the Catholic community by driving out the unconverted must have appealed to both his dynastic and political ideals. The merchants' motives were probably expressed in the same pious terms, though freedom from competition by the skilled and well-organized Jewish businessmen must have been primary.

Despite Philippe Auguste's decree, some Jews remained in the city, and in 1290 a Parisian Jew named Jonathas was convicted of sacrilege by the bishop's court. Under torture, he confessed to stealing a consecrated Communion wafer, stabbing it with a knife, and throwing it into boiling water. He also confessed that the wafer bled when it was pierced and that it floated on the surface. Prosecutions like that of Jonathas were common throughout Europe from the thirteenth century on. It was an era in which miracles associated with the sanctified host were widely and enthusiastically reported, and when anti-Semitism, inspired by the same religious fervor that idolized the host, reached new heights. Jews were accused of abducting Christian children and sacrificing them during Passover. Campaigns to convert the Jews and movements to purge Christian cities of those who refused conversion were widespread.

In the aftermath of Jonathas's trial, a Paris religious order was proposed whose members would devote their lives to penitence and prayer that they hoped would expiate the terrible crime attributed to the unfortunate Jew. In 1299 Pope Boniface VIII approved the foundation of a convent at the site of the sacrilege. Members of the order were known as *billettes*— a heraldic emblem that their distinctive habit called to mind. The monastery continued in existence, though with different orders in residence, until suppression and expropriation by the Revolution. In 1808 the city bought what remained of

42

43

the property. The eighteenth-century church was consecrated for Protestant worship in 1812, and the tiny, forlorn cloister, with its miserable history, now hosts occasional art exhibits.

While Saint Germain des Prés and other monastic foundations were disbanded by the Revolution and their properties sold off, the buildings of Saint Martin des Champs on the north edge of the city were preserved. When the monks were expelled during the Revolution, the monastery buildings were turned into a school. In 1798 the school became the Conservatory of Arts and Occupations (Arts et Métiers), a high-level technical college that provided job training for students from Paris and across the country. The conservatory, now dedicated to adult education, continues in operation today as a national institution. Called the Museum of Arts and Occupations, the former monastery houses objects that illustrate the history of French technology from the age of steam to the age of the Internet. The monastery church can be entered through the museum.

From the outside, the rounded chapels at the church's eastern end plainly declare its Romanesque style. (42) Gothic apses with their peaked chapel roofs are like paper crowns set at the feet of soaring buttresses. The apse of a Romanesque church, with its cluster of cylindrical chapels, looks more like a head of garlic. Fortunately, the Romanesque apse with

its characteristic arched windows cut into the thickness of the wall has
been largely untouched by renovations. In the painted Gothic nave, an
iron scaffold supports a collection of automobiles, while early canvas-
winged airplanes hang from the vaulted ceiling. (43) A model of the Statue
of Liberty stands on a wooden base decorated with the prows of ships.

The cloister of the monastery is also preserved inside the museum,
but it cannot be visited. It is possible to visit the dining hall, or refectory,
which has been converted to a library for the students of the conservatory
(entrance is at 292 Rue Saint Martin). The refectory is a steep, narrow
hall with a row of pillars down its middle, lit
by multiple peaked windows. (44) A pulpit from
which a lector read during meals is halfway
down one side.

While the Romanesque church in the monastery complex served members of the order,
the church of Saint Nicolas des Champs
served the substantial lay community employed
by the wealthy and populous foundation.
Saint Nicolas became a parish church in the
thirteenth century. Though it lay within the
circuit of the walls of Philippe Auguste, the
slow pace of urbanization in this area probably
left the church in a semirural neighborhood
until at least the fifteenth century. Rebuilt in
the sixteenth century to meet the needs of a
parish population that was at last expanding,

44

45

Saint Nicolas is vast and high, its lofty nave flanked by two side aisles and a chain of chapels. The apse is ringed by a double ambulatory and a circuit of chapels. A major chapel behind the altar protrudes from its eastern end.

Elaborate cross vaulting marks the ceiling of the apse and its surrounds, but the rest of the vaults are relatively simple. It is in the nave that the change of fashion from the Romanesque to the Gothic is most apparent. (45) Groined arches spring from Gothic piers, while both arches and columns in the choir are round. The contrast already existed in the seventeenth century, but it was sharpened in the eighteenth century. The choir columns were fluted, Doric capitals were put in place of the originals, an archivolt was traced on the face of each arch, and a fictional keystone was set in its summit.

As a parish church, Saint Nicolas survived the first round of revolutionary expropriations that transformed the abbey of Saint Martin in 1790, but it was not immune to the wholesale shutdown of 1793. While sulfurous chemicals or fodder packed less fortunate institutions, Saint Nicolas was redirected to the thoroughly secularized celebration of marriage in the rational republic. Dedicated to the Roman god Hymen and the personified Fidelity, the old church continued to perform one of its traditional social tasks. It was returned to Catholic worship in 1802.

The church of Saint Eustache was built sometime in the late twelfth century on the site of a little chapel dedicated to Saint Agnes. Spurred by completion of the wall of Philippe Auguste and accelerated by the development of the nearby public market, population in the area surged. The chapel became a parish church and was enlarged in the mid-fifteenth century. (46) In 1532 the provost of merchants laid the cornerstone of a massive new structure. Building began on both the western end and the choir and converged on the old church, which was entirely engulfed by the new building.

The project was so ambitious that funds repeatedly failed and work stopped for years at a time. Church lands, including a nearby cemetery, had to be sold to finance the building. Construction was still going on in the middle of the sixteenth century—not all of it top quality, evidently. Work on two chapels at the western end of the church weakened the foundations. The façade and the first bay of the nave had to be taken down, and funds to replace them were unavailable until the middle of the eighteenth century. At that time a neoclassical façade was placed on the front of what is otherwise a resoundingly Gothic fabric. Closed by the Revolution, Saint Eustache was transformed into a Temple of Agriculture. Fires and structural problems complicated the process of restoration, which continued into the twentieth century.

Unlike Saint Germain des Prés, which is named for a bishop of Paris, the Gothic church of Saint Germain l'Auxerrois, near the Lou-vre, is named for the earlier Gallic bishop who met Saint Geneviève

46

47

and encouraged her vocation. Founded in the sixth century, it was the first church in Paris to be dedicated to this popular saint. An important center during the Merovingian era, it was sacked by the Vikings and rebuilt and fortified in the eleventh century. Archaeological evidence suggests that the base of the small tower at the junction of the nave and the south transept dates from the twelfth century. The choir piers date from the thirteenth, and the rest of the church from the fifteenth and sixteenth centuries. (47)

Its location near the royal palace made the church a Parisian landmark, and during the eighteenth century when revulsion against Gothic taste was at its height, the canons of the church carried out a thorough modernization. The front doors were widened and their sculpture destroyed; milky glass replaced medieval stained glass windows. Fortunately, the tracery that supported the Gothic glass was left intact, and the nave and rose windows of Saint Germain l'Auxerrois are among the finest surviving examples of flamboyant window structure in Paris. In the eighteenth century the choir columns were fluted and their capitals replaced; plaster casings squared off the pier profiles. The Revolution hit just as hard. The church became a barn, then a printshop, before serving briefly as the Temple of Recognition. Restored in the nineteenth century, the church is still a prominent Parisian landmark.

The Gothic porch on its western end is unique in Paris. Three peaked arches are separated by pillars encrusted with small sculptures in richly decorated niches. With the exception of two sixteenth-century statues, the works are all nineteenth-century replacements. The surviving figure of Saint Francis of Assisi has been badly damaged. But the figure of Saint Mary of Egypt, though weathered, is still nearly intact.

For seventeen years, Mary was a prostitute in Alexandria. On a ship crowded with pilgrims, whom she recognized as likely patrons, she traveled to Jerusalem. There, she attempted to enter a Christian church at a time when relics of the Cross were exposed. Whenever she tried to walk through the doors of the church, a strange force repelled her. Perplexed and alone outside the church, she suddenly understood that her sin prevented her from entering. She repented, and when she prayed to the Virgin, the barrier was immediately removed. After her remarkable conversion, Mary accepted baptism in the River Jordan, then wandered alone in the desert for forty-seven years. Nearing the end of her days, she received Communion and told her story to a priest named Zosima, who buried her and published her life.

This remarkable story was written and widely circulated before the end of the fifth century. Mary's desert wanderings represent the earliest kind of monastic vocation—a life of prayer and repentance spent alone in a harsh and inhospitable landscape. The *Life of Saint Anthony* was the best known and most influential text about a Christian hermit; Saint Mary of Egypt is one of very few women saints of this era. The communal monasticism first regularized by Saint Benedict was both inspired by the life of hermits but also structured to give individuals guidance in combating the temptations of the contemplative life.

The statue of Saint Mary of Egypt on the façade of Saint Germain l'Auxerrois shows the saint dressed in an animal skin and carrying three loaves of bread, the only food she took with her into the desert. The sculpture's placement on the porch was intended to remind the faithful of the life of sin that prevented Mary from entering. The chapel dedicated to the Virgin Mary at the far end of the church, on axis with the nave, represents the overcoming of sin through the figure who converted Saint Mary of Egypt.

Chapter Four

FOUNDATIONS OF THE LOUVRE

For generations the powerful dukes of Normandy had acknowledged their subordination and loyalty—their fealty—to the French sovereign. In the beginning of the fourteenth century, however, a succession of English monarchs became inflamed with a desire to incorporate Normandy into English Crown territory. From about 1336 to the midpoint of the fifteenth century, England and France were caught up in the Hundred Years War. This multigenerational campaign was carried on in fits and starts. Periods of high activity, open battle, bloodshed, and brutal pillaging alternated with periods of relative calm. From time to time the English managed to draw Spain and Flanders into the fight in hopes of forcing France to fight a two-front war.

The chain of events that first awakened the long dormant English interest in Normandy began during the short reign of Charles IV, the last Capetian king. Not long after Charles was crowned in 1322, he seized the possessions of the duke of Normandy, who was at that time England's ineffective King Edward II. Edward, who had married Charles's sister Isabella, made the mistake of thinking that his wife would be an advocate for his hereditary rights in France. Instead, the French king and his sister contrived the overthrow of Edward and the appointment of Isabella and her lover, Roger Mortimer, as co-regents of England.

In 1328 Charles died without leaving a male heir. Since neither of Charles's daughters could claim the French throne, the irrepressible Isabella claimed the crown for her son Edward, Charles's nephew. The French invoked the disused Salic law, which ruled out inheritance through the female line, to rebuff her claim. Charles's cousin became king as Philippe VI and inaugurated a new branch of the Capetian dynasty, the House of Valois. Meanwhile, in 1330 eighteen-year-old Edward overthrew the regency of Mortimer and his mother and assumed the throne of England as Edward III. Relations between the two monarchs, Edward and Philippe, were friendly in the first years of their reigns but soon soured.

The French prepared an invasion fleet to cross the Channel; the English destroyed it. The English provoked border wars in Flanders and in the coastal provinces, but during eight years of inconclusive battle they spent a great deal of money with little result. Parliament demanded and received increased control over the national purse. Despite this belt-tightening, King Edward was able to lead a force of fifteen thousand English knights, foot soldiers, and bowmen into Normandy in 1345. The English troops foraged, looted, and burned. King Philippe quickly organized an army and marched against the invaders, who were drawn up at a small town with the memorable name of Crécy.

A force of about twelve thousand English soldiers sat along the brow of a hill overlooking the crossroads where Philippe's forces, estimated at about thirty thousand, were grouping. It was late in a day of heavy rains. The sky had cleared, but the sun was already setting behind the English line. Philippe ordered skirmishers forward to feel out the enemy, but through inexperience, overconfidence, or failed communication a general surge of the French troops began.

A company of crossbowmen were in the vanguard of the French attack. At their approach, the English soldiers came to their feet. The French chronicler Froissart recorded the result. "When the crossbowmen were assembled together and began to approach, they made a great cry to intimidate the Englishmen, who stood still and stirred not: then the crossbowmen made another great cry, and stepped forward a little, and the Englishmen removed not one foot: thirdly, again they lept and cried, and went forth till they came within shot; then they shot fiercely with their crossbows. Then the English archers stepped forth one pace and let fly their arrows all at once, so thick, that it seemed snow. When the cross-bowmen felt the arrows piercing through heads, arms and breasts, many of them cast down their crossbows and cut their strings and retreated. When the French king saw them fly away, he said: 'Kill these rascals, for they will cripple our attack.'

"Then you should have seen the knights on horseback dash in among them and kill a great number of them: and ever still the Englishmen shot wherever they saw the thickest crowds; the sharp arrows pierced the knights and their horses, and many fell, horse and men, among the crossbowmen. And when they were down, they could not get up again, the crowd was so thick that one fell upon another. Also among the Englishmen there were certain soldiers that went on foot with great knives, and they went in among the fallen knights, and murdered many as they lay on the ground, both earls, barons, knights, and squires."

Charging uphill through mud with the sun in their eyes and fallen crossbowmen underfoot, the French knights were at an extreme dis-advantage. For the most part, their armor protected them against the arrows of the English, and few knights were killed outright. But many were wounded, and more were immobilized when their horses fell dead or disabled beneath them; the English foragers with their great knives finished them off. Until this battle, the armed and mounted knight, universally a member of the feudal upper class, had seemed to be the ultimate, unstoppable weapon. While he was of little value in siege warfare, it was accepted that on the open battlefield neither infantry nor archers could stand against him. With a good deal of luck on their side and none on the side of the French, the English bowmen challenged this axiom of medieval warfare.

The broader implications of the battle were not lost on contemporaries. No longer immune to attack from social inferiors, the earls, barons, knights, and squires on both sides were suddenly forced to face disquieting possibilities. These specters became terribly real in the mid-1350s when peasants in war-torn northeastern France and the poor of regional towns and cities, including Paris, combined in a loosely knit revolutionary movement known as the Jacquerie. Robbing, pillaging, and burning as they had seen soldiers do over the preceding decades, the peasants attacked manors and castles, where they tortured and murdered entire families. Terror and outrage among the nobility were so extreme that nobles of France and England united to exterminate the rebels. They violated a truce and seized the rebel leader, whom they tortured and killed. At the battle of Mello on June 10, 1358, mounted knights proved once again that they could ride down and massacre men on foot, especially if the latter were disorganized, poorly armed, and leaderless.

The peasant uprising reflected the turmoil of warfare, but other terrifying forces were stalking the land. Climate historians have identified shifts in the Arctic ice pack around 1300 and related changes in rainfall that destroyed crops and produced repeated famines in France. In addition to these troubles, in 1348 an outbreak of plague swept through western Europe, reducing the population by as much as a third, according to many estimates. No one in the fourteenth century knew how the pandemic had come upon them, and modern biologists are still in disagreement about the exact nature of the disease that swept the continent. Though 1348 was the worst plague year in history, epidemic diseases indistinguishable to medieval diagnosticians flared up again every decade or so for the next two hundred years.

In the medieval period, when faith was nearly universal and theology, not science, was the supreme source of explanation, plague and famine were inevitably seen as judgments from God directed against the established social order. The link between the social order and divine providence which in good times supported traditional hierarchies became a source of chaos and suspicion. The peasants of the Jacquerie must have felt that these terrible scourges were God's incitement to social change. The nobles who fought so viciously against their inferiors may have had doubts themselves that God really was on their side.

After the victory at Crécy, the English army attacked the coastal town of Calais, and in 1356, during the battle of Poitiers, they captured the French king, Jean II. As the peasants' revolt raged through town and country, the English king marched on Reims and headed toward Paris. The campaign was not a success, and in 1360 Edward III signed the Treaty of Calais, which ratified British conquests in Normandy and restored his territories in Aquitaine but did little else. Jean II was released from captivity and died four years later. Charles V (the Wise), who succeeded him, enjoyed a five-year lull in the war with the English, which he put to good use consolidating his control over the barons of his kingdom and fortifying his capital city.

Despite rebellion, endemic warfare, deaths from starvation, and the ravages of plague, Paris had somehow managed to outgrow the walls of Philippe Auguste. The old fortifications were still adequate on the Left Bank, but on the right side the city sprawled well beyond these limits. Growth along the major highways leading out from the city gates and in the shadow of the great extramural institutions—the Louvre, Saint Martin des Champs, and the temple of the Knights Templar among them—had merged into a continuous fabric nearly as dense as that inside the old walls. In the first years of Charles's reign, he began to build a wider defensive circuit on the right bank and to update the old walls on the left. (Map 2)

The new defenses were not just walls but concentric bands of contoured earthworks, one portion of which was faced with stone and punctuated by gates and towers. Structurally, the works began by excavating a moat nearly a hundred feet wide with sloping banks on both sides. The dirt from the moat was piled up on the city side in a long mound. A stone wall set into this mound stabilized it and protected its outer edge. The top of the mound behind the wall was flattened to serve as a roadway along which defenders rushed to secure areas under attack and as a platform from which they could fire on the enemy. Beyond the moat, which was flooded with river water, a second dry ditch with steeply sloping sides kept siege engines at a safe distance. A road at the outer edge of this second moat was continually patrolled in peacetime. Virtually none of Charles V's wall survives, though its trace can been seen in the so-called *grands boulevards* that circle the city

center, following the wall's course. These include boulevards Bonne Nou-
velle, Saint Martin, Filles du Calvaire, and Beaumarchais, among others.

The new defensive circuit was completed in 1420, forty years after
the death of Charles V. The Hundred Years War that had spurred its
creation was still going strong. After a lull in the late fourteenth century,
the English campaign resumed in earnest under Henry V. Shakespeare
featured this charismatic ruler in a series of plays that gradually modu-
lated from high comedy in *Henry IV, Part I* to nationalist hymn in *Henry V.*
Henry's campaign in France was quickly crowned by victory in the battle
of Agincourt in 1415. Though the French king was not captured, the leading royalist nobles of France were imprisoned by the English, who followed
their conquest with a sweep through the Seine valley.

Resistance to the English was hamstrung by outright civil war in
France, because the duke of Burgundy and his followers opposed the
Valois kings. The Burgundians recognized Henry V as king of France and
set up a rival capital in Tours on the Loire River. The two oldest sons
of Charles VI died mysteriously while under the nominal protection of
the duke. In 1418 the Burgundian faction gained control of Paris, and
Charles VI was forced to flee. The walls built to keep out the English
proved to be pointless. The Burgundians simply opened the gates and
invited their English allies inside.

For decades afterward, Paris was a hotbed of virulent and energetic
opposition to the beleaguered French king. Severely pressured by enemies
on every side and broken by exile and the murder of his sons, Charles
VI, who had a history of mental illness, become increasingly unstable. In
1420 he agreed to the marriage of his daughter to Henry V and the Eng-

lish king's succession to the French throne after his own death. This act could easily have spelled the end of an independent France. But a year later Henry V died unexpectedly. Though Charles survived him by only two months, the English monarch's death effectively nullified the treaty. The English regent tried, and failed, to place Henry's ten-month-old son on the French throne. The threat of an English dynasty in France, though still real, had receded.

After the death of Charles VI, his remaining son, the dauphin or crown prince, led the opposition to English dominance. Enemy occupation of Reims, the traditional site of royal coronation, deprived him of claiming his rightful title. In 1428 a young girl from a small French town tradition-ally loyal to the monarchy but located in Burgundian territory began to have visions. Two or three times a week she heard the voices of shadowy figures whom she identified as the warrior Saint Michael, Saint Catherine, and others. The voices urged her to drive out the English and secure the coronation of the dauphin.

She reported these events to her parents, who forbade her to leave the village. But soon the visions became so insistent and so clear that she ran away to find the dauphin's regional commander. He ignored her at first but eventually agreed to send her to the crown prince. Receiving her for the first time, the dauphin blended in among his courtiers, but Joan recognized him anyway. In a private two-hour conversation, she told him a secret that the voices had confided to her and convinced him that she was someone to be taken seriously.

The Middle Ages appear to us to be a credulous age, and we tend to assume that Joan's claims of divine sponsorship were accepted at face value, at least by those whose interests she served. But that was not the case. Joan's voices caused deep concern in the dauphin's court, and she was sent to Poitiers to be examined by theologians. They sent letters to local authorities asking for information about her family and her reputation in the village. They talked with her about the visions she saw and assessed her character. After this formal examination, they prepared a report that was carefully studied at court. In the end, the theologians of Poitiers concluded that Joan was the genuine article.

The dauphin gave Joan (who was often called La Pucelle, the Maid) a military command and assigned her a personal suite appropriate to an officer and a gentleman. Like any officer, she was served by a chaplain, a squire, and two pages. Within a few months she and her family were ennobled. Joan dressed like a man and wore a man's armor. As promised, she spearheaded the liberation of Orléans from the English and Burgundians. She planted the first siege ladder against the citadel there and took an arrow to the shoulder during the successful assault. She also led the attack against the occupiers of Reims, liberating that city and making it possible for the dauphin to be crowned by the archbishop as King Charles VII of France.

In other campaigns she was less successful. In a moment of great irony, she led the royal army in its assault against one of the gates in the new circuit walls around Paris, but the walls defeated her, as they were designed to do. While commanding a party attempting to fill in the moat, Joan was shot through the thigh by a crossbow bolt. She refused to leave the battlefield and had to be carried off by the duke of Alençon. Some months later at the siege of Compiègne Joan became isolated among Burgundian troops and fell into enemy hands.

Here begins one of the most notorious and sickening events of an era studded with brutality. The English bought the prisoner from their

Burgundian allies, but rather than kill her outright they decided to put her on trial and then kill her. The trial would not only legitimate the execution, it would serve an important public relations goal as well. A successful ecclesiastical trial would weaken or destroy Joan's reputation as a visionary patriot and diminish French resistance to English conquest.

Joan was moved to a prison in Rouen, the center of the English occupation, and put on trial before an ecclesiastical court headed by Pierre Cauchon, bishop of Beauvais, and staffed by local clerics and faculty from the University of Paris. Important members of the university hierarchy, rather than resist the Burgundian and English occupiers, had taken their side. From the very first, the chancellor of the university was among Joan's most prejudiced and bitter attackers. The trial transcripts also reveal the prejudice of Cauchon. From the start, he assumed her guilt and saw his duty "as the ordinary judge to institute inquiries and proceedings against this woman who, suspected of heresy, had committed so many misdemeanors against the Catholic faith."

Prisoners of ecclesiastical courts were typically kept under close guard in monasteries, but Joan remained in secular hands. She was guarded by male warders and was at first chained head and foot in an iron cage. Canon lawyers normally spoke for the accused, but Joan was denied representation. She answered the theologians' hostile questions as best she could and repeatedly urged the judges to obtain and read the documents prepared in Poitiers for Charles, which they refused to do. By the end of May the court established to its satisfaction that Joan had been misled by Satanic messengers and was guilty of multiple counts of heresy. The fact that she had worn men's clothing was especially significant and galling to them.

Repeatedly bullied by the court, threatened with brutal torture, and faced with death at the stake, Joan formally accepted the court's judgment and abjured her claims of divine counsel and assistance. Within a few days, however, she was again found to be wearing men's clothes—either voluntarily or because they were forced on her by her English jailers—and she was condemned to death for apostasy. She was burned alive in the Old Market of Rouen on May 30, 1431.

The English and their allied theologians disseminated the minutes of the trial as widely as possible. Not everyone was convinced. Nearly two decades after her death, Charles VII, who had not attempted to ransom or rescue Joan, made an effort to rehabilitate her reputation. English theologians were able to block the review of her condemnation by the papal court, but in 1456 an ecclesiastical hearing sanctioned by Pope Callixtus III reopened inquiries. Joan's mother was still alive, and many others who had known her as a child and a soldier testified to her courage and piety. A quarter century after her tragic death, Joan of Arc was cleared of all the charges brought against her. Responsibility for the vicious misconduct of the earlier trial was assigned to Bishop Cauchon, who was already dead. Since Charles had recaptured Paris by this time, the theology faculty of the university were once again loyal Frenchmen. Those who had condemned Joan were exonerated on the grounds that Cauchon had deceived them. In 1920 Pope Benedict XV declared Joan of Arc a saint.

The threat of English invasion did not end at mid-century. English monarchs held on to the illusion that they were French kings until the Treaty of Amiens in 1802 formally deprived them of the title. By the end of the fifteenth century, though, Paris began to enjoy the benefits of a

de facto peace with England and to recover from the devastation created by invading armies, civil unrest, famine, and plagues. Peace and a
gradually increasing population made farming and industry viable again.
The commerce that nourished Paris and the population that powered it
recovered at the same time. By the end of the sixteenth century, the city
was flourishing. It was the largest urban center not only in France, still a
loosely organized political entity, but on the entire continent of Europe.

As the English threat to the north diminished, French kings began a
series of military campaigns into the far less organized Italian peninsula to
the south. Once united in a single empire, Italy had long been fractured, its
internal political boundaries as complex as the cracked glaze on a Roman
pot. Four major conglomerates—one headed by the papacy and the others
headed by the cities of Milan, Florence, and Venice—vied for supreme
power in the northern end of the peninsula. During their struggles to gain
an edge against one another, the powers built and broke alliances among
themselves. But in the mid-1490s the Milanese made a disastrous miscal-
culation: they asked France for help. The French quickly realized that they
were far more powerful than any alliance of Italian states, and they began a
series of invasions and occupations that stretched over forty years.

The French won and lost territory and carried off the usual spoils of
war, but the lasting victory of the peninsular campaigns was the conquest
of French taste by Italian architects and artists. Italian influence began to
grow as commanders experienced the amenity of Renaissance towns, the
brilliance of Italian painting, and the majesty of neoclassical architecture.
The ascension to the French throne of King François I in 1515 brought a
sharp spike in the power of Italian art over the French imagination. In the
second year of his reign, François invited the aging Leonardo da Vinci to

become a member of his court. Leonardo lived the few remaining years of his life in a small chateau near the royal palace in Amboise, a small town in the Loire valley. According to a romantic but fanciful legend, Leonardo died in the arms of the young monarch.

By the time the elderly painter and polymath reached France, he was well beyond his most creative years. Though he painted little for the French court, he did bring with him works from his earlier life. The most significant of these was the *Mona Lisa,* which became one of the king's most prized possessions. After Leonardo's death, his friend and fellow painter Francesco Melzi took his papers, which were only later bound into the famous notebooks, back to Italy. The master's writings included pages on painting that would have their greatest influence in France, beginning in the seventeenth century.

Even though the new walls of Paris had failed to keep out the English, they had a very important effect on one of the city's key defensive structures, the Louvre. The extended circuit of Charles V's walls had marooned the old fortress inside the city limits. Soon after their construction was under way, the king began to transform the forbidding castle into a royal residence. He enlarged ground floor rooms, created audience rooms, and fitted out a royal apartment, which included a bedroom, reception and dining rooms, and an indoor bath. The palace floors were covered with colored tiles and the occasional carpet; walls were hung with tapestries or decorated with cloth of gold or tooled leather. Charles heard mass in a private chapel decorated with statues of prophets.

A tower in the old fortress was devoted to Charles's library. Under the monarch's supervision, its three rooms, one above the other, were paneled with cedar to protect the books from insects. At a time when a

university professor with twenty or thirty books of his own was unusually well supplied, the 1373 inventory of Charles V's books included
more than nine hundred volumes, on subjects ranging from astrology and
astronomy, through the Latin classics, to works of devotion and theology.
He also owned popular books like the *Romance of the Rose,* an allegorical
medieval love adventure. Though it was written in French, the text had
tremendous appeal not just in France but throughout Europe.

Though Charles's renovations made the fortress more comfortable,
he did not live there full time. In 1528 François became the first king to
announce his intention to spend the majority of each year in Paris and
to make the Louvre his royal palace. To convert the older fortress and its
grounds into a suitable residence, the king proposed a major overhaul.
The round keep was razed immediately. At public expense, the sandy
banks of the river were shored up with stonework, and a broad roadway
was built along the river's edge. The old gateway from the riverside into
the fortress was closed, and the main entrance was shifted around the
corner to the east side of the palace. From then on the royal residence
would face the developing city upriver on the right bank. (Map 4)

In 1546, thirty years after ascending the throne, François I appointed an architect to design an entirely new palace. Pierre Lescot was
born in Paris in 1510. Unlike other French architects of the period, he
was not from a family of masons. His father was a judge in a commercial
court in Paris and, as prefect of Parisian merchants, the city's de facto
mayor. Lescot's turn toward architecture and the source of his knowledge is something of a mystery. His work is strongly influenced by Italian
architecture of the High Renaissance, but no evidence of where in Italy he
might have traveled or studied has come to light—and indeed there is no

direct evidence that he ever set foot there. He is known to have held other important commissions, but his work on them has not survived.

However he learned his art, Lescot was a secure master of Renaissance design whose work on the Louvre contained novelties that Italian architects might have envied. These innovations not only determined the basic form that the palace would take over its long history but they also set a pattern for French architecture that would be imitated for centuries throughout the city and ultimately the world. François I died shortly after ground was broken for the new palace, but his successor, Henri II, continued to employ Lescot to work on the Louvre until the architect's death in 1578.

As originally planned, the Renaissance Louvre would have followed the footprint of the medieval fortress, with work beginning on the west wing. The Italian model that underlay the royal residence and determined its essential shape was the extension to the Vatican palace that Donato Bramante laid out in the early sixteenth century. To give his long, low building liveliness and dignity, Bramante relied on Roman precedent. Roman architects had created buildings of the sort that Bramante needed, but none survived in sixteenth-century Rome. What did survive, however, were rounded buildings—the Theater of Marcellus and the Colosseum— where the sort of vertical wall Bramante was seeking had been bent around circular or elliptical structures. All he had to do was flatten out these curved wall designs and imitate them on his façades.

Following these models, Bramante created variety by dividing his façades into distinct horizontal zones. Each zone had a different form of ornament and a unique horizontal rhythm. In obedience to this tradition, Lescot created a façade with contrasting levels. The original plan called for only two, but at the insistence of Henri II a third story was added. At ground level, Lescot set rectangular windows deep within arched openings framed by Corinthian pilasters that rested on low pedestals and supported an entablature. In his second story Lescot retained the pilasters of the first story but placed windows with alternating peaked and arched tops between them. He also mimicked the pedestals that ran across the bottom of the lower story and the decorated band at its top. The entablature that the second-story pilasters support contains a frieze of organic shapes. The third story appears to be about half the height of the lower two. Its decoration is essentially the same: pilasters that frame small openings. But the floral decoration that begins in the second story has become a dominant motif here. Large floral swags hang from the window frames and create a wavelike pattern across the façade.

Had Lescot stopped at this point, he would have created a harmonious, beautiful, and fully realized adaptation of the prevailing Italian models. But he went further, adding something to those models that made his building unique. Lescot subdivided his façade by pushing out the wall between each group of three bays. Each of these enhanced bays framed a door in its bottom story and a window in each of those above. Lescot set these openings between paired pilasters. On the ground and second floors, niches between the pilasters sheltered sculptures. Ornamental friezes filled the space on the third floor level, and a round cornice framed a heraldic shield. The sculptures were the work of Jean Goujon.

After Lescot's west block—running perpendicular to the river—was complete, plans for the palace expanded again. The south block of the old Louvre facing the river was taken down, and Lescot created a second wing perpendicular to the first using the same design. (Map 4) At the intersection of the two wings he designed a monumental three-bay pavilion facing the

river to serve as the
royal residence.
This became
known as the
Pavillon du Roi,
or King's Pavilion.
At the end of the
sixteenth century,
Henri IV imagined

48

extending the Lescot façade to embrace an area four times the size of the
old Louvre, and during the reign of Louis XIII Lescot's original design was
duplicated to create a double-length west wall. (48) Inspired by Lescot's
King's Pavilion, Jacques Lemercier created the innovative Sully Pavilion at
the center of this extended west wing.

Lescot's original façade overlooks what is now called the Cour Carrée
of the Louvre, and it can be seen only from that inner square. The two
remaining wings of the old fortress that Lescot did not build over were
taken down to ground level, and eventually the Cour Carrée was laid out
above them. During the revamping of the museum in the last decades
of the twentieth century, these substructures were put on public display
inside the Louvre. Access to the excavated parts of the fortress is through
the entresol (basement) level of the Sully Pavilion. Visitors can now walk
along the bottom of the moat that once protected the original fortress and
admire the slanting walls, the flaring bases of the great corner towers, and
the cylindrical bases of the smaller towers that guarded its drawbridge.
(49) They can pass through the walls and stand in the cramped courtyard
that is nearly filled by the vast circular base of the central keep.

49

The old Louvre stood between the walls of Philippe Auguste and the walls of Charles V. Henri II began to see the Louvre as an administrative center, not a royal residence, and he asked Lescot to design a palace outside the city wall that would serve as the private home of the royal family. He also imagined a garden beyond the residential palace. Henri II combined the artistic interests of his father, François I, with political skills that were even more polished. During his brief reign, he won Calais back from the English and negotiated an end to the Italian wars that was confirmed by the 1559 Treaty of Chateau Cambrensis. That treaty called for a marriage between one of Henri's daughters and the son of the king of Spain. As part of the wedding celebration, a tournament was held in Paris on July 1, 1559. In what was meant to be a bloodless joust with the duke of Montgomery, Henri was accidentally struck through the eye by wood from a shattered lance. He remained alive for ten days before succumbing to his untreatable injury.

Henri's successor was underage at his father's death, and control of the kingdom passed into the hands of Henri's queen, Catherine de' Medici. Born in Florence in 1519, Catherine was heir to the vast fortunes of the Medici banking family. After her parents' death, she was brought up in Rome by her uncle, Pope Clement VII. In 1533 the pope arranged her marriage to Henri, the second son of François I. What appeared to be a grand match for a mere duchess was little more than a mercantile exchange—Catherine's enormous dowry secured the deal. Henri's real love interest was his mistress, Diane de Poitiers. Unable to speak French and continually upstaged by Diane, the fifteen-year-old Catherine was powerless and isolated in the French court.

Her fortunes changed overnight when the elder son and heir of François I died in 1536. As wife of the heir apparent, her titles, standing, and importance suddenly soared. But because she was childless, Catherine was in danger of repudiation by her husband, who was now even more eager for a male heir. In 1544 a son was born to the couple. In all, Catherine gave Henri seven children who survived infancy.

Devastated by her husband's sudden, pointless death, Catherine adopted full mourning, which was uncommon at court, and changed her personal emblem from the rainbow veil of the Roman god Iris to the figure of a broken lance and an inscription that means "From this my tears, from this my sorrow." She sold the palace where the fatal tournament had taken place and concentrated her energies on completing a royal residence like the one her husband had envisaged, the Tuileries.

Passing over Lescot, Catherine appointed Philibert de l'Orme, who had spent four years studying architecture in Rome, to design her palace. Completed in several stages, the building with its massive central pavilion, abundant neoclassical architectural details, and sculpture owed an obvious debt to Lescot nevertheless. During the reign of Henri IV at the end of the sixteenth century, the building was extended on the river end to meet up with a long gallery coming from the Louvre. The residence was remodeled and enriched both by Louis XIV and Napoleon, but after it burned in 1871, it was never rebuilt.

As the seventeenth century began in France, the Louvre and the Tuileries were still separated by the wall of Charles V. Early in the new century

50

the wall was moved farther downriver and reconfigured to meet the defensive demands of a new era. (Map 2) Pressed by increasing population from within, the enlarged circuit was adapted to a new kind of aggression from without. During the sixteenth century, gunpowder weapons replaced the mechanical devices that had been the mainstay of siege warfare since the Roman period. Perpendicular walls protected by round towers—state-of-the-art defenses in the Middle Ages—gave way in the Renaissance to sloping walls and angled bastions. Iron cannon balls that would knock down vertical walls bounced off sloping or angled walls. Enlarged bastions gave gunners room to maneuver their increasingly cumbersome weapons.

As soon as the city wall that had separated the two palaces began to come down, plans were made to unite them in a single though very oddly shaped structure. The Louvre itself consisted of Lescot's two perpendicular wings still linked up to the two surviving blocks of the old fortress that are now preserved in the basement. From the junction point of Lescot's two wings, a short gallery headed straight toward the river, where it met the long corridor that paralleled the Seine and abutted the Tuileries at its far end. The whole meandering project looked more like a game of dominoes than the ground plan for a coherent building.

This awkwardness was accentuated by what the windows of the two palaces overlooked. It is hard to imagine that the present desertlike courtyard of the Louvre was once a busy neighborhood crisscrossed with roads and dotted with houses. Some of these were modest; others were the multi-winged residences of influential courtiers. And sitting among them for decades stood a sizeable orphaned chunk of the wall of Charles V. At the far end of the palace complex, where the river gallery joined the Tuileries, there was a formal garden. Between the Tuileries and the extended city wall was a grand and glorious garden designed by the landscape architect André Le Nôtre.

During Louis XIV's long reign (1643–1715), the last of the old Louvre fortress finally disappeared, and the Cour Carrée was closed in by buildings designed by Louis Le Vau and Claude Perrault. (50) Particularly influential was Perrault's design for the long east wing that paralleled Lescot's original structure across the Cour Carrée. The external façade of that wing, which faced toward town, transformed Lescot's formula of pavilions and interconnections into a neoclassical system that set the direction of eighteenth-century French architecture.

Perrault's façade is divided into three sections anchored in a central pavilion and two end pavilions. But there the resemblance with Lescot's work more or less ends. Perrault based his design on a second Renaissance formula also associated with Bramante and first used on important private palaces in Rome. The ground floor of the pavilion is made of heavy square blocks and lit by rounded framed windows. Corinthian columns that support a continuous entablature are the defining mark of the upper stories. In the center pavilion these columns frame a frieze that depicts a winged Victory driving her chariot above the main entryway arch. (51)

51

In the nineteenth century, galleries parallel to the long river corridor but on the inland side were built in a series of campaigns. Construction began with a wing attached to the north end of the Tuileries palace under Napoleon Bonaparte. During the reign of Napoleon III at mid-century, that north wing was extended eastward, and symmetrical structures were built over a portion of the gardens within the now-enclosed courtyard, called the Cour Napoléon. All of these new pavilions imitated the Sully Pavilion at the east end of this vast open space—an influential architectural style adopted worldwide under the name Second Empire.

When the Tuileries palace burned in 1871, the once-enclosed complex suddenly gained an open end. Beyond it stretched the newly remodeled gardens of the Tuileries and the Avenue des Champs Elysées. The destruction of the Tuileries broke down a barrier that had divided two distant triumphal arches—the Arc de Triomphe at the end of the Champs Elysées and the Arc de Triomphe du Carrousel, both commissioned by Napoleon. The latter was based on a surviving original near the Colosseum

52

dedicated to Constantine. (52) At its top was an antique chariot pulled by four bronze horses. The first horses that stood there had come from the porch of Saint Mark's basilica in Venice. They had occupied that prime position since the thirteenth century, when the Venetians had plundered them from

Constantinople. Napoleon acquired the horses, along with a great deal of other art, during negotiations for the city's capitulation to overwhelming French force in 1797. When Napoleon was defeated in turn, Austria took possession of the horses and returned them to Venice, which Austria then occupied. Copies of the horses now replace them.

In 1989 the open-ended Louvre courtyard was resurfaced and a new and controversial monument was placed at its center. Designed by the internationally celebrated architect I. M. Pei, the centerpiece, which now serves as a gateway to the Louvre museum, combines fountains and four glass pyramids. Though the entry complex makes no concessions to the influence of Lescot that dominates the neoclassical buildings surrounding it, pyramids have historic associations with the place. Visionary French architects of the eighteenth century imagined buildings in a variety of pure geometric shapes, including spheres and pyramids. After Napoleon's conquest of Egypt, thousands of Egyptian artifacts were brought to Paris, where they continue to form a substantial part of the collections of the Louvre.

In function though not in form, Pei's pyramids are monumentalized skylights. (53) They identify the entrances to the various pavilions of the remodeled Louvre and light the reception areas beneath the central courtyard that link the multiple collections together. These new substructures add thousands of feet of floor space

53

to the museum and supply it with all those things that modern museology requires: ticket booth, gift shop, cafeteria, conference center, bookstore, cloak room, information desk, restrooms, and so on.

54

In one sense the Louvre Museum is a tangible memorandum of the ambitions of the French nation. Its vast collection of sculpture and inscriptions from the eastern Mediterranean reflect the influence of French politics in that area. The Egyptian collections, which are among the largest in the world, include souvenirs of Napoleon's invasion. Most of the collections, however, were acquired in peaceful ways and represent not so much French political aspirations as the desire of the museum's powerful curators to make the museum the most authoritative assembly of art works in the world.

A small percentage of the pre-Renaissance paintings in the collection were recovered from monasteries seized by the Revolution. The *Pietà* from the abbey of Saint Germain des Prés is one of the most precious and remarkable of these rare objects (Richelieu Pavilion, second floor, Room 7). In the center of the large painting, the dead Christ lies across the dark blue skirt of the Virgin, who lifts his torso into a near-sitting position. The two are surrounded by a group of kneeling and standing figures most remarkable for their sumptuous brocades and velvets. The anonymous painter, who probably trained in Cologne, worked in a style that was characteristic of the great Flemish and German painters of the late Middle

Ages. His figures are brightly colored and brightly lit; there is meticulous detail and subtle dimensionality in the clothing, but little individuality or emotional complexity in the faces.

The most wonderful details of the painting are in the left background, where the painter has represented, with the particularity of a miniaturist, the abbey of Saint Germain des Prés and across the river from it the medieval Louvre, with its surrounding wall, corner turrets, and defensive crenellations. (54) The painter's willingness to fuse the Paris of his own day with the Holy Land of New Testament times represents an important trend in medieval spirituality that has much to do with the rationale of devotional painting of this kind. The aim of the painting is to make the viewer experience Christ's suffering as real and immediate. The message of the painting is that Christ's passion was not just an event of the remote past; it is happening now, in this time and place.

The Louvre's collection of European painting from the thirteenth through the nineteenth centuries is enormous and unparalleled. It began with François I, the last patron of Leonardo, whose taste for what was then modern art embraced significant Italian painters of the High Renaissance and the early Mannerist period. Along with the *Mona Lisa,* François acquired works by Raphael and Andrea del Sarto and patronized the French artist Jean Clouet.

Jean and his brother François were court painters at the Chateau de Fon-

55

tainebleau. Jean's portrait of François I shows the monarch apparently at full maturity (Richelieu, second floor, Room 8). (55) The king is flooded with the same intense light that illuminates the figures in the Pietà from Saint Germain des Prés. Against a backdrop of rich red brocade decorated with various emblems including a crown, the king turns slightly to the right, a posture that emphasizes the extraordinary nose of which he was evidently very proud. Though the portrait conveys some of the character of the king—a certain power of gaze and a determination in the set of his head—the real message is contained in the opulent background and rich clothing. François Clouet's later portrait of Elizabeth of Austria, which entered the collection in the reign of Louis XV, is as preoccupied with brocade, gored sleeves, and jewelry as the king's portrait, but the queen's face is the real center of attention (Richelieu, second floor, Room 8).

Madonna is a title of respect, meaning "my lady." In Renaissance Italy it was commonly shortened to Monna or Mona. Mona Lisa Gherardini married a wealthy Florentine cloth merchant, Francesco del Giocondo, in 1495. She sat for her portrait about eight years after that with Leonardo, whose father had done business over the years with her husband. The small portrait, now only about twenty by thirty inches, was evidently cut down at some time so that the subject, who was once framed by the outline of a window, now has a more enigmatical relation to the fantastic landscape behind her (Denon, first floor, Room 6). That landscape moves from a foreground marked by a road and a bridge or aqueduct into a remote distance where human activity yields to open water and imaginatively molded and eroded rocky peaks. Lisa's body seems to counterpoint this passage; her torso coincides with the part of the landscape that is most human, but her head projects into the realm beyond.

The varnish on the surface of the painting has yellowed with age, and a dark crackle covers the sitter's face and neck. This aging robs the painting of some of the mysterious luminosity that Leonardo gave to bare skin, which he typically highlighted—as he does here—by surrounding his figures with deep shadow or dressing them in black. In his notes on painting, Leonardo talked at length about the nature of direct and diffused light. His figures may seem to glow as if they were lit from within, but they are actually bathed in a unidirectional light from above. The harsh contrast between light and shadow that such a single source would normally create is softened to the suffused radiance of a cloudy day. Evenly caressed by this omnipresent light, Leonardo's figures have a solidity and roundness that is almost sculptural. His treatment contrasts with the floodlit figures and carefully chronicled minutia that marked the German painters at work in Paris at the beginning of the sixteenth century. In their paintings, the light foregrounds each detail, creating a cacophony of objects that compete for our attention. Without ignoring detail, Leonardo establishes hierarchy and focus.

In an age as spiritual as the Renaissance, light of the kind that Leonardo depicted could hardly avoid taking on a metaphysical quality. He heightened that association and its significance by contrasting the omnipresent glow with distinct highlights. As he emphasized repeatedly in his discussion of light and shadow, the highlights on an object shift with the position of the viewer, playing against the objectifying light and emphasizing the unique, subjective point of view of the artist. All this complexity is evident to the viewer, whose eye and brain record and respond to it. It contributes to a sense that the painting exists just beyond the reach of articulation in an intricate region where understanding and mystery touch.

56

Sometime early in the seventeenth century Leonardo's *Virgin and Child with Saint Anne* (Denon, Grande Galerie, section 5) entered the royal collections. (56) This group, portrayed in full sunlight with bright blues and reds, appears uncomplicated at first. Against a rocky background like that in the *Mona Lisa,* Saint Anne, her daughter the Virgin Mary, and the infant Christ sit literally one on top of the other. The three figures form a triangle that rises to the pinnacle of Saint Anne's head, and this compositional formula greatly influenced both Andrea del Sarto and Raphael. The arrangement of the figures is like a stop-motion photograph of someone bending to the left, which gives the picture a restless sense of orderly movement.

Like Leonardo, Andrea del Sarto spent some time in France, and at least one painting in the Louvre was completed there. His *Charity* is a subtle representation of a common theme (Denon, Grande Galerie, section 5). At first sight the picture appears to be nothing more than a portrait of an unusually patient mother trying to nurse her triplets. But in fact, the picture represents the virtue of supreme unconditional love and the distinct human responses to it. One child sucks at his mother's breast, while a second smiles and offers her a small bird. The third child, who is farthest from her breast, turns his eyes away and buries his head in his hands. The same polarity between acceptance and rejection is reflected in the background landscape. Under mature trees, a family sits together in sunlight outside a small walled town on the left margin. On the right, a dark landscape with sheer cliffs and stunted trees represents the world of those who reject divine love.

The great Renaissance painter Raphael inspired the enthusiasm of both François I and Louis XIV. François bought Raphael's *Virgin and Child with the Infant Saint John in a Landscape* (also called *La Belle Jardinière;* Denon, Grande Galerie, section 5). Mary and the two infants are grouped in a triangle. A church in the distance represents the fruit of the devotion that John shows to Jesus. It is the sort of comfortable, cheery Raphael that makes the painter suspect in modern eyes. Louis XIV added darker and more complex pictures to the royal collection. *Portrait of the Artist with a Friend* is a somber and mysterious painting (Denon, Grande Galerie, section 8). The unknown friend, who occupies the center of the picture, turns back to look at Raphael, who is behind and to the left. (57) The play of their glances links to the foregrounded hand of the friend in an oblique triangle that moves back and forth rather than across the picture frame.

57

In the late sixteenth century, dominance in painting moved from Rome and Florence north to Venice. François I was well enough aware of this trend to have his portrait painted by Titian. The Venetian writer Pietro Aretino brokered the arrangement, but the painter and his subject never actually met. A bronze medal that featured the king's profile was sent to the artist. Titian dressed the king in a fur cape and a gored velvet doublet of that particu-

lar Venetian red that the painter and his imitators so admired. He did
not fail to represent the monarch's commanding nose (Denon, first floor,
Room 6).

By the time of Louis XIV, Titian was accepted as the equal of the
masters of the High Renaissance. The king and those who contributed
to his collection—the cardinals Mazarin and Richelieu—bought several

of his paintings.
Napoleon's capture
of Venice in 1798
added still more.
A prominent room
off the Grande Gal-
erie in the Denon
Pavilion is devoted
to Titian and his
followers. Unfor-

58

tunately, the *Mona Lisa,* which has occupied various spots in the Louvre
over the years, is now installed in the middle of this room. As a result, the
crowds standing in front of the Leonardo make it virtually impossible to
see the Titians to whom the room originally belonged. The difficulties are
compounded by the way the paintings are hung one above another and the
evident need of many of them for restoration.

Still, the collection contains amazing works. There are portraits like
the *Man with the Glove,* a psychological study in which head, gloved,
and ungloved hand gain an eerie autonomy as they protrude from the
dark background. The *Pastoral Concert* is an allegory based on the work
of Giorgione, to whom it has sometimes been attributed. Among the

most magnificent and moving Titians that Louis collected is the intensely dramatic *Entombment.* (58) In this dynamic and turbulent picture, Joseph of Arimathea and Nicodemus lift the heavy, pallid, inert body of Christ over the lip of a stone sarcophagus. Joseph looks across the body toward Nicodemus, whose head is completely turned away and enveloped in darkness like that of Christ himself. Behind the sarcophagus the disciple John helps support his right arm and shoulder. As he lifts Christ's dead hand in midair, it curls on itself to mimic the gesture of Adam in Michelangelo's *Creation* fresco in the Sistine Chapel. Christian theology identifies Christ as the new Adam whose sacrifice repaired the damage done by the first man's disobedience and fall.

Marie de' Medici, widow of Henri IV and queen mother of Louis XIII, inspired one of the greatest series of paintings now in the Louvre (Richelieu, second floor, Room 18). In 1621 her agents commissioned Peter Paul Rubens to paint twenty-one large canvases for the Luxembourg palace on the Left Bank. The subject of the series was the life story of the patron herself. The sequence begins with three corpulent Fates spinning the life thread of the future queen, while Jupiter, for once the sole object of his wife's attention, looks on. Juno descends from Olympus to present the child to the personified city of Florence; Apollo and Mercury oversee her education while the three Graces, looking sculpted and fleshy simultaneously, stand by. The following scenes depict Marie's marriage to Henri IV, her arrival as a beautiful young bride in France, and her coronation. In every picture of the adult queen, her distended neck, the result of an iodine deficiency in her diet, is prominent. Though it seems an odd detail to feature, Marie evidently saw her goiter as a mark of distinction, just as François I, it seems, admired his own oversized nose.

In most of the paintings Rubens does a remarkable job with recalcitrant material. The most successful and influential scene in the vast commission is the enormous *Apotheosis of Henri IV*. Henri IV—one of the most agile of the political figures in the second half of the sixteenth century—negotiated the quick turns and counterturns of the civil wars of religion. When the Protestant movement boiled up in the wake of Martin Luther's defiance of Catholic authority, France, like Germany and the Low Countries before her, split into two factions and ultimately into two territories. The province of Navarre, where Henri was hereditary king, was the stronghold of Protestantism, and Henri willingly took command of the forces committed to that religion. In a moment of reconciliation between the two faiths, Henri married Marguerite de Valois, the sister of the reigning Catholic king, Charles IX. Shortly after the marriage, on Saint Bartholomew's Day, August 24, 1572, a massacre of Protestants began. Carefully choreographed, many believe, by Catherine de' Medici, soldiers broke into the houses of Protestant nobles and clergymen and murdered them.

Henri, the most prominent of all, was spared when he abjured Protestantism. He remained a prisoner of the Catholic court for four years before he escaped and returned to his home region and his original religion. In 1584 Henri became heir to the French throne. After the death of the king in 1589, Henri fought against a coalition determined to deny him the throne. In 1593 he reconciled with his former enemies and again embraced Catholicism. It is on this occasion that he said, if he ever did, that "Paris is well worth a mass." Henri IV was gradually accepted and ultimately much beloved as a Catholic king of France—the first of the Bourbon branch of Capetian kings.

His childless marriage to Marguerite de Valois was annulled in 1599, and less than a year later he married Marie de' Medici, a distant relation of Catherine de' Medici who had controlled France as queen and then regent during much of the sixteenth century. Marie's major attraction for the middle-aged monarch, who was quite happy with his official mistress, was a dowry even larger than the one Catherine had brought from Florence to the son of François I.

Despite his successful foreign policy and his reconciliation of Catholics and Protestants, Henri IV fell victim to an assassin in 1610. A provincial Catholic schoolteacher, François Ravaillac, who was almost certainly delusional, stabbed Henri while the royal carriage was stuck in traffic not far from the Louvre. As he awaited trial, the assassin was imprisoned in the Conciergerie on the Ile de la Cité. After his conviction, he was drawn and quartered—the gruesome form of execution reserved for regicides—on the Place de Grève.

Rubens' *Apotheosis* represented the assassination symbolically rather than literally. (59) The left side of the picture depicts the death of Henri IV as a deification. Its sources and allegorical figures are predominately but not entirely classical. Henri, armored in a cuirass and draped with a red cape, is lifted into

59

the air by Jupiter, robed in crimson and resting on his symbol, the eagle, and Chronos, Father Time, who carries an upraised sickle. The trio rise above a twisted fire-breathing serpent—the assassin—which coils around a fallen suit of armor. Dressed in gold and seated next to the armor, an allegorical figure holds a palm frond, one of the conventional Christian symbols of martyrdom. Next to her a half nude winged woman runs toward the viewer with her left arm thrown back behind her head in a gesture traditionally believed to express intense pain or emotion. In her right hand she holds up a Roman trophy of crossed sticks with the full armor of the king raised toward the pale Olympian gods just visible in the background of the scene.

The right side of the picture is devoted to Marie, who upon her husband's death assumed control of the kingdom as regent for her infant son, Louis XIII. Sitting on a throne that is raised on a dais and holding her son in her arms, she is framed by the opening of a Roman triumphal arch. Kneeling at her feet, Minerva presents the globe. On Marie's behalf a servant accepts the globe with her right hand. A serpent coils around her left. This transformed symbol of the assassin represents prudence or wisdom. A throng of anguished courtiers cluster at Marie's feet and raise their arms to her in gestures of abject neediness.

Just as a symbol of Christian martyrdom edges into the picture of the apotheosis, there is a surprising and deeply powerful symbol of Christian orthodoxy on the right. The pillars that surround the throne presumably hold a canopy above the queen, but the pillars themselves are representations of those serpentine bronze columns that Bernini cast to support the baldachin above the high altar in Saint Peter's basilica. These columns represent the last transformation of the assassin serpent. From a figure of chaos and disorder on the left, the serpent has metamorphosed into a figure of prudent rule and orthodoxy on the right. The painting's political argument seems to be that Marie will transform the violence done to her husband into wisdom and authority. The divine right of kings had been an important political tool of French monarchs from Hugh Capet on, but here it gains a modern and very compelling expression. No monarch will take greater advantage of it than Marie's long-lived grandson, Louis XIV.

While royal collectors favored Italian painting, they also made room for the works of two masters who were born and educated in France but lived for a significant time in Italy. Though born in Normandy and briefly trained in Paris, Nicolas Poussin spent the best part of his life in Rome, and like many other painters he adopted the style of Caravaggio in his first works. His *Apparition of the Virgin to Saint James* mimicked the style of contemporary paintings that were the very opposite of everything Poussin would eventually embrace (Richelieu, second floor, Room 12).

In time the painter came to believe that Caravaggio's Baroque style was not the best or the truest form of painting. Along with other artists in Rome, he turned back to the style of the ancients and to those artists of the High Renaissance who seemed most faithful to their vision. Though no important examples of ancient painting were known in the 1630s, Poussin studied the techniques of artists who had created shallow relief carvings in stone. Rome was rich in examples of this work, and as he explored them Poussin began to model his figures and his representation of space on these prototypes where three-dimensionality was necessarily reduced. He also began to study the great neoclassical artists of the century before, most importantly Raphael, whose greatest works were still to be seen in Rome. He was also interested in Leonardo da Vinci, whose few works were harder to find.

Poussin added the study of nature to the study of the past. Along with other artists in Rome, including Claude Lorrain, Poussin spent a good deal of time in the Roman countryside drawing and painting in the openair. In 1633 Poussin became a member of the Accademia di San Luca, a guild-like organization of artists that helped its members with sales and commissions but also encouraged the formal study of art history, theory, and practical methods. All these threads of Poussin's self-education combined to create a new kind of pictorial literalism and a style of linear composition that Baroque painters had repudiated.

In turning against the Baroque style, Poussin and his contemporaries did not forsake its ambitions. Paintings would still tell the great and mysterious stories of the Bible along with the histories and legends of the Greeks and Romans. But both the miraculous and the heroic would find expression in figures whose interactions reflected what the artists believed to be the norms of classical painting. The figures would act in a landscape that was

60

a plausible recreation of the past but based on the familiar features of contemporary landscapes.

Saint John Baptizing is a good example of Poussin's new direction (Richelieu, second floor, Room 14). The foreground is filled with a shallow band of figures in a variety of poses and states of undress. (60) Both their postures and their grouping reflect the style of classical sarcophagi. The figures surround John, who lifts his hand over two semi-nude men kneeling before him. Their strongly muscled backs reflect the anatomical knowledge of bodies in torsion that Baroque painters loved to display, but here

the figures are subdued and static. Color is still important and dynamic, as it was in the *Apparition of the Virgin.* The play of deep blues, golds, and reds moves the eye back and forth across the assembled figures. In the background a small crowd waits on the far shore of the River Jordan. They

61

are nearly lost, however, in a stunning landscape—with its roots in Venetian art—that reaches from bare brown hills topped by a few trees to the deep blue mountain beneath sunset-yellow clouds on the left margin.

The *Plague at Ashdod,* painted in 1630 and displayed in the same room, is an interesting fusion of the principles of Baroque composition and Poussin's neoclassicism. (61) The painting represents the disaster that befell the Philistine city of Ashdod when its soldiers placed the captured Ark of the Covenant in the temple of their god Dagon. The temple stands on the left margin; the Ark of the Covenant seems to hover in midair between the columns on its porch. The statue of Dagon with head and hands cut off, as described in 1 Samuel 5:4, lies on its face on the ground before the Ark. The Philistines are struck by various divine punishments that Poussin represents as plague.

The architecture of the scene is nothing like that of the Philistines. Poussin declares his Roman sources in his representation of an ancient bas-relief on the foundations of the temple in the left foreground. The temple of Dagon with its fluted columns is faced by another public building with a long and wide flight of open stairs. Next to it is a small enclosed building with an ornamental frieze below its roof. A double portico on the next building pairs Doric columns with square piers. Arched niches on both this building and the one diagonally across from it shelter statues of Roman dignitaries. A stunted obelisk stands in the distance at the end of a long street. Apparently Poussin felt that neoclassical architecture of this kind was the most appropriate and dignified form for any time and people. This notion gained official expression in Paris during the reign of Louis XIV.

The intensely dramatic mood of the painting comes from the turbulence of the crowd, but it is also strongly represented in the postures and reactions of the foreground figures. A woman lies with her head toward the viewer; her dead child has fallen to one side of her, while her surviving baby looks to her lifeless breast for nourishment. Her husband reaches toward the child while covering his mouth. Another man entering from the right covers his nose against the smell of death, while a figure on the left turns away. Biblical plagues were a common theme in seventeenth-century painting, as epidemic disease continued to ravage Europe for centuries after its first appearance in 1348.

Poussin's works in the 1630s brought him many commissions, and before the end of the decade a number of his paintings had made their way to Paris. Louis XIII appointed Poussin as royal painter and commanded his return to the capital to begin decorating the newly built wings of the Louvre. Poussin was happy in Rome and content with a career that allowed him to paint on his own terms. He resisted the royal invitation until it was accompanied by veiled threats. Eighteen months after his appointment, Poussin gave in and headed for Paris. He immediately found himself transformed from a painter into a shop steward—the point man in a system of art production that was unfamiliar and uncongenial. As creator-in-chief, his job was to produce compositions and full-sized drawings—called cartoons—for ceiling frescoes in the Louvre and for tapestries to be turned out by weavers at the Gobelins workshop. The actual execution of his designs was left to assistants and apprentices. After two years, Poussin begged for permission to return temporarily to Rome. His brief trip became permanent, and he died in his adopted city in 1665. His paintings continued to be collected by French nobility, by royal advisers Richelieu, Mazarin, and Colbert, and by Louis XIII and Louis XIV.

Poussin's style and the ideals it expressed conflicted with those of the most influential Baroque artworks in Paris, the series created by Rubens to celebrate the legend of Marie de' Medici. The confrontation between the two styles took on a moral tone and then a political significance. When Poussin returned to Rome in 1642, he welcomed a young French painter, Charles Le Brun, to his circle. Le Brun quickly became an enthusiast of Poussin's style, and in a treatise he laid out the principles that, he felt, formed the underpinnings of Poussin's art. He emphasized the study of classical sculpture and the paintings of Raphael that had influenced the master.

Painting, Le Brun argued, is the expression of an idea. Art is primarily intellectual rather than sensual, and beauty is a means to promote understanding, not an end in itself. Human emotions are depicted in art so that they can be examined dispassionately, not for the sake of creating empathy. These principles led Le Brun to a hierarchy of kinds of paintings. Portraits, landscapes, and still-lifes were among the least intellectual forms of painting. The illustration of great historical events stood at the pinnacle of art.

Le Brun's ideas were based not just on Poussin's thoughts and practices but on the writings of Leonardo da Vinci. Poussin was active in the recovery and dissemination of Leonardo's notes, and the first French edition of Leonardo's *Treatise on Painting,* published in 1651, was illustrated with engravings based on Poussin's drawings. It also featured a dedicatory letter to Poussin. With Le Brun as their synthesizer, the ideas of Leonardo and Poussin dominated French thinking about art for two centuries, until the revolt of the Impressionists.

While Le Brun's writings were influential and his paintings continued to sell, he was above all a skilled entrepreneur. Unlike Poussin, who hated the French workshops, Le Brun thrived in just this atmosphere. He was a much better organizer of artists than he was a painter. The French crown recognized this ability by making him director of the Gobelins factory in 1663. In the twenty years since Poussin had reluctantly drawn designs for the weavers, it had been transformed from a prestigious workshop into a state-sponsored industry that turned out luxury goods for all the royal establishments.

In the same year, Le Brun became the first director of the Academy of Painting and Sculpture. While the academy idea grew out of the loose association of painters in the Accademia di San Luca to which Poussin had belonged, the new French academy replaced the informal studio training of earlier generations with an art curriculum taught by certified masters to novice painters and sculptors. It was a full-fledged system of education that Le Brun based on the principles he had codified in his writings.

Le Brun also became the curator of the king's pictures. His views helped to shape a collection of masterpieces that no longer reflected the sometimes quirky taste of royal collectors but exemplified the ideals of painting that the new academy was teaching. The academy moved from place to place on the Left Bank, but the Louvre always remained a focus of study. Until the nineteenth century, ground-floor studios overlooking the Cour Carrée were made available free of charge to chosen artists.

Claude Lorrain was a contemporary and friend of Poussin who also painted in Rome. He arrived in the city about 1620 and died there in the mid-1680s, having returned to France for only one brief period. Nourished in the same environment and sharing some of his friend's beliefs, Claude reflected very different ideals in his most celebrated paintings. The common ground between the two is most evident in Claude's history paintings (Richelieu, second floor, Room 15). In the *Landing of Cleopatra at Tarsus,* he combines a seascape with a landing area among grand buildings decorated with fantastic versions of Roman architecture.

His *View of the Campo Vaccino* is much less difficult for a modern sensibility to appreciate. (62) The painting represents the ruins that surrounded the unexcavated Roman Forum—then called the Cow Pasture. From the platform of the Temple of Saturn and overshadowed by the remaining columns of that enormous structure, the painter looks toward the Arch of Septimius Severus on the left and above it to the medieval Torre delle Milizie. Just beyond is the

62

colonnade of the Temple of Antoninus and Faustina and in the far distance the Arch of Trajan. The three columns and the surviving entablature of the Temple of the Dioscuri stand just to the left of the Saturn columns, overshadowed by a great tree.

The sky above the Forum is misty and sprinkled with small clouds. A soft, warm, late-afternoon sunlight picks out details while it casts long shadows around figures who stand idly around. In the harbor scenes, the sinking sun seems to represent the approaching end of an age of glory. But in the *Campo Vaccino,* rather than suggest an idea, the light creates a mood. Atmosphere, both in the meteorological and psychological sense, is what separates Poussin from Claude Lorrain. Claude is a sentimentalist in the best sense of the word, who again and again recovers the emotional link we feel to cherished places.

Chapter Five

CITY OF LIGHT

The state's direction of painting and sculpture reflected the monarchy's growing interest in sponsoring and regulating public works of many kinds. These ranged from residential developments and sumptuous churches to bridges and public gardens. Some monarchs loved the city; others evidently loathed it. But however they felt about it, the kings of France understood that in a symbolic sense the city was their residence, an extension of their palace. Its size, grandeur, and amenity offered proof of the power and beneficence of its ruler.

Henri IV was the moving force behind the creation of the Place des Vosges, a landmark residential complex in the eastern end of the city known as the Marais. (Map 5) The king's project started with the founding of a factory for weaving opulent fabrics of silk interwoven with threads of gold and silver. A year later, Henri decided to sponsor an upscale development whose residents would be drawn not from those employed in making these expensive products but from people likely to buy them. Henri envisaged a large central square that would be "useful as a public gathering place on holidays and other state occasions." This enclosed square, rimmed by houses and shops, was the first residential project of a kind that other monarchs would imitate as they sponsored what came to be called "royal squares" in areas closer to the Louvre.

63

The main entrance to the plaza was through the royal pavilion. (63) At the opposite end of the square stood the complementary Hôtel de la Reine (the queen's pavilion). The two upper stories of the buildings were subdivided into apartments. Gables in the steep roofs lit the garret quarters of servants or workers. The front façades combined brick with chains of stone block, and behind each pavilion was a walled garden. Though construction was left to individual owners, covenants that remained in force for generations guaranteed uniformity throughout the square.

During the eighteenth century, the development experienced hard times, as the Marais declined from a fashionable district to a working-class neighborhood. A statue of Louis XIII erected in 1639 at the center of the square was, predictably, pulled down during the Revolution. The gardens that once surrounded the buildings were completely filled in with residential properties. But in the mid-twentieth century the Marais came back into fashion, and the fortunes of the Place des Vosges climbed with it. (64) Commercial life on the ground floors around the square is now decidedly upscale. Art galleries, high-end clothing stores, and multiple restaurants fill many of the old boutiques and spill onto the covered walkways. The Victor Hugo house museum occupies one corner. Allées under pruned trees surround open lawns, with a grove of chestnut trees in its center.

At the southwest corner of the Place des Vosges, a passage leads to the back courtyard of the Hôtel de Sully, named for Henri IV's minister who bought the palace and used it as his residence. The front of the building, on Rue Saint Antoine, is a narrower version of a typical early-seventeenth-century façade. What is most unusual about this structure is the material from which it is made. In contrast with the brick façades of the Place des Vosges, the Hôtel de Sully is made entirely of stone, and it is one of the few private houses of the period to be built in this much more costly material. The ends of two wings that surround an inner courtyard flank a grand entryway. At the far end of the first courtyard a façade similar to the one that overlooks the street focuses around a more elaborate center bay.

Sphinxes on plinths stand next to the main entry stairs, and sculpted figures in shallow niches representing Autumn and Winter stand on both sides of the center window on the second floor. A passage through the building leads to a formal garden. At the back end of this garden are the arched openings of a second courtyard, an orangerie. The sculptural program that begins on the inner front façade continues in the second courtyard with representations of the four seasons, signs of the zodiac, and personifications of the four elements. Representations of the seasons on the façade of Notre Dame completed centuries ear-lier depict the labors of the months—the seasonal work that mankind must endure

64

to repair the damage done by the Fall. In the Hôtel de Sully, by contrast, the sculptures suggest harmony with the natural world. Though built by a citizen of Paris rather than a monarch, the building program shows the same desire to harmonize the built and natural environments that is evident in the Place des Vosges and in many other royal projects of the era. The city of Paris bought the building in the 1930s and restored it. It is now home to the National Trust for historic monuments and sites, which maintains a library and an excellent bookstore devoted to monuments in Paris and throughout France. (65)

Diagonally across the street from the Hôtel de Sully, the church of Saint Paul and Saint Louis stands on a piece of land once occupied by the walls of Philippe Auguste. In 1619 Louis XIII donated this property for the mother church of the Society of Jesus. The church had begun its life as a chapel in a private house. In 1582 Cardinal Charles de Bourbon donated the Hôtel Damville to the few pioneering members of this new religious order in Paris, but by 1619 both the palace and its chapel were far too small to serve the dynamic community of priests and their lay followers.

Early in its history the Jesuit order was known for the simplicity of its architecture. But meteoric growth brought tremendous wealth, and during the seventeenth century the Jesuits adopted a style of decoration notable for its embellishment of every available surface with rich materials and highly sophisticated workmanship. While the Jesuit church in Paris never equaled the splendors

65

of Il Gesù in Rome, it was still a large, ambitious, and richly ornamented
structure. A rounded pediment above the first story and the peaked gable
at the top of the three-story façade echo details of the façade of the
mother church. The interior plan is even more clearly indebted to that
model. The nave of both churches is unusually wide, because an unob-
structed view of the altar was essential to the Counter-Reformation ideals
of the Jesuits. Vignola, the designer of Il Gesù, created a chain of chapels
along each side of the church, closing off the aisles almost completely. In
Paris, the chapels in the same position are open to the nave.

Construction began in 1627, and in 1641, with the royal family at-
tending, Cardinal Richelieu celebrated the first mass in the sumptuous
new building. But by the middle of the eighteenth century the fortunes
of the Society of Jesus in France had begun to sour. Religious purists opposed them from inside the Church, while humanists and the philosophi-
cally minded challenged them from outside. During mid-century debates
in the French Parliament, opponents were able to paint the Jesuits as
conspiratorial. To the donations of the pious accumulated over several
centuries, the order had added the profits of colonial industries, in which
they were very active. Their enemies combined to overpower the order's
many defenders in the government. In 1764 Louis XV was forced, much
against his will, to abolish the Jesuits within his dominions. The church
of Saint Louis was handed over to the canons of another Parisian church,
who retained control until the Revolution ousted them. The enormous
church became a depository for books and manuscripts seized from
monastic foundations. In 1802 it was resanctified, and its congregation
merged with that of the nearby parish of Saint Paul, whose church had
been demolished in 1797. (66)

66

Civic development under Louis XIII extended to land reclamation in the River Seine. Upstream from the Ile de la Cité were two undeveloped islands called Ile Notre Dame and Ile aux Vaches. Before a canal was dredged between the two in the fourteenth century, they had been a single low-lying and relatively uninhabited place. Boatsmen who towed barges upstream against the current lived in houses along the shore, and fields in the interior were devoted to pasturing cattle—the *vaches* from which one part of the island took its name—or to open lawns where cloth was stretched out to dry.

In 1614 the nobleman Christophe Marie signed a contract with the young king which called for the contractor to fill in the channel and build permanent bridges linking the new island to both banks of the river. The contract also required the construction of stone quays—which combined flood protection with docks—along the perimeter and the bases of the two bridges, and a grid of streets on the island. In exchange for this tangible investment, the contractor and his partners were guaranteed the profit from the appreciation of island real estate for a period of sixty years.

Work began on Pont Marie (named for the developer, not the Virgin) in the year that the contract was signed. In 1635 this stone bridge with its rounded arches was complete. In order to make the project profitable as soon as possible, the end of the bridge closest to the right bank was lined with two rows of houses. These were already leased to tenants before work on the bridge was finished. In 1658 flood waters carried away the two arches of the bridge nearest the Ile Saint Louis and twenty houses

along with them. More than a hundred people were crushed or drowned in
the disaster. The bridge was rebuilt but these houses were not replaced.
The remaining houses on the bridge were taken down in the eighteenth
century. (67)

The island's streets were laid out in a rational way, more or less in the
pattern of a Roman colony. The first road connected the two bridges and
is still called the Rue des Deux Ponts, street of two bridges. Perpendicular
to this road and bisecting the island lengthwise is the Rue Saint Louis
en l'Ile. The Rue le Regrattier, named for one of the founding partners,
followed the old canal. Its counterpart on the upriver end of the island was
the Rue Poulletier,
named for the third
partner. Like the
walls of a Roman
camp, the quays
traced the outline
of the island. A
continuous road-
way with several
different names
ran along them.
Starting in the late
seventeenth cen-

67

tury, this highly attractive island was home to the palaces of a few wealthy
families and to the far more numerous multistory residences of government
officials and affluent men of business. Smaller houses on the interior roads
were occupied by artisans, merchants, and servants. Despite much rebuild-

68

ing, the long ranks of houses that still ring the Ile Saint Louis are among the most beautiful in Paris.

The wooden bridge connecting the Left Bank of the Seine to the island—the first of many successive bridges still called the Pont de la Tournelle—was a poor relation to the Pont Marie. (68) When the bridge was rebuilt in stone in the mid-seventeenth century, pedestrians were charged a modest tariff to cross, but the rate tripled for men on horseback and quadrupled for carriages. Nevertheless, the Pont Marie and Pont de la Tournelle created a new link between the two banks and eased the flow of traffic across the river.

The pair of bridges that the Romans had built across the Ile de la Cité formed the only connection between the city's two segments until sometime shortly before the Viking invasions. By that time there were two pairs of bridges, one at the downstream end of the island and the other at its center, near the old Roman crossing. Until the seventeenth century, these four bridges were the only form of passage from one side of Paris to the other. (69) The Seine is an unruly river, and flooding over the centuries led to

69

frequent rebuildings. Each new bridge shifted its ground slightly to gain some imagined advantage against the water, and each one had a distinct name and character.

In the late thirteenth century, the long bridge linking the downstream end of the island to the right bank was knocked down and rebuilt twice. The first rebuilding in 1280 produced a structure lined with private houses. These were carried away sixteen years later. The bridge was shifted a bit to the east and rebuilt, this time with the shops of money-changers along both sides. That bridge became known as the Pont au Changeurs, more commonly the Pont au Change, a name that its successor still maintains.

In the late sixteenth century, Henri III set the first stone for what is now the oldest bridge in Paris, ironically named Le Pont Neuf, the new bridge. It was finished in 1604. Though the bridge was built during the French Renaissance

70

and based on Roman models, its ornaments are medieval. In accord with Roman engineering traditions, the rounded arches of the bridge are anchored in piers with sharp edges to divide the water and shed floating debris. Above each pier, the sides of the bridge bulge out like the top of a medieval tower. (70) The parapet that traces these outworks is supported on brackets, each anchored in a stone mask. These decorations transform the neoclassical structure into an object that looks like the walls and turrets of a castle. At the time of its completion, the Pont Neuf was the only Paris bridge without houses or shops built in. Its central location made it a favorite spot for strolling, and the passing crowd attracted every kind of street trade, from jugglers and storytellers to booksellers, pickpockets, and itinerant dentists.

During the next thirty years, the number of bridges more than doubled. Unlike the Pont Neuf and the Pont Marie, both built in stone and open to the public at no cost, most bridges were made of wood, like the Pont de la Tournelle, and sometimes painted barn red. One of these painted bridges connected the two islands, and another connected the Left Bank with the Ile de la Cité. The toll for crossing was a double tournois—a small coin of the period, worth a few pennies—which earned the bridge a name that its successors have maintained, Pont au Double.

Bridges were not just for crossing. The Seine was also a source of energy, and waterwheels on the bridges transferred the power of the current through cogs and gears to grindstones for milling wheat, barley, and rye. But mills and their platforms interfered with commerce on the river, and during floods the mills often broke loose and crashed into downstream structures, increasing the thrust of the current against them and contributing to their eventual collapse. By the eighteenth century the Seine was free of mills. Flour continued to be produced by the many windmills that stood on plots of elevated ground on the edges of the city.

The Seine was also a major source of drinking water for Paris. An aqueduct had served the town in the Roman period, and by the mid-thirteenth century, smaller aqueducts were bringing water from country ponds and streams to public fountains on the right bank. By the end of the six-

teenth century, half of this water was being consumed in the Louvre and
the Tuileries palaces. To increase the city's supply, Henri IV commissioned
a pumping station in the middle of the Seine, just below Pont Neuf. In an
ingenious combination, the river provided both water and the power to lift
it above street level, where it was stored in
a large holding tank. (71) A bas-relief on the
tank depicted Jesus talking with the Samar-
itan woman at the well. The name survives
in the Samaritaine department store a few
blocks away.

71

The pump was supposed to deliver
more than a hundred thousand gallons of
water per day, but it never produced more
than five thousand. Staffing and maintain-
ing the works proved to be very expensive, and major overhauls were
frequent. Despite these difficulties, the city commissioned a second and
a third pumping station attached to a bridge in the last third of the seventeenth century. One of these continued in service until the middle of the
nineteenth century.

Though the water of the Seine was polluted from the Middle Ages on,
Parisians continued to believe that it was not only safe to drink but healthy
and invigorating. In the middle of the nineteenth century Baron Haussmann
encountered the Parisians' stubborn faith in their river water, and for a long
time he was alone in questioning the water quality of the Seine. When the
water was finally tested, at Haussmann's urging, it was found to have four
to five times the acceptable level of microorganisms. It was not only not

72

beneficial but positively dangerous to drink, and a reliable source of cholera and typhoid, epidemic diseases that periodically ravaged the city.

Although Henri IV was not the developer of the Pont Neuf, it is his statue, rather than that of his predecessor, which stands in the center of a small plaza between the bridges. The statue of Henri IV was commissioned by his widow, Marie de' Medici, in 1614, four years after the king's assassination. The bronze figure in full armor, crowned with the victor's wreath of laurel and holding the baton of a marshal of France, was the first equestrian statue ever erected in the city. Designed by a French sculptor, it was cast by Pierre Tasca, whose name is undoubtedly Italian.

The monument itself reflects Marie's Florentine background. Bronze equestrian statues of military heroes made their first modern appearance in northern Italy. The Florentine sculptor Donatello created a mounted image of the Paduan military leader known as Gattamelata in the mid-fifteenth century that inspired many imitators. All of these works, many by Florentines, were based on the ancient equestrian statue of Marcus Aurelius that stood in front of the Lateran basilica in Rome until the mid-sixteenth century, when it became the centerpiece of Michelangelo's redesign of the Capitoline hill. Though the statue of Henri depicts him as an emperor at war, its location near the watermill that he gave to the city was probably not accidental. Water was the frequent gift of Roman emperors, and it seems likely that Henri, or perhaps Marie, had this imperial association in mind when commissioning the waterworks.

The seventeenth-century statue was torn down during the Revolution, melted, and recast into cannons. After the restoration of the monarchy, a new statue was commissioned, and—in an unusual act of artistic revenge— bronze statues of Napoleon were melted down to create the new figure. The sculptor, François-Frédéric Lemot, proved to be a devotee of the emperor, however, and he reputedly placed a small bronze of Napoleon, along with some other seditious artifacts, in the horse's hollow belly. (72)

In 1607 the equestrian king sponsored the creation of a mixed commercial and residential development in the triangular space between the two bridges and the back of the Conciergerie. Called the Place Dauphine, it honored Henri's heir apparent, the future Louis XIII. A narrow entrance between two pavilions led away from the crowded bridges and roadway into a secluded courtyard surrounded by shops at ground level with two stories of living space above them. (73) The house façades were uniform in design and materials—red brick accented with chains of lighter brick. Though lots within the development were of unequal size, the regular façades and a common roof along each row of houses ensured a uniform appearance. The footprint of the development has remained almost intact, though the back end has been razed to make room for the burgeoning façade of the Palace of Justice. But every seventeenth-century building around the tree-shaded plaza has been rebuilt. Only the two pavilions that guard the narrow entrance are original.

73

The downriver end of the island is one of the most peaceful and pleasant spots in Paris. Stairs near the statue of Henri IV lead down to a small
park called the Square du Vert Galant that fills what is now the triangular
stern of the island. The park was created from the consolidation of three
small islands that stood at ground level in Roman times. One was the site
of executions, while another held a mill where water power was harnessed
to stamp the royal coinage. Today, grassplots, benches, and walks shaded
by mature, unpruned trees offer not only a welcome retreat from the city
but an outpost on the river that is unique. (74)

Paris's long history of struggle with the Seine is reflected in the increasingly high embankments that have, over the centuries, sprung up all
along its course. As late as 1910, the river overwhelmed even these pro-
tections and submerged the lowest-lying neighborhoods. Generally speaking, though, Paris, unlike many European cities, actually welcomes the
river that flows through its center. All along the riverside, stairways lead
to wide walkways just above water level. There are benches and promenades where people stroll untroubled by the incessant, maniac traffic
that streaks along roadways up above. On the river itself, water taxis and

74

the famous glassed-
in tour boats, called
bateaux-mouches,
pass up and down
the river, showing off
the city to visitors
and natives together.
(75) Everywhere else,
though, one looks

down on the river from the quays that protect the city from its waters. But
from the Square du Vert Galant, the eye shares the viewpoint of the wide
and fast-moving sheet of water whose powers have driven the city from the
earliest days. The park is unique, too, because it is the place where the
river comes closest to trees and grass—where engineering and technology
are held at bay as much as possible,
and the primitive components of the
landscape are given a tiny space to
assert themselves.

75

The informality of this riverside
park contrasts strongly with the city's
great formal gardens. The first gardens at the Tuileries were uninspired
patchworks of lawns and flower beds
divided by a grid of gravel walks. The
transformation of this two-dimensional canvas into a multilevel and complex grouping of trees, shrubs, lawns, and parterres punctuated by fountains and statues was the work of the great seventeenth-century French
landscape designer André Le Nôtre. Born in 1613, Le Nôtre belonged to
a celebrated family with generations of service and experience in the royal
gardens, including decades at the Tuileries. André's father was apprentice
to the chief gardener there during the reign of Henri IV. Under Louis XIII,
he assumed control and at his death passed the post on to his son.

André first distinguished himself during the reign of Louis XIV by his
designs at the charming but ill-conceived estate of the young king's finance
minister, Nicolas Fouquet. Fouquet's estate, called Vaux-le-Vicomte, is famous in French history as an extreme example of the hazards of ministerial

76

life. When Louis XIV was first invited to the new chateau, his reaction was immediate and disastrous for the proud owner. The estate was grander than anything Louis himself possessed, and it was evidence of the finance minister's extraordinary wealth. A mere subject ostentatiously outdoing the king, though not quite illegal, was certainly imprudent and offensive to his majesty. But the sheer magnitude of Fouquet's wealth also gave Louis pause. Concluding that Fouquet was guilty of diverting state funds to his private use, Louis had the minister arrested on the day after his visit, and his property seized. The men responsible for the creation of the chateau were not punished, however. Instead, the architect Le Vau, the painter Le Brun, and the landscape architect Le Nôtre were all hired to design an even grander residence for the young king in the nearby town of Versailles.

Le Nôtre's gardens at Vaux and Versailles remain among the most celebrated in the world, but his work at the Tuileries is visited and enjoyed by tens of thousands of people every day. Because of the destruction of the Tuileries palace in the nineteenth century, the garden is now fused with the Jardin du Carrousel that originally stood between the Louvre and the Tuileries. Le Nôtre's garden begins at the foot of the broad terrace

where the palace stood. (76) Its first section, called the Great Square,
is a collection of lawns and beds grouped around a central basin and
two smaller ones. The main axis of the garden drives through its center;
smaller secondary axes come in at right angles. Trees line the north and
west edges of this garden, which is dotted with statues and unique speci-
men plants. Elevated terraces on both the north and south, which extend
the full length of the garden, isolate it from the city. The narrower terraces
on the south side offer views of the river.

The Grand Couvert is a tree-shaded garden roughly one and a half
times the size of the Grand Square. Its centerline is a wide open gravel
walkway that ends in an octagonal basin near the western edge. Beneath
the shade of the thick trees are smaller walks lined with benches and a
number of specialized plantings. Since the opening of the garden to the
public in the nineteenth century, children's activities and playgrounds have
been brought into the park. There are model boats for rent and pony rides,
restaurants, and grounds for playing boules. (77) An Orangerie on the south
side and the Jeu de Paume (handball court) on the north have long been
used to exhibit paintings.

Courtiers who flocked to the Louvre and Tuileries relied on their own
wealth and ingenuity to create residences near the palaces. The grandest
of these *hôtels particuliers* evolved
from a smaller house close to the seat
of power. In 1624 in anticipation of
his role as royal counselor, Cardinal

77

Richelieu bought the Hôtel d'Angennes directly across the Rue Saint Honoré from the Louvre and near the fortification wall built by Charles V.

Richelieu, who was destined to be one of the most powerful and famous men in French history, was born in Paris in 1585. At age five he entered the Collège de Navarre. He hoped to become a soldier like his father, but financial pressure forced him into an ecclesiastical career. His political ability and his hard-line orthodoxy—Richelieu was a zealous advocate of the Catholic Counter-Reformation—caught the attention of Marie de' Medici. In 1616 during Marie's prolonged regency, Richelieu became her secretary of state. When the young Louis XIII asserted his right to the throne and banished his mother, he also ousted her chief adviser. In a few years, however, Richelieu won the trust and respect of the young king. In 1622 he was created cardinal and two years later became the leading minister in Louis' government. For the remaining twenty years of his life, Cardinal Richelieu was the most powerful figure in France.

The modest Hôtel d'Angennes quickly proved too small for the king's chief minister. In the 1630s Richelieu took advantage of his appointment as director general of fortifications to have the outmoded wall of Charles V torn down. On the reclaimed land he created a palace with a large garden behind it that stretched halfway to the new city walls. (78) Almost as soon as Richelieu moved in, he ordered construction of a gallery extending from the back of the palace. Behind a row of simple Tuscan columns was a paved sheltered walkway and a suite of small rooms, one of which the cardinal used as a chapel. Like similar structures in Italian villas of the period, this gallery connected subordinate buildings to the main palace and also offered a sheltered viewpoint from which the garden could be enjoyed. When the gallery was begun, Richelieu had just been appointed superintendent of commerce and navigation. Plaques decorated with anchors and ship's prows set into its back wall commemorated this appointment. Called the Gallery of the Prows, it is the only part of the seventeenth-century structure that still stands.

Richelieu donated the house to the monarchy, and the royal family briefly lived there in the mid-seventeenth century, which earned the building its title, the Palais Royal. In the eighteenth century it passed into the hands of the prominent dukes of Orléans. Eager to capitalize on their valuable holdings, the dukes of Orléans lined the back edges of the garden with three-story residences above an open arcade. Richelieu's Tuscan columns became pilasters that stretched from the ground to the top of the second story of each unit. A bracket above each pilaster framed small windows in the third story; a balustrade, above, partially hid dormer windows.

Since the eighteenth century, these beautiful buildings have had their ups and downs. Despite their royal connections, eighteenth-century members of the Orléans family were quite radical. Coffee houses around the garden were the center of revolutionary debate and action. During the nineteenth century, the area was unpopular and dangerous at night. Almost all of Richelieu's palace was gradually replaced by a building that is now home to

78

79

the Conseil d'Etat (Council of State), a government agency which reviews legislation that has constitutional implications.

The most enduring features of the original palace are the gardens behind it and the Gallery of the Prows. The courtyard is separated from the rest of the garden by a transverse arcade modeled on Richelieu's original. This inner area has been transformed into a sculpture garden of sorts where bollards in the shape of column stubs are arranged like checkers on a board. (79) These sculptural columns call attention to the utilitarian pillars that rim the space. In the main gardens of the palace, two long graveled walks between carefully groomed trees surround a fountain and open lawns bordered by flower-filled parterres. The essential topography of the garden was laid out in the seventeenth century, though the fountain, which once stood at the end of the garden farthest from the palace, has been moved to its center. (80) This subtle shift signals the transformation of the garden from something intended to be enjoyed from the prospect of the palace to something self-contained and open to all. Today, the arcade shops surrounding the garden are a mix of celebrated restaurants and upscale boutiques.

Richelieu, patron of the painter Poussin, was interested in the other arts as well. In 1635 he organized the Académie Française, which to this day continues to oversee the evolution of the French language and to honor the achievements of writers and literary scholars. At the time of its founding, the main task of the academy was to create a dictionary of the French language. The Accademia della Crusca founded in the sixteenth century had already produced a second edition of its Italian dictionary by the time the Académie Française was formed, and it would produce a third before the first official French dictionary was printed in 1694.

The task of these academies was formidable. The languages they were attempting to capture in their alphabetical word lists were amorphous, to say the least. France, though united under a single increasingly centralizing ruler, was not by any means a unified culture, and it had no national language. The earliest vernacular dictionaries were not meant to be mirrors that recorded every variant or regional form. Their aim was to create a standard spoken language for the nation, one that lived up to the model of the two languages that all Europeans regarded as fully developed and fully explored, Latin and Greek. According to Article 24 of the academy's statutes, its "principal function will be to labor with all the care and diligence possible at the creation of unambiguous rules for our language and to make it pure and eloquent."

In Italy, where dialect variations were (and remain) even greater than in France, heated literary debates during the Renaissance created a framework for a national literary culture. Formalizing the Italian language was easier because the scholars at work on the dictionary

acknowledged the primacy of three great authors, Dante Alighieri, Francesco Petrarca, and Giovanni Boccaccio. The French language had no comparable literary foundation. French literature was younger and more diverse. Its greatest authors were alive and working in the sixteenth and seventeenth centuries at the same time that the academy was creating its dictionary. In the end, the French Academy created standard French on the model of the dialect of the royal court, which was essentially the dialect of Paris. Its principles of correct usage were fixed by adopting the words and grammatical constructions preferred by contemporary authors.

In addition to purifying the French language and clarifying its grammar, members of the academy were charged with making it "capable of treating of the arts and sciences." Speakers of English take for granted the resources of a language that has hundreds of thousands of words to describe every conceivable thing and a full repertoire of grammatical conventions that permit the combination of words and phrases in ways that set out the most nuanced shades of meaning. In the eyes of Renaissance scholars, no vernacular language had that range of expressiveness; it remained the exclusive property of Latin and Greek. In his *Défense et illustration de la langue française,* Nicolas Boileau discussed ways to expand French and enrich it by borrowing words from the classical languages. He compared the pillaging of these ancient languages to what he regarded as the bold but legitimate capture of Rome by the Gauls in 387 BC.

For most of its long history the Académie Française maintained rigid control of the French language. It chose the words that entered the standard French dictionary, and through its numerous literary and scholarly prizes, first awarded in 1671, it honored those writers whose use of French best reflected the ideals it cherished. In recent years, the dictionary has become more open to variant dialects within France and more welcoming to the multiple varieties of French spoken in former French colonies throughout the world. This open-mindedness among academicians has been greeted by a welling up of slang, regionalisms, and importations from the former colonies. In recent decades, French, which—in part because of its regulation and precision—was once the establishment language of literature, culture, international diplomacy, and law, has become almost as fluid as English.

Along with his interests in the arts and letters, Richelieu was a patron of the drama. In 1636 a theater was built in an area accessible from the courtyard at the front of his palace. A few years later the theater was moved to the west wing. When this performance area was destroyed by fire in 1781, a new theater was built on the site and later linked to the palace. Now called the Théâtre Richelieu, this neoclassical building has been home to the French national theater since 1799.

Originally designed to hold more than two thousand spectators, the performance hall has been scaled down repeatedly since its creation, mostly for reasons of fire safety, and now accommodates about eight hundred theater-goers. In the process the hall, which was originally a deep oval, has shrunk to a shallow semicircle. Its traditional features, however, have not been completely erased. From a crypt-like circular lobby, multiple stairways lead to seats at all levels. Orchestra seats are surrounded by four balconies that trace the curvilinear form of the back wall. The walls are hung with red velvet, and the proscenium arch and the balcony rails are brightly gilded. Tiers of stage boxes are framed by giant pilasters with comic and tragic masks at their tops.

The Théâtre Richelieu has long been associated with the oldest national theater company now in existence, the Comédie Française. The troupe began in obscurity in the seventeenth century and rose to prominence and royal patronage primarily through the work of a single playwright, Jean Baptiste Poquelin, who is universally known by his stage name, Molière. Poquelin was born in Paris in 1622. Though trained as a lawyer and briefly employed by the court, he used money inherited from his mother to form a troupe of actors. The troupe attracted, and lost, many wealthy patrons as it performed throughout the French provinces. On October 24, 1658, the playwright and his company entertained the king in the guardroom of the Louvre. Two years later the company was given the use of Richelieu's theater. In 1665 they were proclaimed the King's Troupe at the Palais Royal and granted an annual endowment.

They remained in that theater for only two years but continued to enjoy royal patronage for the remaining thirteen years of Molière's life. During that period the dramatist wrote his best-known plays: *The Misanthrope, The Bourgeois Gentleman, The Imaginary Invalid,* and *The Doctor Despite Himself.* These benign social comedies poke fun at the extravagances of wealthy middle-class characters. In 1664 Molière wrote a first version of a play that would prove to be his most controversial. Its central figure, Tartuffe, is an ostentatiously pious man who worms his way into the confidence of a naive gentleman. Molière's creation of a villain who is to all appearances a clergyman was controversial enough, but the ending of the play was, if anything, more audacious.

The schemer wins control over the family's wealth and thwarts each attempt to expose his hypocrisy. The victimized family has exhausted every resource, and only a miracle can save them. An officer of the king, who it seems is about to enforce the sentence of a lower court against Tartuffe's victims, suddenly announces the villain's arrest. He explains to the bewildered protagonists and to the audience: "We live under a Prince who is the enemy of fraud, / One whom no imposter can ever take in. / His great soul in its fine intelligence / Turns the eye of justice on every case ... / He gives eternal glory to men of good will, / But his zeal for the good does not blind him / Nor does his love for the truth empty his heart / Of all that creates terror in false men. / Tartuffe was not the man to take him in."

Such blatant propaganda is not typical of Molière's plays or the work of other writers and performers supported by the court. Still, *Tartuffe, or The Imposter,* makes apparent what was always an undercurrent in the official art sponsored by the French court. It would glorify France, its institutions, and its language; it would encourage public respect and ex-emplify morality. At Molière's death his troupe divided, then recombined, and eventually absorbed their great rival, the Theater of the Italians, which performed works in the Commedia dell'arte style. At the time of the Revolution the company split again, this time along ideological lines. They were definitively reunited in 1799 and restored to their home next door to the Palais Royal.

Directly north of the Palais Royal, the Palais Mazarin was home to the second most powerful and most notorious cardinal-adviser to French kings. Born in central Italy in 1602, Giulio Mazarini was educated at the

Jesuit Collegio Romano in Rome. Patronage from the Colonna and Bar-
berini families won Mazarini an appointment as canon of the papal church
of Saint John Lateran in Rome. This prize appointment was soon followed
by two diplomatic postings to France. During the two years Mazarini
served as papal nuncio in Paris, he worked closely with Richelieu. Forced
from office by Spanish cardinals, Mazarini adopted French citizenship and
shortened his name in 1639. Richelieu secured his creation as cardinal in
1641.

Richelieu died in December 1642, and without warning Louis XIII
died the following spring at age forty-one. His wife, Queen Anne of Austria, became regent for the young Louis XIV. She gave nominal charge of
the regency to the duke of Orléans but placed real power in the hands of
Mazarin. Her trust in the cardinal was so great and their contact so repeated and intimate that there were rumors of a secret marriage between
the two. When Louis attained his majority in 1643, Mazarin continued to
serve as his adviser until his own death in 1661. He saw the king through
the final days of the Thirty Years War and two palace rebellions, one led
by judges who protested cutbacks in salary and the second by disaffected
nobles. A pious Catholic trained by the ultra-orthodox Jesuits, Mazarin
guided the regime's handling of both Protestants and Jansenists.

Early in his tenure as cardinal, Mazarin rented a private palace
directly behind Richelieu's Palais Royal on what is now the Rue des
Petits Champs. Called the Hôtel Tubeuf, the building, though frequently
remodeled, still stands. It now forms part of the complex of the old
French National Library (Bibliothèque Nationale). Early in his regency, the
cardinal hired François Mansart to enlarge the building. Though built into

the library complex that began to evolve around it in the late seventeenth century, the Hôtel Tubeuf remains relatively isolated from the rest. A main block and two wings surround three sides of a courtyard. A gateway and low wall guard the main entrance.

The building, structured of red brick decorated with chains of lighter stone, is spare. Its two main stories are separated by a small cornice and lit by multiple windows. There are two rows of small windows below the cornice and a single row of very high windows on the second floor, where the ceremonial rooms of the palace were placed. Mansart's roof, with its steep pitch and alternating round and gabled windows, tops the building. A formal garden stretched out behind the palace, a smaller-scale version of Richelieu's garden at the Palais Royal. What survives is now called the Jardin Vivienne; it is paved with gravel and dotted with statues.

Some of the more than three hundred pieces of ancient sculpture the cardinal collected were displayed on the ground floor of his palace. His painting collection was housed in frescoed galleries that flanked the garden behind the palace and now form the interconnecting link between the Hôtel Tubeuf and the rest of the library complex. The second-floor gallery with frescoes representing scenes from the *Metamorphoses* of Ovid is now called the Galerie Mazarin. The lower-floor gallery decorated with stuccoes and partially preserved *grisaille* paintings is called the Galerie Mansart. Mazarin exhibited some of the hundreds of Italian paintings he owned in these galleries. He also owned almost a hundred French paintings. Like Richelieu, Mazarin was especially fond of Poussin.

The cardinal also collected books. Housed in a separate building near the palace, his collection numbered some forty thousand volumes. From

his earliest years in the Hôtel Tubeuf, Mazarin opened his library to scholars. It is ironic that the Bibliothèque Nationale built around his palace
houses only a portion of the cardinal's own books. The bulk of his collection was moved to the Mazarin Library in the Institut de France directly
across from the Louvre on the Left Bank.

The royal book collection that Charles V had so carefully and lovingly
housed in the old Louvre fared badly in succeeding generations. During
the English occupation, the duke of Bedford acted as agent for the Crown
and bought many of the king's books at fire-sale prices. Succeeding French
kings reestablished the library, housing it in chateaux throughout the kingdom. In the early sixteenth century, when printed books were beginning to
be produced in great abundance, an ordinance of François I multiplied the
library's collection overnight. A copy of every book printed in the kingdom
was to be deposited in the royal collection. François' librarian, Guillaume
Budé, added early manuscripts, including important Greek texts, to the
king's holdings. The fall of Byzantium in 1453 had sent a stream of refugee
scholars to the West, armed with a knowledge of Greek and, often enough,
with a few valuable manuscripts. Greek, which had proved so challenging to
Western scholars of the early Renaissance, became one of the cornerstones
of intellectual life during the sixteenth century.

Henri IV gave eight hundred manuscripts—part of Marie de' Medici's
dowry—to the library and moved it away from the court to a more convenient setting at the Collège de Clermont in the university quarter. Though
the library continued to move around after that, it always remained in
Paris. In 1712 the royal collection was placed in the palace of the duke
de Nevers, and gradually over the next century and a half it expanded to
fill the large city block anchored in the Hôtel Tubeuf.

The Revolution that was so destructive to religious and royal institutions was generous to the national library. Books and manuscripts belong-
ing to suppressed religious orders throughout France became the property
of the national government, and most collections of any significance
found their way to the Bibliothèque Nationale. More than nine thousand
manuscripts were seized from the abbey of Saint Germain des Prés alone,
and the total number of books added to the collection was enormous. The
Revolution renewed the law of François I requiring that one or two copies
of all printed materials—books, music, newspapers, and journals included—be deposited in the library. Innovations in nineteenth-century printing
and the rapid expansion of literacy in industrial Europe produced oceans
of printed matter that the library struggled to store and catalogue.

Napoleon—whose conquests of Egypt, Spain, and Italy enlarged the
Louvre's collections of antiquities, European painting, and sculpture—also
expanded the collections of the national library. A secret codicil in the
1799 treaty of Venice that brought Venetian canvases to Paris also guaranteed the conqueror his personal choice of five hundred manuscripts.
The booty from Rome, again spelled out in detail in a formal treaty, was
even greater. In the decades following Napoleon's defeat, many of these
objects were repatriated, but others could not be returned. The French
conquests in Italy led to the suppression of monastic foundations and sei-
zure of their property. Many of these institutions never reopened. Objects
and manuscripts obtained from them had no advocates demanding their
return and no secure place to return to.

The enormous expansion of the national library's holdings put the
building complex under an incredible strain. Major renovations were carried out in the middle of the nineteenth century, most notably the addition

81

of two great reading rooms. The first, designed by Henri Labrouste and completed in 1868, now bears the architect's name. The Oval Reading Room was begun after 1880 by Jean-Louis Pascal, an associate of Labrouste. It remained incomplete until 1936.

The Labrouste Reading Room on the ground floor is a remarkable nineteenth-century hybrid space created from Romanesque forms that are given unprecedented dimension and complexity by the use of an iron framework. The ceiling of the huge room is made up of multiple intersecting domes each with a skylight at its summit. The intersections between domes are supported on rounded steel girders with ornamental X-shaped braces along their entire length that spring from attenuated iron pillars. The soaring domes are so light and so lightly supported that they seem not to bear down on the floor but to rise from it like air-filled parachutes tethered to the ground by slender cables. (81) Beneath the multiple arcades are double files of desks like rows of pews perpendicular to the long axis of the room and cut though by a center aisle. A bar between facing desks acts as a support for books and holds reading lamps with rounded glass globes that echo the shape of the vaults above.

The end of the room opposite the entry has the shape of an enormous apse. Like the roof vaults, the apse is a common structure in Roman

basilicas, which were the source of ecclesiastical architecture throughout Europe. The focal point of the apse of a Christian church is the altar
where the Eucharist is celebrated. The apse of the Labrouste reading
room focuses on the librarian's desk. In this secular church, the librarian
mediates the exchange of books between the stacks (accessible through a
doorway in the center of the apse curve) and readers. The librarian acts as
a priest presiding over the transmission of knowledge from page to mind.
As the wisdom of past generations is handed over to the present, the
librarian's act becomes a representation of tradition itself. The structure of
this reading room is a well-thought-out embodiment of a culture that has
been continually self-conscious in its own creation, regulation, and pres-
ervation. What the librarian dispenses to the eager reader is the carefully
groomed, well-cultivated tradition of French institutional culture.

The contemporary center of the nation's cultural heritage is a building
directly across the Pont des Arts from the Louvre. Now called the Institut
de France, the building was originally conceived as the Collège des Quatre
Nations. Mazarin left funds to build and endow a college for sixty young
gentlemen. He left his books to the college, along with funds to create
the Bibliothèque Mazarin, which continues in use today as an important
research library. Louis Le Vau was hired to design the structure. The building is a variant on the organizational scheme of the Palais Royal and the
Hôtel Tubeuf. A central pavilion with curving wings reaches out to two side
pavilions as it embraces a wide semicircular courtyard. The main pavilion
features a temple front and a dome. The wings and side pavilions have
arcaded openings on the first level and rectangular windows above. (82)

During the Revolution the college became one of three centralized
schools in Paris. Then in 1805 Napoleon designated it the home of

82

the Institut de France. Originally suppressed by the Revolution, the royal academies were rechartered in 1795 and grouped into a single umbrella organization. The institute now includes five academies: the Académie Française (French language); Académie des Beaux Arts (painting, sculpture, music, and architecture); Académie des Inscriptions et Belles Lettres (literature and the humanities); Académie des Sciences; and Académie des Sciences Morales et Politiques (ethical and political sciences).

The work of the great centralizing idealists of the seventeenth century—Henri IV, Louis XIII, and especially Richelieu, Mazarin, and Louis XIV—transformed the concept of Paris even more than it changed the physical city. By the end of Louis XIV's long reign, Paris was the capital of the kingdom in a far more fundamental sense than it had ever been before. Power had visited the city throughout its long history, but the city had never before asserted its cultural dominance.

From the seventeenth century onward, the language of Paris was enshrined in French dictionaries, making the peculiar intonations of the capital the standard toward which every educated speaker aspired. The literature of an entire country was overseen by an organization committed to rewarding those efforts that corresponded to their very Parisian sense of correctness, elegance, and usefulness. In addition, the royal academy defined art, monopolized the training of painters and sculptors, and rewarded or punished their products according to its own standards, creating fruitful careers full of successful exhibitions and rich commissions or aborting them at will. The theater, which in France had always been itinerant and regional, remained so, but the goal of every actor now was to perform in the capital and ideally to own a share in the Comédie Française. In architecture, the model was the formulaic redeployment of multistory wings and pavilions decorated with columns and crowned with peaked or rounded gables.

Louis XIV is widely recognized as a centralizing leader whose main political strategy was to keep the French nobility occupied in the court. Far from home, their hold on their territories would weaken. It is less generally understood that Louis' cultural strategy, like that of his predecessors, was centralizing as well. Someone once joked that a national language is a dialect backed up by an army. There is certainly truth to that in the case of France. But putting muscle behind cultural activity is pointless unless it gains some political end, and none of the men involved in the organization of French cultural life was either wasteful of effort or ignorant of consequences. Louis and his advisers meant to make Paris the center of French culture because this transformation would reinforce the power and prestige of the court.

Paris became what Athens and Rome had once been, cities that combined political power and cultural preeminence. Like them, Paris made itself the only conceivable place to succeed. From the seventeenth century onward, whatever a person of ability and drive aspired to be was found in Paris. In a certain readily understandable sense, Paris was France. Even a man as brilliant and eccentric as Michel de Montaigne, who spent virtually all of his creative life far from the City of Light, could write: "Paris has been in my heart since I was a child. I am not French except through that great city."

Chapter Six

THE LIMITS OF ROYAL AMBITION

Louis XIV, who broke new ground with institutions governing the French language, literature, and the fine arts, was also a pioneer in the creation of vast public projects that shaped Paris both socially and structurally. Their design and execution give a sense of the guiding principles that the seventeenth-century absolutists would have liked to apply throughout the capital, had conditions been different. The densely settled inner city was almost unapproachable, however, and the only land available for large-scale development lay either outside the city walls altogether or in areas where the obsolete wall of Charles V was being demolished.

Louis' most ambitious public projects came to fruition in semirural areas on the Left Bank. The grandest of these was Les Invalides, an enormous complex designed to house soldiers disabled by wounds, disease, or old age. (Map 6) Charitable institutions of this kind (though not on this scale) were typically the work of religious groups. Monastic orders dedicated themselves to the care of the incurably ill and the aged, while lay organizations under the sponsorship of a church or brotherhood visited the sick and comforted the dying. For the state to assume direct responsibility for the health and well-being of an entire category of the infirm is almost without precedent in the seventeenth century. The scale on which Louis XIV's builders worked and the cost to the regime of caring for the institution's inmates would not

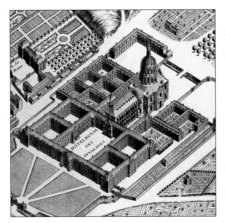

83

be matched elsewhere before the nineteenth
century.

The first architect chosen for the project was
Libéral Bruant. In 1676, with work still incomplete, Bruant's pupil and the grand-nephew of
François Mansart, Jules Hardouin-Mansart, took
over. On a vast plot of former agricultural land
on the Left Bank well outside the city walls,
Bruant laid out an enormous master plan that
combined cultivated meadows with multistory buildings grouped around
courtyards. (83) This fusion of residence and garden was essentially the
design scheme that had defined the Louvre and Tuileries complex, as
well as the Palais Royal, the Hôtel Mazarin, the Hôtel de Sully, and other
hôtels particuliers throughout the city. Each of these great building-garden
combinations occupied a long, narrow city block. Surrounding streets con-
formed to the rectilinear shape and adopted the axes of these structures,
creating areas of order and palatial beauty in the helter-skelter urban grid.

The long axis of the Louvre was the most important of these in the city.
It continued to grow and develop through the centuries, and its extensions
eventually formed the spine of one of the largest and most dynamic organizations of urban space in the world. Laid out in open country on the other
side of the river, the axis created by Les Invalides extended from an inland
complex of buildings across a long esplanade to the banks of the Seine.

The broad north side of the complex is marked by a central entryway
and modest pavilions at each of its long ends. This structural formula was
based on the innovative façade that Lescot invented for the Louvre in the
sixteenth century, a model that was imitated and developed with some

variety and considerable persistence by many other French architects over the years. The doorway of the center pavilion incorporates an architectural form that also influenced the Louvre entryway designed by Perrault. The prototype for both of these designs is the Roman triumphal arch. At Les Invalides, the arch begins at ground level, where it is anchored in twin statues, before it soars upward through two applied columns to a grand vault rimmed with floral friezes and military trophies. At the top of the arch is an image of the sun, and directly beneath it an equestrian statue of Louis XIV—the Sun King—stands on an inscribed plinth with personifications to either side. The high dome of the memorial chapel at the far end of the complex echoes the curve of the arch at a height sufficient to counterbalance the long façade.

The interior of the hospice was divided into a number of courtyards overlooked by the rooms of its thousands of inmates. The disabled were cared for in a hospital, but the other residents were required to work, both to defray the cost of their care and to provide a useful and productive way for the men to spend their time. They made uniforms and wound rope—useful items for military purposes—and some of them created illustrations for books or wove tapestries. The pensioners attended services in a church at the south end of the complex that opened in 1679. Its dedicatee was Louis IX, the sainted member of the French royal family. The vaulted nave of the neoclassical interior is decorated with banners captured in battle from the nation's adversaries.

Behind the altar of this church is an enormous chapel surmounted by a soaring dome designed by Hardouin-Mansart, based on plans drafted by his great-uncle. The chapel has its own outside entry on the south side: a double tier of columned porches that guide the eye toward the

84

entrance of the building and begin the strong verticals that the dome completes. (84) Elevated on an ornamented drum and topped by a soaring lantern, domes of this type were a response to the square towers of the Romanesque and the needle spires of the Gothic. They reached into the sky and staked a claim to absolutist order in that divine dimension, as well as below.

The chapel's form represents one of the great ideals of the Renaissance, a free-standing, centrally planned domed structure. At the center of Hardouin-Mansart's chapel is a perfect circle aligned with the main axis of the pensioners' church and its altar. The circle, which is directly beneath the dome, is extended in each of the four cardinal directions by a short arm. (85) Free-standing Corinthian columns at the corner of each of the chapel's four extensions support an entablature that traces the contours of the cruciform room. This in turn supports the vaulted roof of each extension. Framed by these columns, blind arcades in the walls surround smaller doors that lead to circular chapels at the corners of the building.

The four pendentives supporting the drum are decorated with images of the four evangelists. Twelve windows light the drum of the cupola. Medallions representing twelve French kings above them were restored in

1815. The cupola itself is divided into twelve sections by heavy ribbing; the image of an apostle fills each section. In a second cupola, visible through an oculus in the first, the crusader Saint Louis offers Jesus the sword with which he triumphed over the enemies of Christianity. This triumphant image crowns a decorative program that fuses apostolic and royal imagery. Though the style is new, the message is a familiar one—the kings of Judah and Israel on the façade of Notre Dame tell the same story. It is echoed in Sainte Chapelle, where the crown of thorns and the crown of France are merged into a single image of divinely sponsored rule.

Given the chapel's royal sponsorship and militant orthodoxy, it is no wonder that Saint Louis des Invalides was badly treated during the Revolution. It was briefly rededicated to Mars the Roman god of war, but the rush of events soon presented the building with a new purpose. During Napoleon's first empire, the chapel was transformed into a shrine—a military pantheon—where members of the imperial household and great military leaders were buried. Napoleon's brother Joseph is entombed in the chapel of Saint Augustine. In 1840 the emperor himself, who died in 1821, was buried in an unusual open crypt below floor level in the center of the chapel.

The emperor's tomb is carved of a red quartzite stone that looks like porphyry, the material from which the tombs of Roman emperors were traditionally cut. The floor beneath is marked like a compass rose and inscribed with the names of Napoleon's greatest battles. A circle of piers, each with a caryatid-like Victory on its inner face, supports the

85

86

rim of the open floor above. Like the names on the floor, these figures represent major military successes. On the back wall of the round space behind the piers are bas-reliefs that commemorate achievements in government. (86) While the immediate sur-

roundings of Napoleon's tomb are distinctive, the tomb coexists with the restored imagery of the entire chapel. Napoleon takes his place among these monarchs and adds his story to the symbolism of royal power and piety that the chapel has expressed since the time of its creation. The emperor's body anchors the succession of images that reach heavenward to culminate in the deification of Louis IX.

In the mid-eighteenth century, Louis XIV's successor founded the national military academy, the Ecole Militaire. Rather than continue the street grid established by Les Invalides, Louis XV's designers imitated the complex as a whole. They built an inland institution with a long greensward that met the curving river at right angles. At its back they created a circle with radiating avenues. Streets spawned by this complex gave order to the neighborhood farther downriver that developed in its shadow.

In his systematic remodeling of the city in the nineteenth century, Baron Haussmann used these seventeenth-century axes and developed others on their model to bring order to the metropolis. The axis created by Les Invalides was continued across the Alexandre III Bridge to link with the axis of the Louvre. (Map 7) Their junction point was monumentalized by the creation of the Grand Palais and Petit Palais. Farther west, the Eiffel Tower was erected near the river's edge on the green space created by the Ecole Militaire. Intended at first as a temporary structure, it earned a permanent position on a broad axis that crossed the Pont d'Iéna and terminated at the Trocadéro. (87) This open plaza is flanked by the Palais de Chaillot built for the international exposition of 1937. Its two wings house a naval museum and the museum of ethnology. A circle at the back of that complex links to one of the broad avenues radiating from the Arc de Triomphe.

Like Les Invalides, the Luxem-bourg palace also expresses the ambi-tions and taste of the seventeenth-century absolutists. (Map 6) In 1612 Marie de' Medici, widow of King Henri IV, purchased a chateau on the Left Bank site and commissioned Salo-mon de Brosse to remodel both the building and its grounds. In his plan, a long rusticated arcade and a central gateway ornamented with rusticated columns and topped by a small dome guarded the entrance to the palace on the north side of the building, facing downhill toward the Seine. In a design similar to that of the Hôtel Tubeuf, this wall linked the embracing wings of the palace behind it and closed off the front of an open court. (88) De Brosse borrowed the rustication of the

87

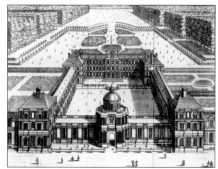

building and other architectural details from
the Pitti Palace in Florence. The Luxembourg
was well outside the city walls in a semirural
setting where rustication made sense. Eventually Florence and Paris grew well beyond their
earlier limits and engulfed both of these country
estates in a tight webwork of urban streets.

88

Marie de' Medici was exiled in 1631 by her son, Louis XIII, and
never returned to France. The building passed to her heirs, the dukes of
Orléans, and then to other prominent courtiers. In 1750 some paintings
from the royal collections at Versailles were transferred to the palace,
where they joined Rubens' twenty-one-canvas cycle illustrating Marie's
life. These works migrated to Versailles a few years later. After 1818 the
Luxembourg palace was the official exhibition space for contemporary art.
The limited gallery spaces still remaining in the building host temporary
exhibits.

Over its long life, the Luxembourg palace was put to many uses in addition to art exhibition. In 1791 the Revolution made the palace a prison.
A marshal of France, Philippe de Noailles, aged seventy-nine, and his wife
were both held there before their executions. The viscount of Beauharnais
and his wife, Joséphine Tascher de la Pagerie, were also prisoners in the
palace. The viscount, accused of insufficient zeal in the military defense
of the city of Mainz, was guillotined. Joséphine survived to become the
first wife of Napoleon Bonaparte, and from 1804 until their divorce in
1810 she was the first empress of France.

Too grand to be an effective prison, the palace was taken over by the
Directorate—the five-man executive branch that ruled the French Repub-

lic from 1795 to 1799. After Napoleon's consulship replaced the direc-
tors, the palace become home to the Senate. At the fall of Napoleon's
empire, it again became a prison, and then home to various ministries.
In 1852 the Senate returned and has occupied the building ever since.
It meets in the D-shaped enclosed space in the center of the palace.
The small annexed palace, called the Petit Luxembourg, which Marie de'
Medici gave to Cardinal Richelieu in 1616, is now the official residence of
the president of the Senate.

Remodeled frequently over the centuries, the building evolved into a
square with pavilions at each corner, connected by short wings. On the east
and west sides, these wings are punctuated by central pavilions; on the
north and south sides, large entryways in smaller pavilions provide access to
the palace. The gardens on the south side form the grounds of the French
Senate. Closely but not obtru-
sively guarded, they are one
of the most popular and con-
genial public parks in Paris.
Unlike the United States
Capitol, which is isolated
from the city and its daily
rhythms by traffic barriers
and armed security forces,
the open lawns and formal
borders of the Luxembourg

89

gardens are a welcoming place to relax. (89) Flowers bloom eight months of
the year, and the circular reflecting pool directly behind the palace provides
entertainment for children, who sail rented toy boats on its surface. Along-

side the formal gardens, paths wind beneath an enormous variety of trees, and sculptures ranging from the traditional to the abstract are scattered about. There are tennis courts and playgrounds for children of all ages.

Acquiring land to build the gardens took years. The final piece was put in place when the property reached uphill to the site of the Paris Observatory. At the middle of the nineteenth century the garden came under direct attack by Baron Haussmann's plans for an updated capital. Despite intense public protest, portions of the garden were sacrificed to widen the Boulevard Saint Michel.

90

Like the Luxembourg palace, the church of Saint Sulpice reflects the influence of Renaissance ideals. Its dedicatee, Saint Sulpicius, was a fourth-century ecclesiastic from southwestern France about whom very little is known. Already in place by the twelfth century, the church was served by monks of the abbey of Saint Germain des Prés and continued to expand as the population of its parish grew. By the seventeenth century, the area was so densely settled that the church could no longer accommodate the multitudes crowding into mass. (90) Rather than see the parish divided and a second church created, the rector undertook a dramatic rebuilding program.

Construction began at the choir end in the middle of the seventeenth century. By 1678 the old church, which had gradually been overtaken by

the new building, was torn down. Four times the size of the original, the
new structure not only exhausted the resources of the parish but created
a debt of more than half a million French pounds, a staggering sum. The
parish defaulted. With the choir, the north end of the apse, and the crossing complete, building stopped for forty years. Work was completed in a
sixty-year campaign that began in 1720.

The new building's façade is divided into two stories by a continuous
Ionic entablature, and the center of each story is marked by a colonnade.
Openings on the first story lead to the five doors of the church, while openings on the second story shelter an open loggia. The two belfries of the
church are rich in classical ornament, but they violate the most fundamental classical principles of harmony and symmetry. They bear no relation to
the structure beneath them and only the slightest relation to each other.

The interior of the church is far more successful. An arcade surrounds
the nave and continues into the choir. Between each of its arches a Corinthian pilaster reaches to the base of an entablature. Arched windows in
the clerestory carry eighteenth-century glass; many in the choir have inset
figured panels. A second arcade separates the side aisles from chapels
along the nave and around the choir. One of the most curious features
of the church is a meridian—a true north-south line—traced by a brass
strip on the floor of the transept that leads to an obelisk at its north end.
Lenses in a south window focus the sun's rays at noon onto points on the
brass line that vary with the seasons. Commissioned in the early eighteenth century by the rector of Saint Sulpice, the meridian line was meant
to aid in calculating the date of Easter, a movable feast that occurs on the
first Sunday following the first full moon after the vernal equinox. (91)

91

The Revolution closed the church in 1793 and transformed it first into a Temple of Reason—a dedication that may have had something to do with the presence of the meridian line—and then somewhat later into a Temple of Victory. Saint Sulpice resumed life as a parish church in 1802. Both before and after the Revolution, many painters contributed to the decoration of the church. In the middle of the nineteenth century, the celebrated painter Eugène Delacroix was commissioned to decorate the Angel Chapel, the first in the south aisle of the nave. By that time religious painting had become derivative and uninspiring, and commissions of the kind Delacroix received, though common in the seventeenth century, had all but disappeared.

Of his three works in the chapel, the circular painting in the ceiling vault is the least inspired. The archangel Michael in armor floats in midair, wings outspread. With his spear he prods a writhing figure of Satan—derived from a classical image of Neptune—and sends him rolling into darkness. The combat of Jacob with the angel is more successful. Against a forest of dark trees evidently inspired by the landscapes of Tintoretto, the patriarch wrestles through the night with the messenger of God. Jacob's clothes lie in a pile in the right foreground, while his family continue their journey in the right middle ground. The episode represented is a significant if enigmatic one. On his way home to meet his elder brother, Esau, whom he has cheated of his birthright, Jacob pauses to meditate and pray. A stranger appears to him, and Jacob is driven for no apparent reason to ask the man's blessing. Convinced that the stranger is no mere mortal, Jacob wrestles with him until dawn, when the angel agrees to bless him, announcing: "Thy name shall not be called Jacob, but Israel; for if thou hast been strong against God, how much more shalt thou prevail against men?" (Genesis 32:28).

The final scene is Delacroix's bravura reinterpretation of one of Raphael's celebrated frescoes in the Vatican palace. Heliodorus was an officer in the army of the Persian satrap. When he attempted to loot the treasure of the Temple at Jerusalem, he was driven out by angels. In both Raphael's fresco and Delacroix's, the plunderer is ridden down by an archangel dressed for battle and mounted on a horse. In the Vatican fresco, two other angels, skimming the ground, float at his side. In Delacroix's version, these angels are fully airborne and sweep into the composition from right and left, swinging flails. The background of Raphael's picture is dominated by the figure of the high priest, who prays at an altar. The pope, borne on his litter, enters from the left, surrounded by courtiers. A crowd on the right of the picture is driven away with Heliodorus.

While Delacroix's image invites comparison with Raphael's masterpiece, the *Heliodorus* in Saint Sulpice is not a great religious painting. Like a book illustration, it successfully captures both the appearance and the emotional charge of its subject, but it fails to interpret that event as anything other than a spectacle that inspires surprise and perhaps awe. In a

92

pattern that is typical of medieval and Renaissance religious paintings, Raphael counterpoised Heliodorus and his fate against the actions of other figures. (92) The solemn high priest prays unmoved at the great altar, while the anachronistic pope looks on at the scene and clearly sees in it a representation of his own sanctity and the divine forces that sustain it. Raphael's painting is theologically, even theo-politically, articulate in a way that Delacroix's is not. (93)

The Pantheon, just to the east of the Luxembourg palace, belongs stylistically to the eighteenth century, but the nature of the project ties it closely to others undertaken in the previous century under the sponsorship of French monarchs. The cruciform building with its soaring dome and classical porch replaced one of the oldest and most venerable monuments in Paris—the Gothic church dedicated to Saint Geneviève. (94) Her role as a patriotic symbol had long protected the shrine, but when revulsion against Gothic architecture spread in the eighteenth century, the importance of the saint became an argument for updating rather than preserving her church.

The event that precipitated the new project was an illness suffered by Louis XV and a vow he took to build a more worthy shrine for the saint if he were cured. The hoped-for cure was realized and the church was begun. Nearly fifty years elapsed before work was completed, however,

and the old church dedicated to the saint was
not dismantled until the early years of the
nineteenth century. The first architect of the
new shrine was Jacques-Germain Soufflot. His
classical porch with its multiple columns and
pediment is an obvious borrowing from Had-
rian's Pantheon in Rome. The dome itself bears
some relation to the one Michelangelo designed
for the new basilica of Saint Peter, and the
drum that heightens it is, somewhat surprisingly, indebted to Christopher Wren's design for
Saint Paul's in London.

93

The interior is structured around a system
of intersecting vaults supported on Corinthian columns and a continual
entablature. Four equal arms meet in a central space beneath the dome.
Each of the arms has a wide central aisle under a longitudinal vault with
a shallow dome inset in its center and narrow side aisles roofed by vaults
perpendicular to the long axis. Demilune windows in these arches light
the interior. From the outside these windows, which conflict with the strict
neoclassical style of the building, are hidden by balustrades. The nave
columns support a balcony. The complex junctions of the building's vaults
and domes create a webwork of intersecting archivolts with much of the
intricacy of flamboyant Gothic tracery.

The building was no sooner completed than the Revolution seized the
property of the monastery and closed its church. The National Assembly
declared the building a national funerary monument that would house

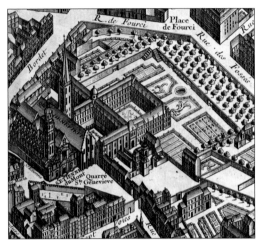

94

the remains of the nation's heroes. An inscription was placed above the main doors that read *Aux grands hommes, la patrie reconnaissante:* To great men, the nation in recognition. The original pediment sculpture representing a radiant cross adored by angels was replaced by an allegory of "France offering laurel crowns to Virtue and Genius; Liberty overthrowing Despotism and Philosophy combating Error." During Napoleon's rule, mass was again said in the Pantheon, but its role as national shrine was maintained. The inscription and pediment sculptures of the revolutionary era were removed under the Bourbon kings and restored under Louis-Philippe. A slightly different pediment sculpture was created that represents the nation distributing laurel crowns to great men whose names History writes down.

The structure of the church was well-suited to its job as national necropolis. Like Saint Sulpice, the church included a labyrinthine substructure with numerous aisles and alcoves where large numbers of people could be buried. Originally intended for members of the order that maintained the church, these vaults are now the final resting place of French cultural, scientific, and political figures. François-Marie Arouet Voltaire, the eighteenth-century skeptic, wit, savant, and author of *Candide,* was among the first to be buried there. His intellectual rival, Jean-Jacques Rousseau, soon followed. (95) Victor Hugo, author of *Les Misérables,* and Emile Zola, who wrote grim novels about the lives of laborers and defended Alfred Dreyfus, a Jewish officer falsely accused of treason, were buried there in the

nineteenth century. Once his inno-
cence was proved, Dreyfus himself
was proposed for entombment in
the Pantheon, but that idea was
rejected. Alexandre Dumas, best
known for his *Three Musketeers,*
was reinterred in the Pantheon in
1902. The remains of Louis Braille,
inventor of an alphabet for the
blind, were placed in the Pantheon

95

one hundred years after his death. Both Pierre and Marie Curie, perhaps the
best-known French scientists, were reburied there in 1995.

The national heroes in its crypt inspired the decoration of the upper
church. Lives of the great men and—despite the inscription above the
door—women of French history are celebrated in large frescoes and canvases by nineteenth-century painters. Their story begins immediately inside the
entrance, where a withered Saint Denis bends down to pick up his severed
head. (96) Saint Geneviève calms Parisians on the approach of Attila. (97)
Clovis and Charlemagne are crowned, and Saint Louis is credited with the
creation of national institutions. Joan of Arc appears in four scenes. In the
first, she hears ghostly voices; in the second, she ensures the coronation of
King Charles VII. She later fights outside the walls of Paris, and in the last
scene faces death by burning in the market at Rouen.

Both Geneviève and Joan reappear in the apse mosaic, where they
kneel at either side of Christ. According to its inscription, Jesus "shows
the fate of the fatherland to the guardian angel of the Gauls." The National Convention, which played such an important part in the revolution-

96

97

ary era, is honored by a sculptural group beneath this mosaic. Debaters on one side of the altar join in a Roman pledge to the goddess Liberty, who stands on a plinth with her left hand resting on a Roman fasces—a bundle of rods symbolizing unity and power—and holding a sword in her right. A small inscription beneath her feet means "Live free or die." Soldiers of the revolutionary army march out from behind the altar.

The most eccentric curiosity of the Pantheon is the pendulum that swings from the center of the dome, a creation of Jean Bernard Léon Foucault. (98) In the mid-nineteenth century, Foucault realized that Newton's law of momentum predicted that once a pendulum was set in motion it would continue to swing in the same plane. He reasoned from this law that a pendulum swinging on a sufficiently long cord would maintain its path even as the earth rotated beneath it, graphically demonstrating the earth's rotation.

Foucault knew that the key to the success of his demonstration would be to hang his pendulum in a sheltered interior space of maximum height. He immediately thought of the dome of a church, but Catholic theologians still had not backed down from their condemnation of Galileo in 1616, and no church was willing to house the unorthodox demonstration. The Pantheon dome was made available, however, and Foucault's pendulum was hung there in the spring of 1851. The pendulum swung in an arc about six feet across and moved about two millimeters with every pass. A marker on its weight traced its course in sand. Late in that year the pendulum was removed. The current version swings across a round table marked with a twenty-four hour clock.

Farther east, another striking urban amenity with a social mission, the royal botanical garden (Jardin des Plantes), was founded in 1635 by Louis XIII, in consultation with his physicians. Its primary purpose was the collection and cultivation of plants known or suspected to have medicinal properties. Like the other great royal institutions of the seventeenth century, the garden was built on the very edge of habitation, where large tracts of land could still be assembled. The Bièvre flowed along one side of the property, while the Seine formed a second boundary.

Within five years of the garden's founding, lectures on botany were established under

98

its sponsorship. In the course of the eighteenth century, some of the most distinguished men of science in France acted as its director. Georges-Louis Leclerc, Comte de Buffon, who theorized a hundred years before Charles Darwin that life forms had changed over time, was associated with the garden. Georges Cuvier, a pioneer of comparative anatomy and the first scientist to document the extinction of ancient species, was one of its directors. Though it was a royal institution (originally named the Jardin du Roi, garden of the king), the scientific research supported by the garden challenged orthodoxy, a characteristic that made it a national treasure during the revolutionary era. It was renamed the National Museum of Natural History in 1793, and the garden's directors were charged with conserving and expanding the collections, fostering fundamental research, both pure and applied, and teaching and diffusing knowledge in the fields of the natural and social sciences.

In addition to its collection of plants, the garden also housed a menagerie. Animals from the royal zoo at Versailles and others seized from traveling circuses formed the core of the collection in the years after the Revolution. These large animals were gradually replaced by small mammals, reptiles, and birds. The zoo's current mission is the study of animal behavior and maintenance of reproductive stocks of endangered species. The garden's pioneering role in biological research, especially paleontology, is highlighted in the Hall of Evolution.

The grounds of the Jardin des Plantes center around an open area of formal lawns, parterres replanted seasonally, and carefully pruned linden trees. Along the outside of the shaded walkways are multiple gardens, including a wonderful rose garden. Pavilions beyond these gardens house permanent collections of mineral and biological specimens. Like the esplanade of Les Invalides and the Ecole Militaire, the formal gardens are anchored in the museum building and extend toward the Seine. But next to the formal gardens are tree-covered winding walks through the natural hilly slope of Mont Saint Geneviève. This pairing of formal and informal landscapes goes a step beyond the grounds of the Luxembourg palace, with its borders and tree-sheltered sculpture garden.

Scattered among the trees leading to Mont Saint Geneviève are several greenhouses where tropical and desert climate collections are exhibited. Like the National Zoo in Washington, DC, the Jardin des Plantes combines research and exhibits of scientific interest and importance within a setting that is pleasant and refreshing. The great difference between the two parks lies in their relationship to their urban surroundings. The National Zoo is carefully segregated from the street grid by the slopes of Rock Creek Park. The Jardin des Plantes draws the urban grid into its garden-equivalent and then moves beyond the grid to create a more relaxed, alternative landscape.

Just to the south of the Jardin des Plantes is the Chapelle de la Salpêtrière, a remarkable and unusual building both in its form and its history. The name refers to the early-seventeenth-century factory on the site where saltpeter was combined with other chemicals to produce gunpowder. The hazardous process, which had originally been carried out on the more populous right bank of the Seine, was moved to the rural fringes of Mont Saint Geneviève, and the business soon failed. When rebellions in the early years of Louis XIV's reign created unemployment and social displacement in Paris, the abandoned factory became a rough-and-ready hospice

for the poor and disabled. Under the sponsorship of the Crown, the
building was greatly improved and new structures added. Libéral Bruant,
first architect of Les Invalides, designed a chapel for the new hospital,
which was dedicated to Saint Louis. It was essentially complete by 1677,
though work continued for the rest of the century. (99)

The entrance to the chapel is marked by a triple arcade with applied
Ionic columns and a small entablature. This neoclassical entryway is set
into a palace-like façade and framed by long wings. The interior of the
chapel is domed, centrally planned, and cruciform, like the Pantheon.
Each of four intersecting arms is equal in length, and each has its own
outside entrance. Four chapels, octagonal in ground plan, open to the
dome between each of the arms. The walls are decorated by large arcades
at ground level, many of them blind, and arched windows above. The ceil-

ing vaults are peaked and made
of wood. The rationale for this
curious floor plan is the mixed
population originally served by
the hospital. At first, only orphans
under the age of four and elderly
women were housed there. But
in the year when construction of
the chapel began, the hospital
became a shelter for former pros-
titutes and women with illegiti-
mate children. These groups were
segregated from one another and

99

accommodated in a separate arm of the chapel. They entered and left in groups through the doors at the end of each section.

During the eighteenth century, mentally ill patients were also taken in. The most violent and delusional were chained to benches in openair, where they endured the attention of curious and sometimes malicious visitors. Prisoners convicted of a variety of crimes increased the inmate population. It was evident to many visitors that the hospital was incapable of serving the large number and great variety of inmates that crowded into it. Conditions were horrible, and the Salpêtrière earned a sinister reputation.

The grim fate of the institution and its population did not improve during the Revolution. In the first days of September 1792 a mob stormed the hospital and liberated many of the young women convicted of moral laxity. The real aim of the invasion, however, was a preemptive strike against presumed enemies of the Revolution. Word had just reached Paris that the Prussian army was nearing the city, and it was widely believed that the invaders would be supported by men and women whom the revolutionaries had jailed. To thwart this entirely imaginary counter-revolutionary attack, kangaroo courts were set up in each of the city's prisons to pass sentence on suspected traitors. For whatever reason, the mock tribunals gave their sentences in code.

On the right bank, at La Force prison not far from the Bastille, those condemned to die were ordered to be released, but as they left the tribunal they were led into an alley already filled with corpses. Their executioners held sabers with which they eviscerated or beheaded their victims. In some cases the accused were beaten to death with mallets. One hundred fifty priests imprisoned in the Carmelite monastery were murdered under similar circumstances. At La Salpêtrière, forty men and women were massacred. These terrible events marked the beginning of a new direction in the Revolution. Originally a protest against the abuses of absolutism, after September 1792 the Revolution became increasingly republican and anti-monarchical.

Chapter Seven

REVOLUTION AND REDESIGN

The Musée Carnavalet, dedicated to the history of
Paris, fills two adjacent *hôtels particuliers* a few blocks
from the Hôtel de Sully and the Place des Vosges.
(Map 6) One of them—the Hôtel Le Peletier de Saint
Fargeau—was built in the last decades of the seven-
teenth century. During the Revolution it was occupied by Louis Michel Le
Peletier de Saint Fargeau, a nobleman elected to the revolutionary National
Convention. He was among a very few aristocratic members of that body
who voted to condemn Louis XVI to death. Within a few days of that fateful
vote—and before the king's public execution—Le Peletier de Saint Fargeau
was himself assassinated while dining with friends in the arcade of the Palais
Royal. The city bought his home in the late nineteenth century, and in 1984
its rooms were reorganized to chronicle life in Paris from the post-revolutionary era to the present.

The Hôtel Carnavalet, from which the museum takes its name, was begun
in the mid-sixteenth century as the home of Jacques de Ligneris, president
of the Parlement de Paris—a judicial rather than legislative body, despite its
name. In the mid-seventeenth century, François Mansart enlarged the building to its present size. After a series of financial scandals, the French Crown
seized the house and rented it to Madame de Sévigné, who ranks as one of
the great, if unintentional, chroniclers of the reign of Louis XIV. In letters

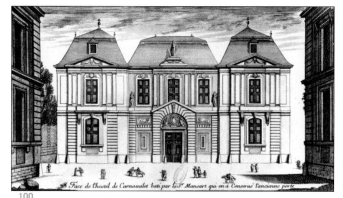

100

Face de l'hostel de Carnavalet bati par le S. Mansart qui en a conservé l'ancienne porte

written to her cousin and to her daughter, Françoise, she described the news from Paris and events in her own life with such vividness and insight that even during her lifetime the letters were copied and shared. After the Revolution, the hôtel passed through many hands until the city bought it in 1866 at the suggestion of Baron Haussmann. (100) Today, it displays collections spanning the period from the Middle Ages to 1800. On its second floor, a suite of rooms sums up the complex history of the French Revolution and its immediate aftermath.

On the eve of revolution in 1788, the government of Louis XVI faced two crises. The nation's debt was enormous, and because both the nobility and the clergy were exempt from almost all taxes, the fiscal burden fell mainly on merchants, workers, and farmers. An acute shortage of food created a second national crisis. Eighteenth-century agricultural production was limited by traditional tools and methods, so most farmers grew only enough to support themselves and their families. Feudal rights and responsibilities also constrained what individual farmers could produce. Under these marginal conditions, crop failures and shortfalls led to frequent famines, and even in years when crops were sufficient, speculation on agricultural products, especially wheat, and manipulations of the market periodically shut down the grain supply.

Both tax inequities and chronic food shortages were long-standing problems, and neither called for a revolutionary solution. What made them causes of revolt was the regime's inability to rethink the premises of absolute monarchy, and the clergy's and nobles' unwillingness to give up their traditional privileges. The king's ministers tried to persuade these superior social orders to allow themselves to be taxed, but the attempt failed. The only recourse was to convene a general meeting of representatives from each of the kingdom's three social classes (called estates) and work toward a compromise.

Despite a general conviction that this was an extreme remedy, the assembly to be convened at Versailles was in reality quite weak. Though virtually every taxpayer could vote, elections, held in multiple rounds, were confined within the three estates. Nobles voted for their representatives, as did the clergy and the third estate, which included about ninety percent of the population. The estates were less segregated than they might have appeared. The count of Mirabeau was elected as a third-estate representative, along with a clergyman, the abbot Emmanuel Joseph Sieyès. Most of the clerical representatives were parish priests, rather than bishops, and about a third of the noble representatives, especially those from Paris, were progressive. But once the assembly convened, the delegates for the most part voted in blocs according to the estate that elected them, so that in effect there was a total of only three votes in the assembly. Added to that, decisions of the assembly were simply recommendations to the monarch, not binding laws.

Tax reform was at the top of the king's agenda, but all three estates understood that tax reform was impossible without broader social reforms.

And social reforms demanded a weakening of absolutist principles. Individual liberty and freedom of the press must be guaranteed. Arbitrary imprisonment by royal warrant must end. Indeed, all royal privileges must be defined and limited by an explicit constitution. Government should decentralize, and customs barriers within the country should be eliminated to encourage trade and lower prices. While the estates were in broad agreement on these and other limitations of the monarchy, each class remained a jealous guardian of its own privileges.

With increasing self-assurance, the third estate articulated its programs and resisted repeated attempts by the Crown to force it to conform to the old order. On June 17, 1789, the third estate, acting alone, declared itself to be the National Assembly. Three days later, meeting in a tennis court at Versailles, the group vowed to give the nation a constitution. The scene is represented in the Musée Carnavalet in a painting by Jacques Louis David. (101) When an officer of the Crown attempted to adjourn the meeting on June 23, its presiding officer defied him and declared, "A nation assembled does not take orders." Within a few days,

members of the clergy and progressive nobles broke ranks with their estates and joined the new National Assembly.

In mid-July a second great force seized center stage in the political process

101

and by its power and energy
accelerated the pace and
direction of change. The
Bastille had been built as the
counterpart to the Louvre, at
the upriver anchor point of
the wall of Charles V. By the
eighteenth century it stood
within the perimeter of the

102

city and played no active role in defense. Though only a few political prisoners were confined behind its high turreted walls in 1789, in the minds of
Parisians the Bastille was still a potent symbol of royal repression. Armed
mobs attacked it on July 14.

Eighty pensioners and a detachment of Swiss guards under the command of the Marquis de Launay garrisoned the fortress. The first wave of
attackers managed to open the drawbridge and surge into the courtyard,
where the defenders shot them like fish in a barrel. Forty insurgents were
killed outright, and many more were wounded. By four in the afternoon,
when members of a newly formed city militia joined the attack, it was
obvious to De Launay that the garrison could not hold out, and he surrendered. On his way to the field headquarters of the insurrection at the Hôtel
de Ville, the marquis was attacked and killed by his escort. A butcher's
boy cut off his head with a kitchen knife and lifted it on the tines of a
pitchfork. When Jacques de Flesselles, the provost of the merchants and
de facto mayor, delayed in arming the crowd, he was shot on the steps
of city hall, and his head soon joined De Launay's. (102) The event is
chronicled in a painting by Jean-Baptiste Lallemand that hangs in the

103

Carnavalet, and in an engraving owned by the museum. One day after its fall, demolition of the Bastille began under the direction of Pierre-François Palloy. Hubert Robert painted the beginning of the process. (103) In a shadowy foreground, curious visitors admire the newly historic building. It takes a moment to realize that the top of every section of wall and every round tower of the massive fortress is teeming with little figures intent on tearing it apart. Robert's canvas, begun soon after July 14, shows a mass of tiny individuals whose antlike determination is bringing down a towering structure.

Under Palloy's direction, blocks from the building were carved into scale models of the fortress and distributed to every French department as official memorials of the event; examples can be seen in the museum. Stones salvaged from the demolition were eventually used to build the bridge that now links the Place de la Concorde to the home of the National Assembly on the Left Bank. Other blocks found their way into the foundations of private houses. Keys to the fortress became precious symbols of liberation. The marquis de Lafayette, commander of the Paris National Guard, sent one to his close friend from the American Revolution, George Washington. It can still be seen hanging in the front hall at the president's home, Mount Vernon. The first Bastille Day was celebrated a year later in a remarkable festival on the Champ de Mars, the large green space in front of the Ecole Militaire.

Despite the violence at the Bastille and the Hôtel de Ville, the king visited the newly appointed mayor of the city on July 17, 1789. He accepted and wore the mayor's gift of a ribbon cockade that combined white, the color of the Bourbon monarchy, with red and blue, the colors of Paris. The king's capitulation to a city government put in place by mob action and paramilitary force showed his appreciation of the power that the city represented. Red and blue became the colors of national revolution, and the three colors united in the French flag remain a continual reminder of the dominant role that Paris played throughout the revolutionary era.

The defiant National Assembly continued to meet at Versailles, and on August 26 they adopted a document entitled *Declaration of the Rights of Man and of the Citizen.* Founded on Enlightenment principles of universal, inalienable human rights, the declaration guaranteed to the citizens of France their right to life, liberty, security, and property. The document defined the nation, not the monarchy, as the source and repository of social rights and recognized the citizens' right to rebel against oppression. The privileges of the nobles and clergy, enjoyed since the Middle Ages, were revoked. Freedom of the press and freedom of religious worship were established. With the adoption of *The Rights of Man and Citizen,* the tremendous work of dismantling the political structure of the old regime was nearly complete.

The king and the congress probably would have continued to work together in the idyllic, isolated confines of Versailles, safely removed from the press of events, if Parisians had not again intervened. This time their action was more than symbolic. On October 5, 1789, hundreds of women met at the Hôtel de Ville. When the newly appointed mayor eluded them, they decided to march on Versailles. Their aim was unclear, but many among them wanted the king to order the release of grain stores and ease bread shortages in Paris.

This dire situation came about because of a panic, called the Great Fear, that had swept through rural France during the previous summer. Excluded from the political process, farm communities were easy prey to rumors that their lands were about to be confiscated by the emerging government or that the nobles whose vast estates spanned rural France were about to launch reprisals against the peasants. With the harvest not yet complete, speculators withheld what little grain there was and drove bread prices to unprecedented levels.

By the time the crowd heading for Versailles passed through the city gates, it had become large and unruly. Merchants in towns along the road hastily closed their shops, and leaders of the march negotiated with them for wine and food to keep the marchers going. The protesters reached Versailles in mid-afternoon and made their first appeals to the assembly. Early in the morning of October 6, the crowd surged into the courtyard of the palace and killed two guards. Then they stormed the apartments of the hated Queen Marie Antoinette, who saved herself by running to the king's apartment.

When Louis XVI came to the balcony overlooking the courtyard, the crowd screamed, "To Paris!" The feckless king, who had nearly fled to Normandy the night before, agreed to their demand. A cortege was formed with the National Guard at its head. Soldiers, some with loaves of bread impaled on their bayonets, were followed by carts full of grain. The royal guards, without their weapons, came next, followed by the king's carriage, with Lafayette riding alongside. The crowd of triumphant women brought

up the rear, screaming for all to hear that they were bringing "the Baker,

the Baker's wife, and the Baker's boy apprentice" (the dauphin) back to

Paris. Two weeks later the National Assembly followed the monarch to the

capital, giving the Paris crowd and the city government leverage over both.

The king and his family moved into the Tuileries palace, where they were

both protected and confined by the National Guard. (Map 7) The National

Assembly found temporary quarters in the archbishop's palace next to Notre

Dame, before moving into the Royal Riding School at the Tuileries, where

they too were guarded by Lafayette's soldiers. For most of the following year

the city and the national leadership got along well together. Despite the

Great Fear, when the harvest finally came it was enormous, and the price

of bread fell sharply. The king agreed to uphold the constitution, and the

infrastructure of a new form of national government was put into place. The

country was divided into administrative districts called departments. The

new nation would be an organization of departments and municipalities.

The most radical actions of the National Assembly extended the old

third estate's control over the other two. Titles of nobility were outlawed,

and church property that was not in public service was confiscated and

sold. This was partly an effort to weaken the power of the clergy, but it

was also a way to raise money for a government that was still short on

cash. The effects of these policies, and of the more stringent ones that

followed in 1793, are visible in every pre-revolutionary church and monas-

tic foundation in Paris and throughout France.

Despite his capitulation to the demands of the assembly, Louis, who

was no enthusiast of constitutional monarchy, was increasingly haunted

by the peril in which he and his family lived. Yet as the danger intensified, he lost focus and energy. Marie Antoinette stepped into the role the French imagination had already assigned to her—that of power-broker, deal-maker, subversive-in-chief. The queen and her advisers accelerated their secret contacts with émigré nobility and foreign royalty, especially the court of Austria, where Marie Antoinette's brother reigned as Emperor Leopold II.

On the morning of June 21, 1791, Louis' valet awoke to find his master gone from the Tuileries. In disguise, the royal family was making slow progress toward the fortress of Montmédy on the Belgian border. Lafayette immediately sent couriers in every direction with orders to find and arrest the king. Recognized in the town of Chalons sur Marne when he paid for bread with a coin bearing his own image, the king and his family were finally taken prisoner in Varennes about forty miles from safety. Louis himself declared to his captors, "France no longer has a king."

National Guard troops surrounded the carriage and escorted it in slow procession back to Paris. When they reached the city gates, the guardsmen turned their rifles upside down, the protocol for a funeral. Thousands of Parisians watched the arrival of the royal family in stony silence: the municipality had posted signs all along the Champs Elysées—the quickest route from the edge of town to the Tuileries palace—which read "Those who hail the king will be beaten; those who insult the king will be hanged."

The king's attempted escape created an enormous public relations problem for the National Assembly. Two years after the Revolution had begun, sympathy for the dissolution of the monarchy and the creation of a republic was still limited. To resolve their difficulties, the assembly came up with an official fiction. The king, they declared, had not fled; he had been kidnapped by foreign agents. Lafayette's National Guard had rescued him and returned him to his palace and his beloved people.

At first the Cordeliers, one of the many political clubs that had sprung up in Paris during the revolutionary years, were alone in refusing to go along with this fabrication. They circulated a petition calling for a public debate on the founding of a republic. On July 17, on the Champ de Mars, a crowd of Parisians came to hear the group's ideas. Convinced that "a troupe of fifty thousand brigands was about to march on the National Assembly," the delegates dispatched the ever-faithful Lafayette and his troops to restore order. When the troops reached the Champ de Mars, they were pelted with rocks. The soldiers opened fire, and fifty in the crowd were killed.

This debacle ended the political influence of the marquis de Lafayette and of the then mayor of Paris, Jean-Sylvain Bailly. Overnight, these revolutionary leaders became reactionary royalists in the eyes of Parisians. At the same time, the image of the king underwent a terrible change. Camille Desmoulins, one of the instigators of the storming of the Bastille, labeled the king an "imbecile, a wild boar with a crown, an animal king." Caricatures of Louis with all these attributes were in wide circulation. Public defacement of the symbols of monarchy became commonplace in Paris. Still the legislators carried on as before. They even revised the constitution to give the king control of government departments and a veto over legislation.

In early spring 1792 Louis reluctantly signed a declaration of war against Austria, whose leaders had conceived a military campaign to invade France, suppress the Revolution, and return Louis to the throne as an absolute monarch. In July 1792 the assembly declared the "Fatherland in danger" and began to recruit volunteers for a national army. The king vetoed recruitment, but no one paid any attention. Volunteers came from all over the country to protect the capital.

Battalions from the Mediterranean port city of Marseille arrived singing a catchy tune they had taught to sympathizers on their long march north. An army engineer and amateur songwriter named Claude-Joseph Rouget de Lisle had composed the anthem at the request of the mayor of Strasbourg. No one knows how a regiment from far-away Marseille came to hear it. Its first verse called on the "sons of the fatherland" to oppose tyranny and to fight against the coalition soldiers, who "come into our very arms intent on slitting the throats of our women and children." Though the gory song is all about the perils of 1792, "La Marseillaise" became the French national anthem, and remains so today.

In July a royalist newspaper in Paris published a declaration to the nation signed by the duke of Brunswick, leader of the coalition army raised by the emperor of Austria and the king of Prussia to invade France. Article Eight of his manifesto ordered the citizens of Paris to submit to the king "immediately and without delay" and to ensure his safety and that of the royal family. Though signed by the Prussian general, the manifesto had been drafted by an émigré French noble and secretly approved by Louis XVI. It went on to spell out the consequences of disobedience: "If . . . the least violence or outrage is committed against their Majesties . . . the King of Prussia and the Emperor of Austria will exact a vengeance that will never be forgotten. The city will be destroyed and its citizens eradicated. Those who have acted against the king or the coalition army will be subjected to those tortures they deserve."

Not surprisingly, the manifesto backfired. Hatred of the king rose higher than ever, as radicals found new audiences. At the Jacobin Club on the day after Brunswick's decree was published, the radical leader Maximilien Robespierre called for the king's deposition. On the night of August 9 the revolutionary council of the city, known as the Paris Commune and led by Georges-Jacques Danton, seized power from a faltering National Assembly. For the next two years—the most turbulent and violent of the Revolution—Danton and Robespierre along with Jean-Paul Marat would be the real rulers of France. All are represented in paintings in the Musée Carnavalet.

Among its first acts, the Paris Commune summoned the current mayor, the marquis de Mandat, to the Hôtel de Ville, where they removed him from office and turned him over to the crowd outside, which tore him to pieces. Huguenin, president of the Paris Commune, demanded the king's deposition and the election of a new assembly. After only two hours of debate, the cowed assembly capitulated. They deposed the king and ordered that he be held as a hostage in the Luxembourg palace. The commune demanded instead that Louis and his family be held in the fortified tower of the Knight's Templar, to which they were moved on August 13.

Ten days later, coalition troops overwhelmed the French fortress of Longwy near what is now the Belgian border. On September 2 word reached Paris that enemy troops had encircled Verdun. Brunswick's path to Paris seemed open. Popular suspicion and hatred, fanned by the commune, led to massacres of supposed anti-revolutionaries during that night and the following day. The forty victims at La Salpêtrière were among them. Ironically, this first night of terror was also the high-water mark of the coalition's drive to take Paris. By early November French armies had driven back the combined forces of Austria and Prussia.

On November 20 looters came upon a secret closet in the king's old apartments in the Tuileries and broke into it. There they discovered copies of letters between the royal family and what public opinion could label only as the enemies of France. After two weeks of debate, the assembly decided to try the former monarch, now known officially as Louis Capet. During debate, two factions emerged. One group, called the Girondins, opposed the king's execution. The Girondins developed the habit of gathering to the right of the presiding officer. On his left, the implacable faction called the Mountain urged the monarch's death and the expansion of radical reform. Louis appeared before this divided chamber to answer charges of treason. The king's trial lasted until January 17, 1793, when a guilty verdict, a triumph for the Mountain, was pronounced. On the morning of January 21, the king and his confessor were brought in a closed carriage to the tall scaffold on which the guillotine was mounted.

Though it is a symbol of the most violent epoch of the Revolution, the guillotine began its bloody career as a humane alternative to the grotesquely theatrical punishments that commoners had suffered under the monarchy. In December 1789 a prominent member of the National Assembly, Dr. Joseph Ignace Guillotin, proposed that decapitation—the capital punishment for nobles—be extended to commoners as well. He also proposed the substitution of a swift and sure mechanical device for the vagaries of the headsman's ax. Work was carried on over the next year and a half, and the first execution by the machine called—much to the doctor's dismay—La Guillotine took place in Paris in April 1792. The new device satisfied all but one of Guillotin's requirements. He had intended a private death for condemned criminals. The Revolution insisted on publicity.

The king was executed in the public space that the revolutionaries had renamed the Place de la Révolution (now called the Place de la Concorde). Designed during the reign of his grandfather, Louis XV, and named after him, this square—sited directly on axis with the Louvre and the Tuileries—was a gift from the city of Paris to honor that monarch. Rather than encircle the square with buildings, the designer, Jacques Ange Gabriel, left it nearly open. Its only buildings were set along the northern edge where they would not interfere with the long space that stretches across the Tuileries gardens and beyond. Louis XV's statue stood for less than thirty years in the center of this square before the revolutionaries pulled it down in 1792. During the next three years, the guillotine towered over it. An obelisk that the English viceroy of Egypt offered to King Louis-Philippe, a later Bourbon monarch, now stands in the center of the square on a long elliptical island with fountains at either end.

Accounts of the king's death are contradictory, and the differences reflect the political views of each eyewitness. Monarchists reported that the king was calm and dignified and that he succeeded in making a short speech from the scaffold, in which he pardoned his people for the crime they were committing against him. In republican accounts, the monarch was fretful and afraid; his remarks were drowned out by soldiers drawn up around the scaffold. Unsympathetic witnesses reported that he struggled against his executioners, twisting his body and kicking his feet in an hysterical effort to escape the guillotine, and that he screamed from the moment he was strapped down until the blade fell.

Both sides agree that the executioner lifted the king's head by the hair and displayed it to the crowd who yelled, "Vive la République!" They also agree that those directly in front of the scaffold put their handkerchiefs on the ends of bayonets and walking sticks to wet them in the king's blood. Then the accounts diverge again. For some, these bloody tokens became symbols of republican triumph over tyranny; for others, they were precious relics dipped in the blood of a martyr.

Killing the king created intense hostility against France in every European country and provoked keen opposition at home. Many who had supported the revolutionary cause backed away, though stalwarts remained. The revolutionaries declared war against Austria and Holland in February. A widespread, heavily armed royalist uprising began in the French region called La Vendée in March. Major cities in the south and west, including Bordeaux, Toulon, and Lyon, changed sides. Even Marseille, whose troops had played such an important military and symbolic role in the battle against coalition forces, revolted against the regime. As early as August 1792, when the royal family were attacked in the Tuileries, the composer of "La Marseillaise" had resigned his commission in the revolutionary army.

To make matters worse, bread was once again in short supply, and the value of the new national currency had dropped sharply. Yet in Paris, despite all the forces working against it, the Revolution continued to thrive. The Mountain, masters of political extremism, exploited the dire situation to their advantage. Robespierre, who merged leadership in the Paris Commune with a principal role in the newly formed national legislature, became head of a Committee on Public Safety. This small group functioned as the virtual executive of France, and from this vantage point Robespierre ruled supreme.

The committee called for an organized "despotism of liberty to crush the despotism of the kings." Their regime, which would become known as the Terror, promised to "be terrible for conspirators, a goad to public servants ... the protector of the downtrodden and tireless against oppressors." In reality, their policies translated into a round-up of presumed enemies, including the relatives of those who had fled, government officials who had lost their jobs, indigents with no visible means of support, and anyone else whose public declarations or writings made them "advocates of tyranny."

The queen was guillotined in October 1793. Surviving members of the opposition party, the Girondins, were executed at the end of the month. Military victories abroad and the capitulation of counter-revolutionary towns and cities throughout the country improved the situation for the extremists. But as the pressure of external events lessened, the justification for the Terror slipped away. Even the founders of the Revolution were growing sick of it. Robespierre and his closest followers were executed in July 1794. The Revolution had, in the words of Pierre Vergniaud, devoured its children.

Provisional governments of one form or another ruled a country suddenly relieved of many of its burdens. In 1795 a new form of government, the Directorate, with a five-man executive and a bicameral legislature, came to power. A year later a young, unknown general was appointed its director of internal security. Napoleon Bonaparte's ambitions were boundless and his political connections strong. One of the key players in the Directorate, Paul de Barras, had spotted the young soldier in Toulon, and with his help Napoleon obtained command of the French army in northern Italy. Through victory after victory, he drove the Austrians eastward across the top of the Italian peninsula. In his correspondence with the directors,

Bonaparte was careful to underline his own skill and ability. He also created a press office in Paris that guaranteed widespread publication of his successes. Through its efforts, the young general crafted an image of himself as a man of action who was virtuous in his private life and crowned with victory on the battlefield.

In 1798 Bonaparte launched a combined archaeological and military campaign against the Ottoman sultanate of Egypt. While Napoleon was in Egypt, the continental reaction against republican France sparked the formation of a new international coalition. French elections at about the same time gave the revolutionary party founded by Robespierre a majority in the assembly. Fearing a return of the Terror, the directors plotted a coup d'état. The man they relied on to take the reins of power into his own hands and to win the good will of the French people was the general. Leaving his soldiers to fight alone against resurgent Egyptian forces and British troops, Bonaparte made a quick trip back to France.

The young military leader soon proved himself a skilled and inventive politician. He managed the paradoxical task of portraying himself as the heir of the royal and orthodox tradition on the one hand and the revolutionary, rationalist strain on the other. As consul, and soon emperor, he achieved what succeeding French administrations have repeatedly struggled to recreate, a government that balanced the tradition of centralizing, absolutist control with the constitutional, social, and economic reforms demanded by the Revolution.

In hundreds of ways, both large and small, the Revolution lived on. One of its most lasting innovations was the substitution of the decimal-based metric system for the chaotic measures of weight and distance under the old regime. The system was first proposed in 1791, and in 1799 a standard

meter and a standard kilogram were deposited in the National Archives. After some revisions in the early nineteenth century, the system was accepted
throughout France and ultimately throughout most of the world.

Another lasting action of the Revolution was an administrative
decision with little ideological significance. In 1795 Paris was divided
into twelve districts called arrondissements. When the city limits were
expanded in 1860, the number of arrondissements rose to twenty. These
divisions remain in place today, and those who know the city well habitu-
ally refer to parts of the city by number rather than name. Both in the
present numbering system and in the earlier one, the first arrondissement
included the center of government in the Louvre and Tuileries palaces.
From that starting point, the current arrondissements are numbered clock-
wise in two rings that spiral out from the center of the city. The boundaries between the rings are for the most part defined by the great avenues
that follow the traces of long-vanished walls. (Map 2)

Napoleon restored the government's relationship with the Vatican and
the Catholic community that the Revolution had severed. This reconciliation
is celebrated in a fresco by Jules Claude Ziegler, a pupil of Ingres, in the
church of Saint Mary Magdalene (La Madeleine), which sits on axis with the
Place de la Concorde and the National Assembly. The church was founded
in the thirteenth century when the city began to grow toward this part of the
periphery. In the mid-eighteenth century, the architect Pierre Conant d'Ivry
was charged with creating a new building able to accommodate a rapidly
growing congregation. His design was expected to conform to the neoclassical style of a projected square to be called Place Louis XV. Plans for this
square, with the church at its center, were far-reaching. A National Library,
the Commercial Courts, and the Bank of France would all be sited around

104

it. This ambitious masterplan was first suspended, then annulled, by the Revolution.

In 1805 Napoleon revived the project for the church but reconceived it as a secular Temple to Glory. A contest to design this monument was announced, and the prize was awarded. Napoleon rejected both the winning design and its creator in favor of a plan by Barthélémy Vignon. After Napoleon was defeated and exiled in 1814, his vanished glory required no monument. The unfinished structure was rededicated to Catholic worship and to the Magdalene. Despite the change of dedication, Vignon remained in charge of construction until his death.

Finally consecrated in 1842, the Madeleine is virtually indistinguishable from a large Greek or Roman temple. It rests on a raised platform and is completely surrounded by a Corinthian colonnade. (104) A double row of columns on the west side at the top of sweeping stairs lead to the main entrance. Above the entrance, the Last Judgment—traditional for the west end of a Christian church—fills the pediment. Inside the building, Corinthian columns spaced along the nave create shallow alcoves where pairs of smaller columns surround miniature temple fronts. Like the chapels in the side aisles of more traditional churches, these aedicules frame paintings of saints. Arches springing from the columns create demilunes that are frescoed. Three shallow domes lit by skylights are inset into

the ceiling. The semicircular choir is also ringed by small columns that
support a decorative band.

The fresco in the curved space above the altar represents the history
of Christianity, but also the effort to reconcile the twin forces at work
in the building's genesis. (105) The Magdalene, identified by a banner
that proclaims *Delixit multum,* "She has loved greatly," kneels before
Christ. On the viewer's left, a parade of figures represents the history of
the church in the east. Constantine, who embraced Christianity and also
transferred the capital of the Roman empire to Byzantium, is a logical
presence here. Many of the men and women who follow were crusaders,
including Louis VII, Richard the Lionhearted, and Saint Louis. Godfrey of
Boulogne, leader of the First Crusade and for a time king of Jerusalem,
appears, along with the blind octogenarian doge of Venice, Enrico Dan-
dolo, whose soldiers sacked Constantinople and sent a host of artworks
and relics—including the crown of thorns—streaming toward the west.

The corpse in the foreground represents modern Greece, which in
1837 was still partly occupied by Muslim Turks. Modern crusaders bent on
liberating Greece fill the left foreground. The figures on the right include
many saints and heroes from
French history. Clovis baptized
by Saint Rémi d'Auxerre, along
with Charlemagne and his
chronicler Einhard, are joined by
Pope Alexander III, who laid the
cornerstone of Notre Dame cathedral, and Joan of Arc. Henri IV,
Louis XIII, and Cardinal Richelieu

105

stand in for the seventeenth century. And finally, the figures grouped in the foreground represent the signing in 1802 of a treaty between Napoleon, who then held the rank of first consul, and Pope Pius VII. By its terms, the Revolution's systematic repudiation of Catholicism was reversed.

Under Napoleon, the recklessness and rage that the Terror expressed were not subdued but channeled into military campaigns. The means if not the source of domestic violence became an international force of impressive strength and ability. A truly national army in an age of professional soldiering, Napoleon's troops transformed warfare. Conscription during the First and Second World Wars are the direct heirs of the *levée en masse* during the Napoleonic wars.

But Napoleon's stunning successes in Austria, Prussia, and Spain were checked by a disastrous campaign in Russia in 1812. Well beyond the reach of his supply lines, his massive army was defeated by a strategy the Gauls would have recognized and approved. The Russians burned every resource that the French might have used, and then gnawed away at the weakened army as it straggled back home to France. Napoleon lost power and was exiled, regained control for one hundred days (during which he abdicated in favor of his son), and then suffered complete and final defeat near the Belgian town of Waterloo. The treaties of Paris and the Council of Vienna restored a Bourbon king, Louis XVIII, to the throne of France in 1815, but the country was not partitioned and no reparations were required.

Louis and his successor ruled until 1830, when Charles X made the mistake of thinking that Paris's revolutionary spirit was dead. He dissolved the Chamber of Deputies, suspended freedom of the press, and disenfranchised three fourths of French voters. When Parisians revolted, the army joined in, forcing Charles to abdicate. His own son was bypassed, and the duke of Orléans became King Louis-Philippe. During the 1830s there were short-lived outbreaks of revolutionary fervor, such as the street fighting of June 5–6, 1832, that forms the climax of Victor Hugo's *Les Misérables*. Generally speaking, though, the so-called Citizen King or Bourgeois Monarch, though widely caricatured, managed to survive in office until the late 1840s.

Then, in what has been called the Year of Revolution, 1848, social unrest spurred by disastrous crop failures, declining industrial wages, and spikes in the cost of living led to violence throughout Europe. Spontaneous uprisings among members of the working class in Prussia, Austria, Poland, Hungary, and Italy inspired Karl Marx and Friedrich Engels to hastily write and publish their *Communist Manifesto*. By far the greatest and most important of these revolts took place in France, and Paris was its center. Terrified of sharing Louis XVI's fate, the Citizen King hastily abdicated and fled in disguise to England. On November 4, 1848, France initiated its Second Republic.

The elected president of the new republic was Louis-Napoléon Bonaparte, nephew of the deposed emperor. For three years he used his position to place his supporters in key government and military posts. On December 2, 1851, the anniversary of his uncle's 1804 coronation, the president declared his intention to restore the Consulate. A national plebiscite approved his choice, and exactly one year later the first consul took the not-surprising step of declaring himself emperor. As Napoleon III, he reigned for almost eighteen years. And under his sponsorship, both the French nation and its capital were reshaped.

In the course of the seventeenth and eighteenth centuries, successive monarchs had sponsored royal squares—harmonious buildings surrounding an open area with a statue of the sponsoring ruler at its center. The Place des Vosges was one of the earliest, and the Place Louis XV (Concorde) was another. Like the aborted square around the Madeleine, the Place Vendôme, just to the southeast, was originally imagined as a monumental government center. (Map 7) Financial pressures forced Louis XIV's hand, and in the end the buildings surrounding the great square were leased to commercial and residential tenants. These buildings were similar in style to the grand colonnaded entryway Perrault had designed for the Louvre, a resemblance that gave them an official appearance even after they lost their official function.

Despite the residential character of Place Vendôme, a colossal image of Louis XIV loomed over it until the Revolution. The statue was pulled from its plinth and melted down in 1792. A historiated column like those that commemorate the heroic actions of the emperors Trajan and Marcus Aurelius in Rome was set up in its place. It describes events of Napoleon's military campaigns between the years 1805 and 1807. A statue of Napoleon dressed as Caesar stood on top of the column until 1814, when it was melted to remake the statue of Henri IV that stands at the end of the Ile de la Cité. A copy of the emperor's statue was replaced on the Colonne Vendôme in 1874.

Despite the beauty of aristocratic enclaves like the Place Vendôme and the grandeur of the city's many churches and palaces, mid-nineteenth century Paris was not in general a healthy or appealing place to live. Typical accounts describe its narrow, winding streets, steep houses, inadequate water supply, and primitive sanitation as survivals of the medieval period. Paris was partly an old city that had fallen into ruin through a natural process of decay, and partly a relatively new one that had suffered

insurrection, occupation, vandalism on an unprecedented scale, and prolonged neglect. It suited the spirit of the age to treat the city as something
that time had delivered to the restorers, rather than something that bore
the marks of a still contentious political history.

The great rebuilding campaign that began during the reign of Napoleon III is probably the best-known urban renewal project ever carried
out. Baron Haussmann, who conceived of much of it and directed all of
it, is also well known and justly celebrated. Georges Eugène Haussmann
was born in Paris in 1809. He studied at the Collège Henri IV near the
Pantheon, then went on to do advanced work in both law and music. In
his thirties he held a number of administrative posts in small French cities. In 1853 Louis-Napoléon appointed Haussmann prefect of the Seine,
the administrative department that includes Paris. For the next seventeen
years he directed nearly every aspect of civic life.

The baron's intent in reshaping Paris has been debated almost since
his work began. The simplest explanation, and one that has been repeatedly advanced, is that his main concern was defensive. This explanation looks
to the great roadways that are the most noticeable feature of Haussmann's
new Paris. It characterizes that network of wide, straight passageways as a
set of access roads allowing the quick and easy deployment of troops into
any rebellious neighborhood. The city's violent history during the Revolution and its record of urban uprisings characterized by barricade fighting
during the first half of the nineteenth century certainly favor this view, but
it is too limited and ignores the many other reforms the baron carried out,
as well as the multiple purposes that his roadways served.

The radical opening up of the Ile de la Cité, for example, served no
defensive purpose, but it did remove the centuries-old maze of roads and

bridges that linked the two banks of the Seine. Under Haussmann's direction, the Boulevard Saint Michel displaced the Rue Saint Jacques as the major axis on the Left Bank. Crossing the Ile de la Cité as the Boulevard du Palais, it joined up with the Rue de Rivoli/Rue Saint Antoine to form a grand intersection with the same symbolic weight and unifying purpose as the junction of the old Roman cardo and decuman.

Haussmann himself repeatedly characterized his work in the city as hygienic. Bringing fresh air and light into neighborhoods where multistory houses overhung narrow roadways was for him as meaningful a source of public health as bringing clean water or removing sewage. Whether increased air and light improved the health of urban people or did not, a supply of uncontaminated drinking water and the removal of disease-fostering waste—the true cause of cholera—certainly did so.

Paris had sewers before Haussmann stepped in, nearly a hundred miles of them. Nonetheless, waste of all kinds filtered into the ground water or passed through the streets before reaching sewers that channeled it into the Seine, still the city's primary source of drinking water in the late nineteenth century. Haussmann increased the length of the Paris sewer system by a factor of five. He buried all the sewers and provided for periodic flushing and cleansing of the system. He also revolutionized the city's water supply by piping in clean water from far beyond the city limits. Eventually a system of aqueducts and underground channels rivaling the system that had watered imperial Rome served millions of Parisians.

While sanitation was primary, Haussmann had his own notions of the city as something to look at, and much of his master plan can be understood only as a desire to create a cityscape that was picturesque and visually stimulating. His ideas of how to do this were adopted from Paris's eighteenth-century planners, and they embody a principle that was seized on again at the end of the twentieth century. The greatest and most successful projects of the absolutist monarchs were those like Les Invalides or the Ecole Militaire where important buildings were the anchor points of long axes. Rich and powerful as they were, the absolutist monarchs lacked the funds and the political clout to create axes of this kind in the built-up fabric of the old city. With the full backing of Napoleon III and the power to condemn property and seize it for public purposes, the prefect of the Seine did just that.

The city's eighteenth-century planners had carried out their work in neighborhoods reserved for nobles and the rich. Haussmann's avenues plowed through poor quarters of the city but also through the barriers that had sheltered wealth and privilege in the eighteenth century. His transformation of the once-aristocratic Place des Victoires, located not far from the Palais Royal, was no different from his approach to the meanest neighborhood. This *place* was designed in the late seventeenth century by Jules Hardouin-Mansart to commemorate the military triumphs of Louis XIV's army. Until the Revolution, a statue of the monarch surrounded by defeated enemies stood at the center of a circular arrangement of buildings. Under the restored monarchy, an equestrian statue of Louis XIV was erected to replace the one destroyed in 1792. Haussmann cut away buildings and opened avenues into the circle, so that the statue suddenly dominated the prospect not just of the square but of every street radiating from it. The newly opened square became a link in the complex chain of interlocked avenues that embraced the entire city. Communication on this scale cannot be one-sided. Whatever its motivation, unrestricted access is by its nature a democratic force.

106

Buildings facing the new streets were governed by strict standards for height, setback, and architectural style. These mandates were enforced by building inspectors who approved plans and monitored construction. The city itself owned many building lots and was especially rigorous in supervising its own projects. But all of this would have been less effective or nullified entirely if the new architectural style had not won wide popular acceptance. Buildings that fit the code became models to emulate, and there was a tendency to complete blocks in a conforming style.

In nineteenth-century Paris the Bois de Boulogne (Boulogne Woods) on the city's northwest perimeter was the appropriate place to ride in a carriage with family and friends, to see and be seen by others who could afford horses, drivers, and leisure. (Map 2) Haussmann created this huge public park and the even more spacious Bois de Vincennes to the east, along with other smaller green areas, to be the "lungs of the city." (106) In the evening, before and after the theater, a larger and more diverse city crowd paraded along the *grands boulevards* that traced the outline of vanished city walls. In extending the network of wide streets of this kind, Haussmann, in his critics' eyes, did little more than extend the range of idle men and women of privilege. But for Charles Baudelaire, one of the greatest poets and critics of the time, the crowd in motion along these avenues was a prime expression of the city's power and energy. Baudelaire's ideal artist was a *flâneur*—a wanderer, who walked the boulevards of

Paris not with indifference or idle curiosity but with exhilaration and high purpose. The *flâneur,* whom Baudelaire also called "the painter of modern life," draws his inspiration from the moving crowd.

"The crowd is his habitat as the air is the bird's or the water the fish's. His passion and his profession is to wed the crowd. For the perfect wanderer, the passionate observer, it is an immense delight to make his home in the many, in the surge of its movement, in the fleeting and the infinite. To be away from home and to feel at home everywhere; to see the world and be at the center of the world ... The lover of the world makes the crowd his family ... He is an 'I' insatiably hungry for what is not himself, who, at each moment represents and expresses the other in images more vivid than that life itself which is always unstable and fleeting" (from "L'Artiste, homme du monde, homme des foules et enfant"). In the twentieth century these ideas would be given a Marxist reformulation in the so-called arcades project by the German critic and philosopher Walter Benjamin.

Haussmann's interlocking grid of avenues could take a wanderer anywhere he might choose to go within the city. Along each avenue he could look forward and back at significant buildings that had been freed from the tangle of encumbering streets. In such a network, the wanderer's path was no longer an inconsequential one. Every step was directed toward some monumental goal, and whether the wanderer cared or not, each monument represented some force or moment in Parisian history. As long as the wanderer followed one of Haussmann's avenues, she was never out of touch with the central institutions of Paris—and, by extension, of French culture. For generations, the city had been a welter of structures that represented a host of discordant ideals. Haussmann's plan put all these monuments in the public eye, placing them on the same plane and forcing them into visual dialogue with one another. This is as close as a planner can come to creating an urban fabric that acknowledges every historical moment as it strives to frame their reconciliation.

Each of Haussmann's monuments sat alone like a fat spider at the intersection of a web of avenues. One of the most significant was the Opera House. (107) Its prominent place in a skein of grand avenues, including those that had skirted the Renaissance ramparts, and its own fabulous grandeur marked it as the center of contemporary Parisian life. Opera was invented during the Renaissance more or less as a revival of Greek theater, where singing, dancing, and dramatic dialogue were all combined. But it really came into its own in the nineteenth century, when the greatest composers in the genre—Verdi, Puccini, Massenet, and Wagner among them—flourished. In its heyday, opera seemed to combine all the arts into one extravagant coordinated production.

An operatic performance is a work of art manufactured by a highly coordinated and finely differentiated work force. At the top of the ladder of skill,

107

prestige, and compensation are the principal voices, along with the orchestra conductor, the ballet master, the composer, and the impresario. Each artist bears responsibility for guiding the production, through either talent, example, or managerial skill. Below this level, in a carefully ordered hierarchy, are others

who are assigned appro-
priate roles on the basis
of their abilities. The
ensemble functions as
a well-ordered factory of
the nineteenth-century
variety—before the in-
vention of the assembly

108

line—in which master craftsmen directed production and distributed tasks
according to their sense of each worker's capacity.

The Opera House itself was well designed to support this complex
enterprise. It was divided into discrete halves. Behind the scenes, the
theater was a vast machine, as intricate as a weaver's loom. The backstage
was filled with removable screens and panels suspended above, while
beneath the stage were multiple platforms that could be raised or lowered.
Hundreds of ropes and pulleys, counterweights and cleats, secured these
objects or moved them into place. Among historic parallels, the one closest to this complex is the multimasted sailing ship, which at mid-century
was already being replaced by more efficient, simpler, and less labor-
intensive steam-powered vessels. The stage crew was organized into its
own hierarchy, with the stage manager as its commander.

The other half of the Opera House—the public part—was formal,
ceremonial, and sumptuous. The main entryway was heralded by a grand
façade with arcades on its first story providing multiple entrances. The
second story featured a colonnade made up of Corinthian columns in
pairs—a nod to Perrault's Louvre façade—that enclosed rectangular windows with round ports above them. (108) Small pavilions at either end of the

façade stepped forward, and their columns were crowned with a rounded pediment. Great winged figures decorated the attics above each one.

Once inside the building, the audience stood in a great central hall that was both a reception area and the jumping off point for magnificent stairways that served the theater's many levels. (109) The performance hall itself echoed the same design tradition that had given form to the Théâtre Richelieu. It was a horseshoe-shaped auditorium with the stage at its flat narrow end. Rows of seats on the raked floor were surrounded by tiers of boxes along the side walls. (110) Each spectator could see the stage, but the spectators, especially those in the boxes, could also see one another.

It was this visibility that made the opera an important social institution. Like the carriage ride or the promenade, appearance at the opera was

a way of establishing and maintaining social standing. The prominence, clothes, and social connections of each spectator were on display throughout the performance, and the genteel struggle to assert power and prestige was visible night after night. But the privilege that the Opera House put on display was distinctly up-to-date, fully reflecting the complexities of post-revolutionary France. The opera crowd represented the multiple paths to wealth and social standing that were open in the second half of the nineteenth century. Nobility was no longer a guarantee of status. A poor noble-woman could not afford to be seen at the opera, while a nouveau-riche businessman

109

without family con-
nections could easily
do so.

The triumphant
display of afflu-
ence that the Opera
House encouraged
was fed by, and
fed on, other in-
novative structures

110

nearby. The building is ringed by the *grand magasins,* the world's original
department stores. Invented in the mid-nineteenth century in Paris, where
the new rail system brought goods in enormous quantities, department
stores offered a new kind of shopping. The stores had fixed prices, and
merchandise could be returned; clerks enjoyed fixed wages and employment guarantees. Though far from the earliest of these buildings, the
Galeries Lafayette building at 38–46 Boulevard Haussmann is the most
characteristic survivor. This iron-framed building is unimpressive from the
outside, but the inside is dominated by a great open atrium under a dome
that combines clear glass with a kaleidoscopic center medallion, brightly
colored rays, and lower rim. Arches below the dome frame balconies on
each of the building's floors. From below, a shopper has a sense of the
inexhaustible range and opulence of the merchandise on display. (111)

The rule of Napoleon III, most of it under the Second Empire, lasted
through two decades. Its endurance is compelling evidence that the regime held the contrary forces of French political life in check. That equi-
librium collapsed and the empire failed not because of domestic dishar-

mony but through an ill-conceived military venture. In 1870 France was manipulated into a declaration of war against Prussia. The mastermind of this twisted plan was Count Otto von

111

Bismarck, chancellor of the North German Confederation, whose covert purpose had little to do with a desire to conquer France. Bismarck's real goal was to rally or bully the smaller German states into a confederation that he could mold into a nation. Even at this relatively late date, Germany and Italy both remained unconsolidated, and in both cases France held the key to national integration.

The Prussian battle plan had been developed by the legendary General Carl von Clausewitz. In his *Art of War,* written in the wake of the Napoleonic campaigns, he described two strategic goals: destroy the French field armies, and capture Paris. In 1870 allied German troops let by General Helmuth von Moltke quickly achieved the first half of this mission. After a series of small victories, Moltke's troops confronted a French army of over a hundred thousand, led by Napoleon III himself. In the battle of Sedan the French were defeated and forced to surrender. Among the prizes taken was the emperor himself. In the second phase of operations, Moltke laid siege to Paris. The city—defended by a ring of virtually impregnable fortresses and a modernized wall—was able to withstand his attack for many months. (Map 2)

The simple scenario that Clausewitz had imagined soon degenerated into chaos, largely as a result of the Germans' own success. Without the emperor at its head, the French nation had no government with whom the Germans could negotiate. Having achieved a sudden and overpowering military victory, the Germans found themselves in a messy political situation. An armistice was declared during which French national elections could be held. A National Assembly was convened and a provisional Third Republic proclaimed. The new national government negotiated an end to the war and agreed to pay heavy reparations. To ensure their payment, Prussian troops remained in France. The capital, which had suffered from months of famine, cold, and neglect during the siege, found itself alienated from the national political temper, opposed to the peace treaty, and increasingly isolated. In March 1871, when the government troops attempted to disarm a city militia, a popular revolt began.

A new Paris Commune, modeled on the unrestrained movement of 1792–1794, seized power in the city and governed for three months. Karl Marx saw the revolt as the prototype of a proletarian revolution. Both the French people and the German government seemed to agree with him, but they were not happy about it. With the complicity of the Prussian occupiers, French troops entered the city in May and rounded up and executed many of the so-called Communards. The labor movement, which had been so active in the commune, suffered repression for years afterward. Among the few lasting effects of the Paris Commune was the arson fire that destroyed most of the Tuileries palace. That symbol of royal and imperial rule was never rebuilt.

The Third Republic was a hasty replacement for the Second Empire, cobbled together quickly in the wake of the battle of Sedan. Despite its shaky foundations, it survived until 1940, when a new German occupation of Paris and the northeastern half of France led to the formation of the much-despised Vichy government. The Third Republic rested on a legislative base of two houses: a Chamber of Deputies directly elected by the people, and an indirectly elected Senate. Together, the two bodies chose the president, whose term was seven years. The president appointed the cabinet and had the power to dissolve the assembly.

The present government of France is organized under the similar constitution of the Fifth Republic ratified in 1958. The Chamber of Deputies reclaimed one of its most venerable names from the revolutionary era, the National Assembly. Delegates to both it and the Senate, which are now large bodies, are directly elected, as is the president, whose term was reduced in 2000 from seven to five years. The president names a prime minister and a cabinet. In cooperation with the two chambers, he also names the Constitutional Council. An Economic and Social Council elected by professional associations and trade unions forms a semi-independent branch of government.

Paris is the center of the French national government, but within Paris there is no cluster of purpose-built structures containing its various agencies, as there are, for example, in Washington, DC. Like the monuments that represent the eclectic forces of post-revolutionary France, the buildings that house the French government are dispersed throughout Paris. The Senate has been housed in the Luxembourg palace since the Third Republic. Across the Seine from the Place de la Concorde, the Palais Bourbon and the annexed Hôtel de Lassay together host the National Assembly and its president. Built in the mid-eighteenth century, the Palais Bourbon was confiscated during the Revolution. To accommodate meetings of the Council of Five Hundred, one of the short-lived legislative bodies of the protean Revolution, a semicircular meeting room was built within it. In the 1830s that room was enlarged into a raked theater with a colonnade along its curved back wall.

Connecting the palace axially with the Place de la Concorde and the church of the Madeleine beyond, the National Assembly building was the work of the Napoleonic era. The original palace was set at an odd angle to the river and its merger with the Hôtel de Lassay extended it downriver in a way that made the linkup even more difficult. The architect's solution was a neoclassical façade modeled on the pediment of the Madeleine that paralleled the river bank and effectively masked the meandering structure behind. The words Assemblée Nationale are inscribed above its colonnade.

The official residence of the French President is the Palais de l'Elysée just west of the Place de la Concorde. Like the Tuileries palace, the Elysée combined a grand residence with a large garden. The palace was designed by Armand Claude Mollet and completed in the early 1720s. The main façade of the building is on the Rue du Faubourg Saint Honoré, facing north. It was one of the first buildings in that area and helped to anchor the growth of what quickly became one of the most prestigious neighborhoods in the city.

Behind a wall and arched gateway, the street entrance to the palace opened into an unusually large courtyard. At its far end stood the three-story main block of the eighteenth-century palace. This area enclosed reception rooms grouped around a central vestibule that stood on axis with the main gate and looked out toward the center of the long garden. Two lower wings at either side of the palace held domestic apartments and a private bath. These wings have been expanded to enclose secondary courtyards. The gardens of the palace stretched from the back of the main block south toward the Champs Elysées. In the original plan, a round fountain encircled by gravel walks completed the long axis that began at the gates of the palace. In the late eighteenth century, the formal gardens were replaced with scattered trees, meandering shaded paths, and sheltered lawns in the English or Romantic landscape style.

The circumstantial history of the mansion exemplifies the rapid and continual reversals of power and fortune that have dominated French political life in the last two centuries. Louis XV inherited the house but used it only as a guest residence for distinguished foreign visitors. During the Revolution the palace was home to the Commission for the Promulgation of Laws and its printing presses. The duchess of Bourbon, evicted in 1793, regained possession of her home in 1797. Impoverished by the Revolution, she divided the palace into apartments, and her ground-floor tenant transformed the reception rooms into a ballroom. Dancing was very popular in the waning years of the eighteenth century, and there were many places in Paris where, for a small sum, couples could dance through the night. None was more popular or more crowded than the Elysée ballroom, with its sumptuous decoration and romantic shadowy garden.

Napoleon Bonaparte's brother-in-law, Joaquim Murat, bought the palace in the early years of the nineteenth century. In 1808 when the emperor named Murat king of Naples, the newly minted monarch ceded all his property in France to Napoleon. The palace, much transformed since its ballroom days, was renamed the Elysée-Napoléon. From 1812 it was the emperor's official residence. He signed the act of abdication there in 1814 before leaving for exile in Elba. During the coalition's occupation of Paris in 1815, the palace hosted the tsar of Russia and the duke of Wellington.

After the first Bourbon restoration it became Crown property and continued to serve as the national guest house. In 1848 the palace, renamed
the Elysée Nationale, became the official residence of the president of
the Republic. The coup d'état that transformed the Second Republic into
the Second Empire left the palace without an official occupant. Creation
of the Third Republic brought the palace back into use as the official
residence. When the French government fled Paris in June 1940 ahead of
Nazi forces, the palace was closed, not to be reopened until 1946, when
a duly elected French president again made it his official home.

The gardens of the Palais de l'Elysée are on axis with the Petit Palais on
the opposite side of the Champs Elysées and, continuing across the river, with
Les Invalides. The Champs Elysées began its long and fabulous life as a royal
road. In the early seventeenth century, Marie de' Medici had a sheltered drive
created for herself from the Tuileries to the Seine parallel to the first leg of
the road to Versailles. Despite the royal example, the drive did not catch on
and the road remained unused. In 1666 Louis XIV moved into the Château
de Saint Germain en Laye, west of the city, and the project to create a royal
drive was revived. The designer of the Tuileries gardens, Le Nôtre, conceived
the idea of a great roadway that would extend the axis of those gardens up
a gentle slope to the height
of land in the distance. (112)
There, it would climax in a great
star-shaped intersection of eight
roads. At about its midpoint
the road would pass through
a circle—a *rond point*—where
two additional roads came in.

112

The projected roadway was extraordinarily wide, its triple carriage lanes separated by parallel rows of elm trees. Much of Le Nôtre's landscaping was destroyed during the Revolution. A few years later, the occupying armies of the coalition against Napoleon set up camp in open areas along the avenue and ruined what was left. In 1834 Jacques-Ignace Hittorff drew up new plans for the area between the Place de la Concorde and the first *rond point,* but rather than treat the whole area as a single unit bisected by the grand avenue, Hittorff divided it into smaller blocks that echo the urban grid with which the garden is closely connected. In each of these areas he placed trees, open parterres, fountains, and pavilions. Among the surviving pavilions are two restaurants rebuilt in the late nineteenth century and two small theaters. In recent years, children's playgrounds have been added as well.

Beyond the *rond point,* the Champs Elysées remains a wide but more conventional urban avenue. Its central roadway is lined with trees, and the wide sidewalks that replaced the original parallel roadways are crowded with wanderers. In the nineteenth century the avenue featured a mix of shops and residences that gave way to exclusive boutiques and offices in the twentieth century. Within recent decades, Parisians have awakened to an alarming trend. Rents in the area have risen sharply, and the shops that once gave the avenue its distinctive Parisian character have been replaced by the stores of multinational corporations.

The Champs Elysées reaches its dramatic high point in the world's most glamorous traffic circle, the Etoile, now officially known as the Place Charles de Gaulle. Haussmann in typical fashion cut many roads into the circle, bringing the total up to twelve. At its center stands one of the most recognizable monuments on earth, the Arc de Triomphe. (113) In 1806

Napoleon commissioned Jean-François Chalgrin to design the arch to commemorate the military successes of the imperial armies. Chalgrin's model was the Arch of Titus in the Roman Forum. That arch is about fifty feet high; Napoleon's architect scaled his copy up to more than three times the size of the original. The arch remained incomplete when Napoleon's empire came to grief, and work was not resumed until 1823. Thirteen more years were required to finish the monument.

Four sculptural groups stand on high plinths at the base of each of its major supports. As one faces the arch from the Champs Elysées, the group on the right, sculpted by François Rude, is the most widely celebrated. Known as the *Marseillaise,* it commemorates the departure of the French armies in 1792 to confront Prussian and Austrian invaders. The other large groups celebrate Napoleon's victory of 1810 and the general themes of resistance and peace. The shallow reliefs higher up on the pillars commemorate other Napoleonic victories. The frieze that rings the monument represents the French army on the march. The names of victorious generals, most from the Napoleonic era, are written around the top. The shields between the triglyphs in the attic story of the arch carry the names of the most important battles of the revolutionary and imperial armies.

113

At the end of World War I an unknown soldier was buried underneath the arch; an eternal flame marks his grave. Victors, not all of them French, have passed through the triumphal arch and marched down the Champs Elysées. Prussian troops in early March 1871 and Nazi soldiers putting on a show of force in the final days of the German occupation during World War II were the most notorious. Hitler visited Paris on June 23, 1940, just a week after the city, abandoned by the French army and the national government, was occupied by his troops. Rather than stage a triumphal parade, however, he preferred to tour the city in his open car. The sites he visited were those on the standard bus tour. He did a little dance (captured on film) on the plaza overlooking the Eiffel Tower. Despite his evident enthusiasm for Paris, Hitler ordered its destruction by mines, field artillery, bombers, and V2 rockets throughout July and August of 1944. The city was saved from annihilation by the repeated refusal of *Wehrmacht* officers, especially General von Choltitz, the military governor of Paris, to follow orders.

On August 26, 1944, Charles de Gaulle relit the flame on the grave of the unknown soldier while sporadic fighting continued in the city. Ignoring the threat of snipers and a German air strike, the triumphant leader of the Free French and the 2nd Armored Division marched from the arch to the cathedral of Notre Dame. A memorial mass there was broken up by sniper fire. Despite this interruption, the parade reclaimed the city, which had endured four years of Nazi occupation, for the people of Paris and France. A statue of De Gaulle striding purposefully toward the Elysée palace stands on a large plinth near the Grand Palais. Its inscription reads: "Paris outraged, Paris broken, Paris martyred, but Paris liberated."

Chapter Eight

PARIS ON THE EDGE

Perched on the top of Montmartre high above the
city center, the basilica of Sacré Coeur is visible from
almost every part of Paris. (Map 8) The church was originally intended to be a votive gift to the Virgin for success in the Franco-Prussian War. When the French lost
the war, the project was not abandoned but redefined. The site was a very
significant one, with deep roots in the history of Paris and the entire French
nation. Montmartre—the mount of the martyr—is the traditional location of
the beheading of Saint Denis. As his legend records and as the grisly painting
in the Pantheon depicts, after his head was severed, the saint bent down and
picked it up. While the head in his arms preached a sermon, the saint walked
to the site of his chosen shrine and burial place, the abbey of Saint Denis on
the north side of Paris.

When the Second Empire fell and the French army suffered embarrassing
defeat, the city and the nation chose to reassert their "penitence, gratitude
and devotion" on this most sacred mount. In 1873, three years after the rout
and only two years after the disastrous Paris Commune uprising, the state
assumed sponsorship of Sacré Coeur. Design of the structure was awarded
to architect Paul Abadie. Born in Paris and educated at the Ecole des Beaux
Arts, Abadie was an enthusiast of the medieval revival style. He collaborated
with Viollet le Duc and Lassus in their first joint campaign to restore Notre

Dame. From that starting point he went on to an independent career as a restorer of significant medieval churches in the French provinces.

Abadie's most important restoration influenced his design for Sacré Coeur. The cathedral of Saint Front de Périgueux, begun early in the twelfth century in the northeastern corner of the province of Aquitaine, is an anomaly among French churches. For reasons that remain obscure, its builders turned to distant examples for inspiration. They modeled their church either directly on the Apostoleion in Constantinople or its near imitation, Saint Mark's basilica in Venice.

Like its models, Sacré Coeur is cruciform in plan. Four vaulted arms extend from a central space, and five domes rise from its roofs, though their disposition is unique. The central dome is lifted far above the crossing by an extended drum belted by a colonnade. And the four subordinate

domes rise from the corners of the building rather than from the intersecting arms where historical examples would place them. Each dome is stretched upward a little and topped by an attenuated lantern. (114) The pure white marble of the basilica's exterior increases the visibility of Sacré Coeur.

Though built at almost the same time, Paris's other most visible landmark, the Eiffel Tower, ignores or repudiates much of the tradition enshrined in the church.

114

The accidental symbol of Paris, the tower was meant to stand for a year or so and then be taken down when the Universal Exposition of 1889 was over. (115) Its designer, Gustave Alexandre Eiffel, was born in Dijon in 1832. After graduating from engineering school, Eiffel found a job with the railroad and was assigned to supervise construction of a major bridge near Bordeaux. From that beginning he went on to a spectacularly successful and well-rewarded career that included the design of bridges throughout France, then Europe, and finally South America and Asia. While Bartholdi may be the

115

French sculptor best known for his work on the Statue of Liberty in New York's harbor, it was Eiffel who designed the iron framework that supports the statue's thin membrane of sculpted copper.

In Eiffel's era the world's most exciting technology was the railroad. The increasingly large and powerful engines that pulled trains were obviously the most dynamic component, but the railroad lines themselves posed complicated problems. And nothing in the building of the roadbed was more difficult or risky than the design of bridges. The physics behind the construction of such objects is called statics, but in fact bridges are continually in motion, especially when trains are crossing them. Keeping a bridge in stasis requires a delicate balance of powerful forces. In an age when French engineers relied on the newly perfected slide rule to make their calculations, analysis of the complex interactions of wind, water, and the shifting weight of a moving train was exceedingly challenging. The design of a foundation and superstructure that could bear these stresses with economy and a certain physical grace was enormously complex, and building them was just as difficult.

Eiffel became a master in the design and construction of agile cross-braced iron skeletons that could do their job with a minimum of fuss. In the Garabit Bridge in central France completed in 1880, he added a new element to the rectilinear cross-braced pylons and caged roadways that had become his trademark: he constructed an arch out of the same ironwork. In designing the Eiffel Tower, he put both of these support systems—linear and curvilinear—to work in an object that celebrated the utilitarian style of railroad architecture while elevating it from an unnoticed underpinning of commerce to an object commanding universal attention.

Four concrete plinths, their bases buried deep in the ground, anchor four sloping piers that soar one by one from the earth until they lock together at the four corners of a square platform two hundred fifty feet above the ground. The first great challenge posed by the project lay in these four widely spaced supports. Each massive pillar started out as a separate job site, sharing a common store of materials and techniques but isolated from its neighbors. The tiniest deviation from specifications in any one of the towers could mean a failure to link up with the other three when the projects finally intersected. From their first point of union to the second platform, the towers were again isolated projects, though more closely aligned with one another and somewhat easier to coordinate. The last third of the tower would have been the easiest of all, since it was built from start to finish as a single frame, but it began more than six hundred feet above the ground, where wind and weather were a constant menace.

Purely ornamental ironwork was kept to a minimum, most of it in the great looping fringes that form the curve of the arches between the four legs. Basically the tower is a matched group of railroad bridges stood on end. It is an engineering marvel, not an architectural one, and the reaction of some contemporary critics was harsh. In the first sentence of a book on travel, the French writer Guy de Maupassant, who is best known for his short stories, wrote, "I left Paris, and then France because the Eiffel Tower finally just irritated me too much ... How is it that all the newspapers have dared to talk about 'modern architecture' in relation to this metal carcass, when architecture, the least understood and the most forgotten of the arts today, is also the most aesthetic, the most mysterious and the art richest in ideas? Throughout the centuries architecture has had the privilege of symbolizing so to speak each epoch, of summing up in a small number of typical monuments the pattern of thought and feeling, the dreams of a nation and a civilization" (Maupassant, *Carnet de voyage*).

What is most striking about this invective is the author's perception of just what the tower was about. Though Maupassant raised the notion of a monument that symbolizes its epoch only to reject the Eiffel Tower's claim to be such a monument, history has shown that his intuition was far ahead of his judgment. Better than any other structure, the Eiffel Tower expresses the ambition and inventiveness of nineteenth-century engineers. The monument looks both backward to the transformation of Paris carried out by Haussmann, a man with the soul of an engineer, and forward to the utilitarian rather than ornamental aesthetic that would dominate building in the twentieth century.

In a less than obvious way, the tower also fit in with the rest of the structures built to house the fair's tens of thousands of exhibits. They too were temporary buildings, though they had elaborate façades that combined grand pavilions and long arcades. Many were domed. Maupassant may have been more receptive to these pavilions because they made more obvious references to historical architecture. What held the pavilions up, however, and made their tremendous scale possible, as well as their viability as temporary structures, was the same iron framing that he hated when it was revealed so conspicuously in the Eiffel Tower.

116

Though all the pavilions from the 1889 exhibit were taken down, architecture of a very similar kind played a major part in the Universal Exhibition of 1900. Two buildings from that extravaganza were preserved, the Grand Palais and the Petit Palais. (116) These two palaces combine stone façades in the academic style known as Beaux Arts neoclassicism with internal iron frameworks which, in the Grand Palais, support acres of glazed roofs. The elaborate façades recall the architectural traditions of France that are anchored in the Louvre, in both Lescot's Renaissance design and in Per-

rault's neoclassical entrance
façade to the Cour Carrée.
The fusion of this tradi-
tional architecture with the
most dramatic contemporary
work is best seen in the Grand
Palais, where a neoclassical
exterior leads into vaulted
rooms. The main pavilion is
especially successful. At the

117

point where a long and wide roof, entirely glazed, intersects a shorter one,

a glazed dome rises above. Fields of glass flood the interior with light and

solve a problem that plagued the builders of Roman basilicas as well as

their imitators who adapted the basilica for Christian churches. Until the

nineteenth century, the Gothic building with its huge windows in soaring

walls had been the most successful solution. Replacing the roof with a

transparent material was the final step. (117)

The Grand Palais and Petit Palais are showplaces, but they are not

that much more glorious than the several train stations that began to serve

Paris in the second half of the nineteenth century. Napoleon III was a

great patron of the railroad, and Haussmann gave train stations promi-

nence in his plan for the modernization of Paris. They stood well inside

the city walls but still on the fringes of the most densely built-up areas.

On the north side of the city were stations named Gare Saint Lazare, Gare

du Nord, and Gare de l'Est. To the east were the Gare de Vincennes and

Gare de Lyon. The Gare d'Austerlitz stood just across the Seine near the

Jardin des Plantes, and the Gare de Montparnasse occupied the south-

118

west fringes of the Latin Quarter.

The Paris stations shared a common program. A gigantic façade with roots in a traditional architectural style introduced a building that was for the most part an assembly of iron-framed halls. (118) The Gare du Nord is a neoclassical building with a massive central pavilion, long wings to either side, and smaller pavilions at each end. The debt to traditional French architecture is obvious in the divisions of the long front, but the exploded scale and the enormous windows are evidence of a new building technology. With its heightened center bay and smaller framing bays, each topped by a slanting cornice, the central pavilion suggests nothing so much as the façade of a Christian basilica. (119) American train stations of this era tend to be modeled on Roman imperial baths, but in Paris train stations identify themselves as secular cathedrals. Ionic pilasters and colossal statues along the roofline and on pedestals in front of the windows bring the building into comfortable coherence with the architecture of its neighbors.

119

What is now the west wing of the Gare de l'Est is the oldest railroad

terminal in Paris. It was designed by an engineer and an architect in

collaboration and completed in 1850. In the early twentieth century the

station doubled in size, and the old façade was cloned on the east. The

original façade is a fanciful assembly of distinct architectural styles all

with strong Parisian roots.

Access to the station is

through an arcade em-

braced by two wings that

reach out from the main

façade and enclose a court-

yard. (120) The arcade and

wings reflect a Renaissance

Revival style. The evident

model for their ground plan

120

is upscale domestic architecture of the seventeenth and eighteenth centu-

ries. Behind the arcade, the main façade of the building is plainly rooted

in church architecture. There is a peaked roof ornamented with pensile

arches—a hallmark of the Gothic—that look like icicles. A demilune win-

dow with elegant tracery fills the space below.

The Gare d'Austerlitz shares the architectural approach of the other

grand Paris stations, but its history is marked by one of the darkest events

of the twentieth century. Soon after the German occupation during the

Second World War, the Vichy government promulgated a series of new

laws directed against the Jews of both the occupied and unoccupied

zones of France. Any person with two Jewish grandparents would belong

by law to the "Jewish race" and therefore be ineligible for public employment, for the practice of medicine or law, or for an official position in any corporation.

The law also took measures to segregate Jews, denying them access to public school and parks, even forbidding their use of public telephones. In 1942 French Jews in the occupied zone were obliged to wear a yellow star on their clothing. There was no Jewish ghetto in Paris, but many of the city's Jewish families lived in the Marais, the Renaissance enclave that had long since become a working-class district. This concentration made it simpler for the authorities—both French and German—to enforce the law and control the population.

The Monument to the Deportation occupies the upriver end of the Ile de la Cité. From its location and its dank simulated cells, a visitor might conclude that the deportees were taken from the city in boats, but this was not the case. When arrests began in 1941, many Jews who were rounded up in the Marais may have passed through the Ile de la Cité, but their immediate destination was the Gare d'Austerlitz. On May 14, 3,700 Jewish men were seized. Between July 19 and July 22, 7,800 men, women, and children were swept up.

They were taken by train from the Austerlitz station to internment camps within France hastily thrown together in Pithiviers and Beaune-la-Rolande. On March 27, 1942, adult and adolescent detainees were shipped from French detainment camps to Auschwitz. The deported left behind some 3,000 children, who were shipped en masse to a third French detention camp at Drancy, where they remained until August before they were taken in six trains to Germany. Not one of these Jewish children survived. During 1942—the worst year of the war for French

Jews, and particularly for citizens and residents of Paris—some 42,000 people were deported to Auschwitz in forty-three railroad convoys.

Though the French police and railroad workers collaborated with the Germans in capturing and deporting France's Jewish citizens, the rest of the nation was not complaisant. French clergy protested against the deportations, and in 1943 the Vichy government pulled back from its earlier policy. When the Germans continued to round up Jewish citizens and increase the pressure on Vichy, the government soon came around. Official policy notwithstanding, many French men and women sheltered Jews and helped them escape the roundups. Still, a quarter of the more than 300,000 Jewish citizens and residents of France did not survive the war.

Of the Paris rail stations, the Gare d'Orsay, which was built to bring visitors to the Universal Exposition of 1900, made the deepest intrusion into the urban fabric. (121) In the 1980s its rail connections were cut off and the building was transformed into a museum dedicated to French art of the nineteenth century. Creation of the new museum brought back to Paris paintings and sculpture that had first been exhibited in the gallery at the Luxembourg palace. Designated as the official gallery for contemporary art in the early nineteenth century, the Luxembourg was replaced in that role by the Palais de Tokyo on the north side of the Seine in 1937. For most of its life as a gallery, the Luxembourg had passed its best contemporary paintings along to the Louvre, but after World War II the Louvre began to focus on earlier periods. Its late-nineteenth-century paintings

121

were removed and exhibited in the Jeu de Paume in the Tuileries gardens, while less celebrated paintings were exiled to provincial museums. In the Musée d'Orsay, items from all these widely dispersed collections have been regrouped and put on display.

Despite the tremendous upheaval in the structure of national life that the Revolution brought about, the academic control of art remained intact. Kings and nobles lost their heads; the Catholic church was disestablished and for a time shut down; the days of the week, the months of the year, and even the beginning of historical time were recalibrated. Through all of this, with only a brief interruption and a change of name, the Ecole des Beaux Arts continued to teach the pre-

122

revolutionary curriculum, to award the Prix de Rome to the best students, to grant official commissions, and to put on exhibitions—called salons—which were thronged year after year. The Musée d'Orsay chronicles the life of the post-revolutionary academy and the multiple rebellions that finally liberated French painting from its control and in the end destroyed the academic ideal worldwide.

Most paintings are hung in small galleries that hug the walls of the vast building. The central spaces of the former train station have been left open for the exhibition of sculpture, for architectural objects, including

a model of the Opera House, and for large paintings. (122) Works in the
first galleries of the ground floor illustrate the achievements and limitations of the academy in the early to mid-nineteenth century. Art in that
era was dominated by the circles of students that formed around each of
the painters who were members of the faculty of the national art school.
Though never a formal requirement for admission to the school, atten-
dance at the private classes of one of the masters was a practical necessity. And while all these instructors subscribed to the basic ideals of the
academy, they approached their work in distinctive ways that their pupils
were advised to adopt.

Two paintings in Room 1 reveal important aspects of the academic
tradition. The modest painting of a Roman villa by Achille Benouville
represents the day-to-day work of a young artist who has been successful
in his bid for a Prix de Rome. Jean-Léon Gérôme's far more striking and
elaborate *Cockfight* is the work of a painter who tried and failed to achieve
the same honor. (123) In an attempt to convince the judges that they had
underestimated him, the
young painter created this
work, which began life as a
study of a popular sculpture
in the Louvre. From this
starting point the composition developed slowly to
include a second figure of
a young woman. A classical
sculpture in the midground

123

and a pastoral landscape in the distance presented the figures in an appropriate antique setting. Fighting cocks added color, contrast, and movement and gave the pair a common focus.

Gérôme exhibited the finished painting in the salon of 1847. The influential art critic and reviewer Théophile Gautier saw in it "prodigies of drawing, animation and color." The modernist Baudelaire, on the other hand, was unimpressed. He declared the painting overly meticulous, sterile, and artificial.

124

In the short run, Gautier's judgment prevailed and the painter became an overnight sensation. In the wake of this success, Gérôme forgot about the Prix de Rome and began a lucrative professional career.

Also exhibited in the salon of 1847, Thomas Couture's massive *Romans in the Age of Decadence* was both a historical painting of the ancient world and a commentary on contemporary art. (124) An impeccable classical portico overlooks and bears down on a wild orgy. Sculptures of illustrious and sober ancestors survey the scene. Two crowned men look on with dismay and disapproval from the right; a second seated figure peers from the left. Couture's notes for the salon catalogue declared that not war but vice destroyed the Roman empire. When Romans forgot the virtues and achievements of their ancestors, they lost their way and ultimately their imperial power. Contemporary painting, he implied, has also lost its way, and only a return to the rigorous classicism of the seventeenth and eighteenth centuries could save it.

What Gérôme and Couture's paintings represented, however, was not salvation but its opposite. Both men were brilliant technicians whose art still can give pleasure and satisfaction. But along with the many others whose works surround and echo theirs, these two artists seem to be mining an exhausted vein, where brilliant technique ironically highlights aridity of theme. Both Gautier and Baudelaire observed the same qualities of meticulous and hyper-realistic representation. Gautier saw them as impressive; but in Baudelaire's view they were pointless and sterile.

Paintings like these—triumphant products of studios that became featured exhibits at the very popular annual salons—stood at the pinnacle of the academic system. But as the century progressed, more and more artists began to produce works that were unacceptable to the academy and so were excluded from the salons. The pressure to display these works reached a climax in 1863, when Louis-Napoléon authorized a show of paintings barred from the official exhibition. The epochal Salon des Refusés (Exhibit of the Rejected) included works that ignored or violated the rules of academic painting.

None of the entries in the Salon des Refusés was more controversial in 1863 or more celebrated today than Edouard Manet's *Le déjeuner sur l'herbe (Lunch on the Grass)*. Everything about it was wrong from an academic standpoint, and it is easy to see why it was refused. The modeling and coloring of the figures are flat, almost one-dimensional. (125) Academy jurists assumed that Manet did not know how to paint people. The artist's subject was neither historical nor allegorical. A painter, his friend, and

125

his model share a picnic on the lawn. Female nudity, however provocative, was welcome in French art if it served an idea, but a naked woman having lunch with two men was not just unconventional, it was obscene.

Manet, of course, saw things differently. He was fully aware of his so-called failings as an academic painter. He saw every one of them as a strength. Like Couture, Manet believed that painting needed to be reanimated by a return to its roots. He even agreed with the academics about what those roots were. The academic tradition rested on twin pillars: the observation of nature and the study of the history of painting. Manet felt that the academic tradition was stifling nature, and that painting could be reformed only if artists re-engaged with the real world of daily life outside the studio. While academic painters transformed life drawings into historical compositions within their workshops, Manet reversed the process when painting *Le déjeuner*. He melded two traditional sources—a painting in the Louvre then attributed to Giorgione and an image of Raphael's—into a scene made vivid by the observation of nature. He transformed an image from art history into a scene from daily life.

Among the many artistic movements that resisted or rejected the academic tradition, the best known is the Impressionist school. Men and women associated with this movement began to emerge in the last decade of the reign of Napoleon III. For a month in the spring of 1874 they mounted a show of 165 works in the former studio of the photographer Nadar. The group, organized as a corporation, called themselves the Société Anonyme des Artistes, Peintres, Sculpteurs et Graveurs (The Corporation of Artists, Painters, Sculptors, and Engravers). The list of exhibitors included a

number of artists unknown today, along with several of the most resonant names in modern art. Paul Cézanne, Edgar Degas, Claude Monet, Berthe Morisot, Camille Pissarro, Jean Renoir, and Alfred Sisley all exhibited multiple paintings at Nadar's. Manet was invited to participate but declined.

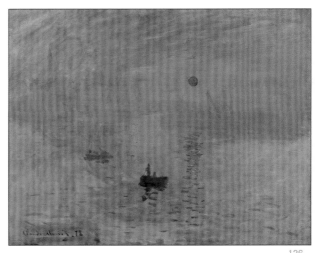

126

Among Monet's works on display was one called *Impression: Sunrise,* which gave the group its popular name, *les impressionistes.* (126) The members themselves assumed this label in 1877.

The group was united by a common practice and a common commitment. Painting what they saw where they saw it was the group's most consistent ideal. *Plein-air* or on-site landscape painting had always had its place in academic training, but in Le Brun's ranking it could never rise above second-best. The Impressionists made landscape the focus of their work, and they gave special emphasis to the delicate and ephemeral response of surfaces to changes in light. The "impression" captured in their name referred to what the artist saw when looking at an object under varying conditions of natural light, not to the conventionally objective truth created under the controlled light of a studio.

Technology played a part in freeing the Impressionists to explore the outdoors. Manufacturers of paints had recently begun selling oil colors in tubes that were easy to transport and ready to use anywhere. Light-weight substitutes for the ponderous studio easels also became available. Painters could carry their materials and paints wherever they chose.

A few thousand people saw the show in Nadar's studio, and some of the works were sold. There were further Impressionist exhibitions in the following decades. The critics responded predictably. Some savaged the art, while others thought there might be something of value in it. Four of the canvases from the show are now on exhibit at the Musée d'Orsay. Like the works bought by François I that formed the core of the Louvre collection, these paintings have a special place as founding objects not just of Impressionism but of what we call Modern Art itself.

Berthe Morisot, the lone woman in the group, showed a painting called *The Crib*. Like much of her work, it is a vivid treatment of a simple domestic scene. Cézanne, who would later break with the Impressionists, showed three canvases, of which two are in the museum. Most of the critics responded to his work with outrage. One of them decided that Cézanne must be insane. Camille Pissarro's *Gelée Blanche (White Frost)* drew the most sarcastic comments. The critic Louis Leroy imagined a dialogue among viewers: "What's that?" one asks. "Don't you see it's white frost on deeply plowed furrows. Here are the furrows and here is the frost," the other responds. "But those are palette scrapings uniformly spaced on a dirty canvas. There's neither head nor tail, top nor bottom, front nor back."

Like painting, sculpture was dominated by the academic system. But these works were much more expensive to produce than paintings, so sculptors were even more dependent on official commissions. Auguste Rodin, who in many minds epitomizes the revolt against the academy that transformed nineteenth-century art, began like many others not as a rebel but as a reject. He was denied admission to the academy, and his early work was turned down not only by the salon juries but even by the organizers of the Salon des Refusés. The work that reversed his fortunes is a curious male nude in the Musée d'Orsay called the *Age d'Airain* (*Age of Bronze*). Its title refers to the most heroic of the four ages of man associated in descending order with the

127

metals gold, silver, bronze, and iron. Originally intended to hold a spear in his extended arm, the figure seems about to step forward, while he shields his half-closed eyes with his right hand. (127)

A cast of the work was first exhibited in Belgium, where the critics were generally enthusiastic. Only a single phrase sounded a note of dissent. One observer suggested that the work had not been crafted by the sculptor but cast directly from the model. Such a casting, had it occurred,

would represent a shocking violation of the rules of the academy, and
Rodin was forced to defend himself. The commission appointed to review
his work seems to have overlooked all the evidence Rodin presented. The
work was accepted at the Paris salon in 1880, but it was shown in a dark
corner of the exhibit space. With the help of friends, however, Rodin was
able to turn this disaster to his advantage. For an admiring public, the
accusation became a tribute to Rodin's extraordinary ability to model the
human form. From this low point, the sculptor became a dominant figure
whose works the *Burghers of Calais, Balzac,* and the *Gates of Hell* are
universally recognized.

The ideal academic artist was a person of unquestionable talent and
often flamboyant originality, whose fame rested on his technical brilliance, which was on view in the salons year after year. There it received
the approval of the juries and the support of the state, which bought the
most important works for the Luxembourg museum. Art critics, who usually applauded the jury's decisions, also played a key part in establishing
reputations and ensuring lucrative private sales and commissions. The
ideal Bohemian artist, on the other hand, was poor but charismatic. His
talent was innate, and his paintings expressed his genius. He lived close
to the people and was surrounded by talented friends just as impoverished
and unrecognized as he. Puccini's 1896 opera *La Bohème,* set in Paris
during the revolutionary year 1830, gave this myth its widest circulation.
Mimi, the painter's beloved, succumbs to a fatal disease, in part because
she cannot afford heat or medicine.

In later elaborations of the Bohemian myth, sickness becomes a driving force in the life of the artist himself. Henri de Toulouse-Lautrec, who

has been the subject of many books and movies, seemed to embody this type of post-Impressionist Bohemian artist. He was the son of a southern French aristocratic family with a long pedigree but reduced resources. As a child, Henri was plagued by several diseases, and after he broke each of his legs in a succession of accidents in early adolescence, they became stunted while his torso continued to grow. Popular biographies of Lautrec emphasize his drinking and whoring and attribute both to the constant ridicule he endured. The same biographies see his art, which centered on bars and brothels, as the inevitable consequence. In reality, Lautrec was an exceptionally talented painter and printmaker whose skills were refined by study with one of the most successful and widely regarded academic painters of his era. Many of his finest works can be seen in the Musée d'Orsay.

Because he was poor, Lautrec lived in Montmartre, where he supported himself in part by working as a commercial artist, creating designs for menus, sheet music, and theater programs. Rents were cheap in the hilly streets around Sacré Coeur, far from the center of Paris. Though officially a part of the metropolis, Montmartre was isolated both from the pressure of urban land prices and from the watchful eyes of the law. In 1889 a music hall called Le Moulin Rouge opened in the neighborhood. French law had been changed in the 1860s to permit singing, dancing, and acting outside the licensed theater, and the main attraction at the Moulin Rouge was wild, exhibitionistic dancing. In its earliest years, a young woman named Louise Weber and her partner Jacques Renaudin were the stars of the show. Weber, who is better known by her stage name La Goulue (the Glutton), and Renaudin, who was called Le Desossé (the Boneless),

128

performed a dance called *le chahut,* which within a few years would become a chorus turn renamed the can-can.

In his first poster for the music hall—created in 1891—Lautrec put La Goulue, whose name appears in black, in the center of his composition. (128) She wears a red dotted blouse and lifts her white skirts to reveal lacy pantaloons and red stockings. In the foreground her partner is profiled in pearly gray. In the background a group of onlookers in complete shadow frame the pair. The brilliant colors, the graphic simplification, and the virtual abandonment of three-dimensionality mark the poster as a triumph of post-Impressionism. It set a stunning new standard for advertising and at the same time brought the graphic arts into the mainstream of innovation and creativity.

In the early years of the twentieth century, the Moulin Rouge transformed itself from a dance hall into a musical theater. The Folies Bergère, founded in the same era, went through a similar transformation. The shows became more carefully choreographed and the productions increasingly elaborate. Featured performers eventually included Maurice Chevalier and Jean Gabin. But the best known and the most popular were women. Mistinguett was a star in the years before the First World War. Between the wars, Josephine Baker, whose race made her a second-class performer in America, achieved extraordinary success in Paris. From the early decades of the twentieth century, black performers in general, especially jazz musicians, found a welcome in Paris and a lifting of the racial barriers that tormented them in the United States. From the mid-1930s until her death in 1963, Edith Piaf was the best known French performer. The writer Colette began as a *petite femme nue* in revues at the Folies Bergère.

While French music halls have always been noted for their risqué acts, these theaters also played a pioneering role in the development of modern dance. In the early 1890s an American dancer whose stage name was Loie Fuller began performing at the Folies Bergère. Fuller had transformed what was then a standard burlesque turn called the skirt dance. In the conventional skirt dance, the dancer reveals and conceals her body as she moves within a diaphanous slip. Fuller made the costume her focus and invented new kinds of stage lighting to heighten its effects. As she danced, the filmy outfit changed form and color to suggest butterflies and flowers. Fuller was lionized by poets, and the organic contours of her costumes influenced designers in the Art Nouveau movement. Fuller also played a major part in introducing Isadora Duncan, one of the great pioneers of modern dance, to Paris audiences. Ruth Saint Denis, who performed as a skirt dancer early in her career, followed Fuller and Duncan's example and played Paris to great acclaim early in the twentieth century.

Montmartre was incorporated into Paris in 1861, when the boundaries of the city were extended to reduce crowding. (Map 2) The new city limits comprised thirteen square miles, an area three times larger than before. This had the immediate statistical effect of reducing population density from 90,000 people per square mile to 45,000, but in reality low density at the periphery balanced out the high density at the center. Actually taking advantage of the breathing room that the extended boundaries offered would require a viable system of urban transportation. And it would have to include far-flung neighborhoods like Montmartre, whose hilly streets were too steep and narrow for horse-drawn trolleys to navigate successfully.

Residents were not the only ones inconvenienced by the state of Paris's transportation system. The many train stations that ringed the city in the late nineteenth century served different regions of the country, and the capital sat at the hub of this system. Traveling to or from Paris was easy and efficient. Traveling *through* Paris on the way to somewhere else, though not impossible, was slow and inconvenient. A passenger might have to change not only trains but train stations in Paris. For freight, the situation was even more critical. Loading and unloading are among the most time-consuming, expensive, and precarious parts of any freight shipment. It did not require much imagination on the part of people traveling through Paris to realize that a link among all the rail stations would be a good idea.

Parisians needed a mass transit system to relieve congestion in its streets and connect the center with the periphery; the French government needed something that would make the city less of an obstacle to national rail transport. These two ideas came into immediate conflict, and the deadlock persisted until the Universal Exposition of 1900, when it was clear that a national purpose, as well as local convenience, would be served by a mass transit system in Paris.

But still the debate continued, this time between partisans of an elevated tramway and partisans of an underground railroad. A tramway required no new technology, and it would be relatively inexpensive and easy to build. The problem of course was aesthetic. Elevated trains are noisy eyesores that plunge the streets beneath them into perpetual semi-darkness. In retrospect it seems inevitable that the underground would be chosen, since for many of its most progressive nineteenth-century initiatives—water, sewer, and even urban burial—Paris had turned to its subsoil for a solution. The bedrock of Paris was the nineteenth-century frontier.

The first line of the Paris Metro still bears the number 1. It now runs from the Chateau de Vincennes on the southeastern edge of the city to the Défense complex in the northwest. Its original boundaries were two gates in the city wall, the Porte de Vincennes and Porte Maillot. For a brief period when the line was first opened in 1900 it served only eight stations. Within months an additional ten were opened. Before year's end, the line carried more than a hundred thousand people each day. The first trains had only three cars with wooden benches for second-class ticket holders and leather seats for first-class. Crowding quickly pushed the railroad to double the number of cars on each train.

Building the underground tunnels was a multistage process that, in its first steps, differed little from mining coal. A square shaft was dug along the course the line would follow. The top of the shaft corresponded to the height of the arc that would ultimately form the tunnel's ceiling. As they moved forward, the excavators shored up the ceiling with wooden supports. When the shaft was completed, workers began carving away at its sides, roughing in the curve of the ceiling and widening the floor beneath it. Next, masons replaced the excavators and built a stone vault to hold up the roof. In the final phase of construction, the excavators came back to dig a deep channel in the center of the floor where the trains would run.

The greatest technical challenges the Metro builders faced were the passage of line 3 under the Canal Saint Martin on the eastern edge of the city and the far more audacious and hazardous passage under the Seine and the Ile de la Cité. The first was accomplished on an accelerated schedule while the canal was temporarily drained. The tunnel beneath the Seine was built in stages from prefabricated iron caissons. Each caisson was floated into place, filled with water, and then submerged. Still entirely self-contained, it was linked to the caisson in front of it and emptied of water. After workers removed the dam that separated this section from the rest of the tunnel, they prepared to submerge the next section. The work was exceedingly dangerous, not just because of the threat of flooding but because the air in the tunnels was pressurized to prevent leaks. Like deepwater divers, workers were subject to decompression sickness, which was called caisson disease before it became known as the bends. Though fatal only in extreme cases, the condition produced severe crippling and chronic pain.

The Metro stations were lined with white tiles to reflect light and make them bright and welcoming. Decoration of the line continued above ground. In 1896 the architect and artist Hector Guimard was commissioned to design entrances for the lines that would go into service in the year of the Universal Exposition. Guimard worked in a new style of decoration that combined calligraphic line, organic forms, and the arcs and elaborate tracery of the Gothic. The style was grounded in the work of English designer William Morris as well as similar work by Belgian artists. Guimard's creations helped to popularize the style and give it a French name, Art Nouveau.

His subway entrances combined steel, iron, and glass in organic and fluid forms that had never been seen before. Fences of cast panels looked

as if they were covered with viney tendrils.
Lamps looked like bending tulips, while
glass panels spread like the wings of dragon-
flies. (129) Not everyone admired Guimard's
constructions. They were compared with
disdain to a "prehistoric skeleton," a "plate
of noodles," a "whiplash," "an assemblage
of thigh bones." The designer was also
criticized for his allegiance to English and
Belgian design. Some felt that the green he
preferred was excessively "Germanic."

129

   The first task of the Metro lines was
to speed communication within the
expanded city limits. Beginning in the
1930s and accelerating after the Second
World War, the lines reached out farther
into the periphery, beyond the old walls that had finally been dismantled in
the 1920s. This was the first trace of a regional rail system. Aborted by the
war, the project was reinvigorated in the 1960s. The Réseau Express Ré-
gional de l'Ile de France, the RER, was devised as a system for integrating
intracity mass transit with train lines into the city's outskirts—*la banlieue*.
This plan finally accomplished what politicians in the 1850s had hoped to
bring about, a railroad intersection under the heart of Paris. Unfortunately,
while the RER integrated the periphery and central Paris, the system further
reinforced the isolation of individual suburbs from one another.

   The rail hub now exists at the Châtelet–Les Halles station, where three
of the five RER train lines intersect underground. (Map 8) Just above that

intersection is one of the few missteps in the postwar history of development in Paris. Since the twelfth century, the city's central provision market, Les Halles, stood on this site, just west of the Cemetery of the Innocents. Les Halles was the hub from which produce made its way to many openair markets that distributed fresh food and produce to individual shoppers. But equally important, as a wholesale market it supplied the kitchens of the thousands of restaurants which, since the beginning of the nineteenth century, have been among the most distinctive landmarks of Paris.

In the eighteenth century a *restaurant* was not a place but a restorative drink, usually bouillon, and shops vending *restaurants* in this original sense of the word existed throughout Paris. Late in the century the term embraced a new way of dining altogether, and after the Revolution this novel concept expanded in Paris, though it remained uncommon elsewhere. One of the distinctive and attractive qualities of the city's restaurants was their form of service. Earlier public eating places, like inns and taverns, generally offered the same meal to all comers and seated everyone together at large tables. Restaurants, on the other hand, offered choices and prepared their meals to order. Diners could be seated and served whenever the restaurant was open.

Though many inexpensive restaurants offered little in the way of elegance or exotic foods, others were far superior. Haute cuisine expanded its reputation and its clientele through the restaurants of Paris. Many cooks and others working in the most ambitious restaurants after the Revolution had been trained in aristocratic houses; the foods and forms of service they introduced had the cachet of nobility. Early in the nineteenth century, diners would most likely be served "in the French manner." The items in each menu category—appetizers, entrees, desserts—were brought to the table in order, and diners took their choice from an array of dishes. Service "in the Russian manner"—where each diner chose a single dish for each course— soon displaced the earlier style. This is still one of the hallmarks of French dining. Elaborate individual place settings created by the French porcelain industry increased its elegance and amplified its appeal.

As early as 1803, Grimod de la Reynière published a guide that rated Paris restaurants according to their cuisine and service. In 1858 Charles Monselet edited *Le Gourmet,* a weekly journal of restaurant reviews. To-day, some 8,000 restaurants in Paris offer a range of foods to suit almost any palate, from fast-food outlets and pizza shops through bistrots to the ten restaurants which in 2007 were awarded the top rating of three stars in the *Michelin Red Guide.* (130)

Traffic congestion was always a problem in the area of Les Halles, and as the city grew outward, a thicker and thicker barrier of narrow, populated streets separated the farmland at the city's boundaries from the thousands of customers who shopped every day at the market. In 1961 the municipal authori-ties moved the market to the edge of the city at Rungis. At first the relocation left a symbolic hole in the center of the city. Iron-framed glazed sheds that once sheltered butchers and fish,

130

fruit, and vegetable vendors suddenly stood empty. The permanent businesses that had grown up around them seemed to have lost their purpose
as well.

Over the succeeding years, however, restaurants like Au Pied de
Cochon and restaurant suppliers like Dehillerin have remained in the area
and recovered their customers. But the glass sheds that once sheltered
the vendors were not so lucky. Projects to convert them to other uses were
examined and abandoned in favor of outright demolition, and in the early
1960s the market sheds were torn down one by one. For a long time the
site, with the glorious Gothic church of Saint Eustache hovering in the
background, remained an excavation, called *le trou des Halles*—the Les
Halles hole.

In the late 1970s a new complex took the place of the old market,
though it did not in any sense fill the void. The Forum des Halles is a
largely underground shopping center linked with the Châtelet–Les Halles
RER station and the intersecting Metro lines. At ground level, the complex

features rectilin-
ear buildings with
rounded edges, droop-
ing or creeping white
ironwork, meandering
tubes, and stubby tow-
ers, all with a heavy
tinge of the technolog-
ical future imagined
in French science
fiction movies of the

131

era. (131) From its opening in 1981, the project was vilified. The mayor of Paris has called it "a soulless, architecturally bombastic concrete jungle" marked by repeated business failures, the ascendancy of fast-food restaurants, and strolling drug dealers.

Several architectural competitions have been held with the goal of replacing or remodeling the Forum des Halles. A garden project was approved in 2004 which will give the piecemeal landscaping around the complex a more coherent and traditional theme. The latest redesign calls for the open plaza that leads to the center of the complex to be spanned by a computer-designed glass canopy with a vaguely avian profile. Like a handkerchief laid on the face of a corpse, the canopy will both shelter the forum's open plaza from the weather and shield it from view. It will inevitably recall the vanished vaults of the nineteenth-century marketplace.

If the Forum des Halles at last shows some promise of finding common ground with its neighbors, the other great project in the area remains defiantly unreconciled. The Beaubourg, also called the Pompidou Center, remains what it was always intended to be, a cultural institution's attempt at a countercultural statement. The building looks like a permanent construction site. Its rectilinear exoskeleton recalls nothing so much as scaffolding that is never taken down. The project's architects, Renzo Piano and Richard Rogers, may have had Michelangelo's notion of the *non-finito*—the dynamically incomplete—in mind, but a more apt comparison might be made with those state-sponsored Italian building programs sheathed in scaffolding that are always in progress yet never finished.

Like the Forum des Halles, the Beaubourg owes some debts to French science fiction, but otherwise it is difficult to find a connection with any structure anywhere else in the city. Almost immediately, younger archi-

132

tects turned against a building which in their view manifested nothing so much as a naive utopianism coupled with deficient professionalism and a style as deceitful as it was nostalgic. Overdone on the outside, the building is a resounding failure as an exhibition space. Its main function has been to serve as backdrop to the endless street theater that takes place in the large plaza around it. (132) As the years pass, the sense that any of this constitutes meaningful public expression grows dimmer.

The Beaubourg commemorates the presidency of Georges Pompidou, who served from 1969 to his death in 1974. He approved the project, though the winning design was not at all to his liking. But Pompidou, like the center, was a product of his era. He believed that the future of Paris lay in her suburbs, and that the greatest force for urban transformation in the postwar era would be the automobile. His urban models were New York and Los Angeles, cities in great turmoil throughout the 1960s where the affluent were fleeing decaying centers and establishing new communities in old farmlands, their flight aided by the construction of new roads. Had Pompidou lived longer, Paris might well have been transected by elevated superhighways.

Proclaiming a "new French architecture," the next French president, Valéry Giscard d'Estaing, rejected the internationally inspired policies

of his predecessor. The architecture he advocated exemplified "humil-
ity, continuity and proportion," and repudiated transatlantic models
that appeared cold, impersonal, and deliberately imposing. During his
administration, the public oversight of architecture, which had remained
obstinately self-regulating, became the responsibility of the Ministry of
the Environment. The reckless creation of suburbs was halted and an
integrated plan of urban development, first mentioned in the 1950s, was
reintroduced. Giscard d'Estaing declared that no superhighways would
crisscross the urban landscape of Paris, and no skyscraper would intrude
into the historic fabric of the city center.

François Mitterrand, a socialist who ran unsuccessfully against Gaullist
candidates for more than a decade, was finally elected president in the
second round of voting in 1981. While his political enemies pilloried him
as an irresponsible populist, in the realm of urban policy he remained true
to his predecessor's commitment. He is widely recognized as one of the
greatest and most insightful builders of modern Paris. His *Grands Projets*
(Great Projects) have assumed a prominent place among the monuments
of the city. The best known of these are the Louvre pyramids by I. M. Pei.
In awarding that contract, Mitterrand bypassed the established process of
architectural competitions. This was a singular exception, however, and the
rest of the buildings sponsored by his administration were commissioned in
the routine way. These include the Opéra de la Bastille designed by Carlos
Ott, the new Bibliothèque Nationale de France by Dominique Perrault, the
Institut du Monde Arabe designed by Jean Nouvel (133), the Ministry of
Economy and Finance by Paul Chemetov and Borja Huidobro, and the Cité
des Sciences et de l'Industrie by Adrien Fainsilber.

133

These projects have little architectural unity, and because they are part of a general shift of government business toward the near-periphery of the city, they make almost no impression on a visitor. The same cannot be said of another Mitterrand project, the Arche de la Défense. It too is part of a drive to extend the effective limits of the city center, but no one would say it is inconspicuous. The Défense complex takes its name from a *rond point* at one of the old gates in the outermost and last city wall. At its center stood a personification of the defense of Paris by its citizens during the Franco-Prussian war.

The Défense complex is a group of imaginative, large-scale buildings sited around an esplanade. These buildings house government offices and the headquarters of national and international companies. The centerpiece of the complex and the building that ties it directly to the grand axis anchored in the Louvre and traced by the Champs Elysées is the building called La Grande Arche de la Défense or Arche de la Fraternité. (134)

This remarkable building, which opened in 1989, was designed by the Danish architect Johan Otto von Spreckelsen, who did not live to see it completed. Built of concrete, marble, and glass, La Grande Arche is an enormous cube pierced through the center. The sides surrounding the opening are angled back, giving it the look of a giant free-standing picture frame. At ground level this bevel incorporates a monumental staircase that leads into the center of the complex. A vast tent suspended by cables from the interior walls shelters an entry way. Behind and above it, a free-standing skeletal elevator shaft serves the upper floors. The sides of the building that overlook the central opening are divided into square coffers and are glazed. The view from the top of the building, which is open to the public, looks back down the long axis toward the historic center.

To the west of La Défense and a few kilometers beyond the city limits is the town of Nanterre, which is home to L'Université de Paris X, an extension of the Sorbonne. This was a new campus in the 1960s, whose focus was (and remains) law, humanities, and the political and social sciences. Its distinguished faculty has included some of the most influential French intellectuals of the late twentieth century. Though hardly household words in America, professors like Jean Baudrillard and Paul Ricoeur are widely known throughout the Francophone world. Yet the university at Nanterre is best known not for its faculty but for its role in *les événements de mai*—the events of May—that took place late in the 1968 academic year. The university's role in the widespread student-led unrest of that season earned it the nickname

134

Nanterre la folle (Mad Nanterre), or more commonly *Nanterre la rouge* (Red Nanterre).

Actions that would culminate in widespread riots the following May began in November 1967, when ten thousand students and faculty staged a strike in opposition to a streamlining and restructuring of higher education throughout France. Protesters argued that the reforms diminished the role of the humanities and the social sciences and exalted the hard and applied sciences. They believed the new policies aimed to substitute a practical, technocratic education for one based on the liberal arts. When the minister of education came to Nanterre in January to explain the reformed system to assembled students, he was challenged by Daniel Cohn-Bendit (who later would become a German delegate to the European Parliament). Since Cohn-Bendit was a foreign student, the university and the ministry thought that the best way to deal with him was to expel him and revoke his passport. Students who rallied to his support were confronted by police, whose presence on campus became another issue in the rebellion.

In mid-February, the revolution-in-the-making took a sudden step sideways when male students occupied women's dorms. Throughout March the situation at Nanterre became increasingly tense. Students held a series of outdoor meetings on the deficiencies of the university system. The faculty voted to close the university while the meetings continued. On May 3 a similar meeting was announced at the Sorbonne, the most prestigious of the country's universities. Because protesters from Nanterre were scheduled to attend, the minister of education and the rector of the Sorbonne agreed that police should be stationed on campus. Rather than creating order, the police outraged students, who felt, however naively, that the campus was their province. When five hundred students were arrested, the crowd lost control. Paving stones were lifted from the streets and hurled at police, who responded with riot clubs.

Demonstrations, marches, and small-scale riots spread throughout the university system. Though the leaders of the country's labor unions refused to support the students, workers throughout France joined the protests. On the evening of May 10, demonstrators marching toward Paris's right bank were blocked by police from crossing the bridges. The crowd shifted its focus to the Rive Gauche and at about 9 p.m. began building barricades throughout the Latin Quarter.

The spontaneous participation of workers finally moved union leadership to declare solidarity with the students and proclaim a general strike in their support. On May 13 more than half a million students and workers marched in Paris. After May 16, employees of the Paris Metro, the national rail system, teachers, postal workers, bank clerks, and miners joined in shutting down the nation. Daniel Cohn-Bendit, more the poster child than the leader of the rebellion, was expelled from France on May 21. His deportation unleashed another wave of marches and riots. With eight to ten million workers on strike, the nation faced near paralysis.

Charles de Gaulle returned from an international visit the following day, and late in the afternoon he gave his first radio address on the situation. Weary from the journey and insufficiently briefed, the president gave a speech that even the most sympathetic interpreted as out of touch with the national mood; the least sympathetic found it disdainful and arrogant. Violent protests that night led to intense confrontations with police. Two marchers were killed, the Paris Stock Exchange was set on fire, and barricades were erected in the streets for the second time.

On May 27 De Gaulle disappeared from Paris. Some believed he had fled the city just as Louis XVI and Louis-Philippe had done. Others anticipated the president's resignation or even suicide. Two days later, after consultations at a NATO air force base, De Gaulle returned to France and at 4:30 p.m. on May 29 he again addressed the nation. It was a take-no-prisoners speech. He would not resign; he would not dismiss the prime minister; he reaffirmed his orders to all national forces to reestablish control of their jurisdictions. His sole concession was to dissolve the National Assembly, clearing the way for a national referendum on the policies of his government. De Gaulle blamed the crisis on the political parties of the left, which opposed him anyway.

The following afternoon, supporters of the president in numbers variously estimated between three hundred thousand and one million staged a national march of solidarity in Paris. After this, the revolution slowly petered out. The students' grievances were, after all, exclusively campus issues: curricular reform, relaxed parietal rules, absence of police on campus. They offered no basis for a truly national movement. As time passed, the month of rioting came to seem more an expression of high spirits and unfocused discontent than the starting point for political revolt.

De Gaulle's whipping boys, the leftist parties that had belatedly and grudgingly supported the students, fared poorly in the June 1968 elections. The Gaullist party won a majority, and the president was returned to office. But less than a year later, in April, after a major legislative defeat, he resigned, and Georges Pompidou won election the following June. On November 9, 1970, Charles de Gaulle—leader of the Free French, founder of the Fifth Republic, and president of the country for more than a decade—died suddenly at his home.

In 2005, the worst unrest to strike the country since the student riots of May 1968 began on the northern periphery of Paris. Late in the afternoon of October 27, three Muslim boys evaded a police identity check by hiding among the transformers of an electrical substation. All three received severe shocks, and two of the boys—Zyed Benna, who was seventeen, and Bouna Traore, who was fifteen—died. Rioting broke out that evening in the suburban community where the boys lived, Clichy-sous-Bois, in the administrative district of Saint Denis. Three nights later, as police battled rioters, a tear gas bomb exploded inside a mosque. The deaths of the two boys coupled with the apparent assault on the mosque galvanized the Muslim community and caused widespread vandalism and rioting in towns all around Paris. From this beginning point, rioting spread to some three hundred French towns and cities. The government proclaimed a state of emergency that continued in effect for three months, though the rioting was of much shorter duration.

Paris had always attracted émigrés, but ethnic communities grew dramatically during the twentieth century. Russian aristocrats flooded to Paris in the aftermath of the revolution. Italian socialists and other dissidents fled Mussolini's brown-shirt thugs. Many Spaniards came to Paris in the Franco era. In the decades after World War II, tens of thousands of émigrés from the former French colonies found new homes in France. Many came from Indochina following the French debacle at Dien Bien Phu in 1954. That stunning defeat of a European colonial power by irregular forces had an immediate effect in other French colonies, especially those in North Africa.

France had invaded Algeria in 1830, and for more than a century it considered the North African nation to be not just a colony but an overseas division of France itself. When isolated acts of rebellion broke out there in November 1954 and escalated during the following fourteen months, the shock to the French national psyche was extreme. During seven years of brutal violence, the two sides fought not just for the independence of a colony but for the civilized soul of France. Governments fell through their failure to respond to the crisis. De Gaulle's own Fifth Republic was nearly engulfed. The war and its aftermath spurred thousands to emigrate from Muslim North Africa; many of them settled in suburban communities around major cities. Paris suburbs like Saint Denis became mostly Muslim communities that the European French viewed with distrust or contempt.

Parisians traditionally believed that the martyred Saint Denis had carried his head to a Gallo-Roman cemetery at this site, far from the center of third-century Paris. In the fifth century, Saint Geneviève sponsored creation of a commemorative chapel on the spot, and in the seventh century King Dagobert was buried there. Dagobert offered the chapel more than his earthly remains. He made the monastery that served it a royal abbey, and he created an annual trade fair that enriched not just the monks but the lay community that grew up on its fringes. Over the centuries his gifts and his example transformed the modest chapel into a rich and powerful abbey. The town grew wealthy from the proceeds of the fair and from serving the many pilgrims who came to visit the royal necropolis.

Beginning in 1144, Suger, abbot of Saint Denis and counselor of Louis XII, began work on a new royal basilica. A brilliant and innovative

organizer and politician,
Suger was also an enthusiast of the newest trends in
architecture, stained glass,
and the decorative arts in
general. Under his leadership, a building that would
be rivaled only by the
Gothic Notre Dame cathe-

135

dral came into being. Behind its entryway modeled on a Roman triumphal
arch stood a massive fabric in the new style with vertical supports grouped
in piers separated by groined arches and outer walls pierced by vast windows glazed with glass in the richest and most jewel-like colors. Over the
centuries, the tombs of successive French kings filled the chapels. (135)

The royal favor that ensured the success of Saint Denis through twelve
hundred years marked the building as a prime target for the Revolution.
The basilica was restored during the nineteenth century, and its history was
reconstructed during a series of archaeological investigations in the late
twentieth century. Though the fabric was repaired, the role the basilica had
played as the economic engine driving the town of Saint Denis ended with
the Revolution. Around the turn of the century the town became home to
a factory that produced printed fabrics. In the decades after the Revolution, more and more factories moved into the community. In the 1820s a
canal linked the village to the Seine and made shipment of raw materials
and goods faster and cheaper. Two decades later the railroad arrived. The
once-royal suburb became one of the most heavily industrialized towns on

the Paris periphery. After the war, heavy industry melted away, and unemployment spread throughout the district. As industry fled, housing prices
dropped and the community became affordable for immigrants.

But unlike many communities with similar stories, Saint Denis caught
the attention of the national government. Urban renewal projects revitalized
the center during the 1990s, and some private industries, like the Christofle
silver factory, continued to employ workers in the area. The new employer
of choice, however, was the service industry, much of it government-spon-
sored. The Stade de France—the stadium that hosted World Cup soccer in
1998 and World Cup rugby in 2007—was built there. Perhaps because of
less unemployment and less despair, the 2005 rioting that originated in the
cités (housing projects) of Saint Denis was less intense than in surrounding
communities, and it peaked and petered out much faster.

The character of the 2005 riots throughout France was uniform. All
involved young men, many of whom were of Arab or African descent and
most of whom were residents of *cités* on the urban periphery. They were
caught up in what the official report of the French Center for Strategic
Analysis called "a triple crisis that was social, political and institutional."
Those most affected were adolescents and young adults who lacked
professional training and had little chance of finding a job. In many cases
their lack of work forced them to live with parents who themselves survived on or below the poverty line. Because of their ethnic backgrounds,
the rioters had experienced discrimination.

The political dimensions of the crisis were more elusive. Many of
those interviewed for the report described frequent, gratuitous harass-
ment by police. The inflammatory rhetoric of the parties on the right also
contributed to the rioters' sense that they were despised by the European

French. Nicolas Sarkozy, minister of the interior and later president
of France, referred to the rioters with a word that can be translated as
"scum." He and his political allies suggested throughout the rioting that
the solution was to expel the "foreign agitators" responsible for it. In reality, most of those arrested, though ethnically African, were French citizens
born in France.

The acts carried out by rioters in most cases were the same. Trash cans
and phone booths were set on fire, and when police confronted the rioters
they responded with volleys of stones. On rare occasions sporadic rifle shots
were heard. But the signature act of the rioters was to burn cars. Night after
night the television news showed young men racing through streets fitfully
lit by cars in flame. November 6, 7, and 8 were the most destructive, with
more than a thousand cars burned each night. Arrests peaked in the same
period, with over three hundred people detained on each of those nights.
Police casualties reached their height on November 7, when thirty-four officers were wounded in confrontations throughout the nation.

In late November 2007, rioters in some of the same suburban communities repeated their protests. This time the demonstrations were
sparked when a police car crashed into a motorbike carrying two minority
teenagers. Though they quickly ended, the riots were more focused and
more dangerous. While rioters set trash cans and cars ablaze as before,
they also targeted security forces directly, and many of the rioters were
armed with shotguns.

The deportation of Parisian Jews by the Vichy government is remote in
time and tragic intensity from the expulsion of Daniel Cohn-Bendit in
1968 or the cries for extradition of foreign agitators during the 2005

rioting. A common thread runs through these events, however, and they highlight a recurring problem of self-definition. France is a nation founded and refounded since the revolutionary era on *The Rights of Man*—on abstract principles of liberty, equality, and brotherhood. It is a nation with historical ties to the Catholic faith, but also one that has for two hundred years repeatedly loosened any official links between church and state. As an abstraction, it is secular and free from discrimination based on race or gender. Official France has committed itself to granting full participation to former colonial citizens at the same time that government has insisted on their integration into the secular system of the European nation. Laws have been passed prohibiting clothing that is a mark of religious identity in public schools, and there has been renewed insistence on the legal equality of men and women, a sore point with most fundamentalist communities.

France is also a historical entity, a European nation with deep ties to its past and the particular ethnic identity that both united it with, and distinguished it from, its European neighbors. In the nineteenth century, national identity was rooted in ethnic distinction. The French were Gauls; the Germans were Teutons; the English, Angles and Saxons; the Scots, Picts; and so on. Everyone knew that these tribes had surged all across Europe and that each nation must be an admixture of several heritages, but the lines of ethnic distinction, however artificial, remained uppermost in people's minds. They helped to justify and explain the political lines drawn on maps.

The present doubt about the exact location of the Gallic colony from which Paris began is one symptom of a growing uncertainty about identity that the city and the nation must now face up to. Genetic research is overturning many of the ethnically based histories of Europe. The underlying continuities between Teuton and Gaul, Saxon and Scot are much more evident in these findings than the long-accented differences. It was language and cultural history that distinguished the Germans from the French, not their biological heritage.

Many in Paris and in France continue to cherish a concept of nationhood and national identity that is rooted in these long-taught and long-asserted ethnic characteristics. For these people, Paris is the capital of a nation that cannot be defined adequately by its adhesion to core humanitarian values—a contractual nation like the United States, open to all (at least in theory) who accept its creed. France for them is, rather, a community defined by experience shared over multiple generations. Its members, properly so-called, are white, European, and sentimentally attached to the Catholic Church, from which they are also resolutely estranged. For people who define their nation this way, the true citizen of France is not dark-skinned, observant, or Muslim. With varying degrees of intensity, French politicians on the right voice these distinctions. Without equivocation, French men and women of African descent feel them in their daily lives.

Paris itself is divided. Its predominately European core is ringed by a band of outer neighborhoods and suburban communities where an African heritage predominates. The tension between idealistic and ethnic definitions of nationhood is preserved in this division. A full integration of the city will require a reconciliation not just of abstractions and ideals but of two communities with distinctive characters and fates. This is unlikely to occur in the near future, and the city may continue to experience outbreaks of unrest like those of 2005 and 2007. But the ideals of the Revolution are sound, and the political process in France is vigorous, wide-ranging, and outspoken. The long arc of the city's history encourages the hope that diversity can produce cohesion and build strength, rather than disintegrate into further ethnic and religious strife.

INFORMATION

This book, like others in the From the Ground Up
series, is organized both chronologically and geographi-
cally. With a minimum of backtracking, visitors to Paris
can move through the book chapter by chapter, as they
move through the city on foot or by Metro. The first
chapter is the most abstract, and much of what it describes in its early pages
is evident from Map 1. The most revealing window on the earliest surviving
vestiges of Paris lies in the archaeological exhibit beneath the pavement in
front of Notre Dame cathedral.

The Ile de la Cité, site of Notre Dame, was the center of a Roman colonial administration that shaped the city for generations after the fall of Rome
and anchored its institutions. A bishop's palace and a cluster of churches
were the home of religious leadership and authority. Notre Dame cathedral,
which is explored at length in Chapter 2, was the third and by far the largest
church to occupy this central site. The Sainte Chapelle, built by the sainted
King Louis IX, is one of the very few remnants of successive palaces that
housed the secular government of both Paris and the country of France.

Paris has always been divided as well as united by the Seine, and
development on each side of the river has been distinctive. Chapter 3 describes the rise of the Paris colleges and universities on the Left Bank and
the monastic foundations and parish churches that served the city and its

large population. Many of these churches were founded before the Viking raids of the ninth century, but none survived their onslaught intact. What survives are new and rebuilt churches, a few in the Romanesque style and a great number in the Gothic style. Beginning at Saint Germain des Prés, the chapter follows a counter-clockwise path through significant Left Bank churches, with a special stop at the Musée de Cluny, devoted to medieval art and culture. Early churches of the right bank include some in the commercial center of medieval Paris and others on its northern fringe. The circuit ends at the church of Saint Germain l'Auxerrois, and Chapter 4 begins directly across the street at the Louvre.

Chapter 5 focuses on royal attempts to make the city a worthy capital and the increasing success of absolutist monarchs in transforming the arts into an instrument of political action. The Place des Vosges, where the itinerary begins, is at the edge of the fashionable district called the Marais on the right bank, a short walk from the Bastille Metro stop. The itinerary includes the Ile Saint Louis, the Seine bridges, and palaces of the two most influential cardinals in French history, Richelieu and Mazarin.

The following chapter begins at Les Invalides (Metro stop Invalides). It traces the edge of habitation in the pre-revolutionary period, where monarchs and princes constructed great public institutions devoted to charity, military training, and public piety. After passing through the public garden, the Jardin des Plantes, it ends in the nearly abandoned chapel of a seventeenth-century hospital.

Paris is filled with monuments to the Revolution, but the collection of the Musée Carnavalet in the Marais offers the most thorough and most engaging picture of the chronology and key figures of this complicated watershed event in French history. The museum's collection also offers a wonderful introduction to the efforts by nineteenth-century politicians, engineers, and architects to reshape the city—subjects explored in Chapter 7.

The final chapter of *Paris from the Ground Up* is about the expansion of the city in the last century, the revolution in transportation that has united it, and the population changes that have transformed and enriched it. It begins at the basilica of Sacré Coeur in Montmartre where Saint Denis was martyred, and ends in the suburb of Saint Denis where the martyr was buried and a great medieval church rose in his honor. Like many suburban towns around Paris, modern Saint Denis is home to a large Islamic community. Their treatment at the hands of French authorities and their integration into French life have created the most dynamic and active faultline in the contemporary life of the city.

FURTHER READING

Adler, Kathleen, et al. *Americans in Paris, 1860–1900*. Washington: National
Gallery Press, 2006.

Asensio, Paco, and Llorenc Bonet. *Gustave Alexandre Eiffel*. Dusseldorf:
teNeues Books, 2003.

——— *Jean Nouvel*. Dusseldorf: teNeues Books, 2002.

Ayers, Andrew. *The Architecture of Paris: An Architectural Guide*. Stuttgart and
London: Axel Menges, 2004.

Brillat-Savarin, Jean Anthelme. *The Physiology of Taste*, trans. M. F. K. Fisher.
Washington, DC: Counterpoint Press, 1999.

Brooks, Peter. *Henry James Goes to Paris*. Princeton: Princeton University
Press, 2007.

Collins, Larry, and Dominique Lapierre. *Is Paris Burning?* New York: Simon and
Schuster, 1965.

Doyle, William, ed. *Old Regime France: The Short Oxford History of France*.
New York and London: Oxford University Press, 2001.

Flanner, Janet. *Paris Was Yesterday*. New York: Viking, 1972.

Goubert, Pierre. *Louis XIV and Twenty Million Frenchmen,* trans. Anne Carter.
New York: Random House, 1970.

Gowing, Lawrence. *Paintings in the Louvre*. New York: Stewart, Tabori and
Chang, 1987.

Higonnet, Patrice. *Paris: Capital of the World*. Cambridge: Harvard University
Press, 2002.

Hobbins, Daniel. *The Trial of Joan of Arc*. Cambridge: Harvard University Press, 2005.

Jordan, David P. *Transforming Paris: The Life and Labors of Baron Haussmann*. New York: Free Press, 1995.

Lefebvre, Georges. *The Great Fear of 1789,* trans. Joan White. New York: Schocken Books, 1973.

McGregor, James H. S. *Rome from the Ground Up*. Cambridge: Harvard University Press, 2005.

———— *Venice from the Ground Up*. Cambridge: Harvard University Press, 2006.

———— *Washington from the Ground Up*. Cambridge: Harvard University Press, 2007.

Poisson, Michel. *Paris Buildings and Monuments*. New York: Abrams, 1999.

Reid, Donald. *Paris Sewers and Sewermen*. Cambridge: Harvard University Press, 1991.

Schama, Simon. *Citizens: A Chronicle of the French Revolution*. New York: Knopf, 1989.

Seigel, Jerrold. *Bohemian Paris: Culture, Politics, and the Boundaries of Bourgeois Life, 1830–1930*. Baltimore: Johns Hopkins University Press, 1999.

Shack, William A. *Harlem in Montmartre: A Paris Jazz Story between the Great Wars*. Berkeley: University of California Press, 2001.

Singer, Daniel. *Prelude to Revolution: France in May 1968,* 2nd ed. Cambridge: South End Press, 2002.

Trubek, Amy B. *Haute Cuisine: How the French Invented the Culinary Profession*. Philadelphia: University of Pennsylvania Press, 2000.

ACKNOWLEDGMENTS

This book is dedicated to my wife, Sallie Spence, who has shared Paris with me, and to my sons, Ned and Raphael, who have not been there enough. As From the Ground Up has grown into a series, each book has become more and more a collaborative effort. Author, editors, designers, mapmaker, and photographers have worked together to create a book on Paris that does not fully belong to any one of us. I am grateful to Lindsay Waters at Harvard University Press for sponsoring these urban histories, and to Phoebe Kosman for assistance during the review phase of publication. Jill Breitbarth, Eric Mulder, Abby Mumford, and Anne McGuire brought their expertise to the book's production. I am especially beholden to Susan Wallace Boehmer, whose comments, suggestions, and excisions have made the book leaner and better able to go the distance. Finally, Wendy Strothman, as always, offered wisdom and comfort when it was needed most.

ILLUSTRATION CREDITS

Adolphe Alphand, *Les Promenades de Paris* (1867–1873): 106 (Charles
    Weber); 112 (E. Grandsire)

Alinari / Art Resource, NY: 92

Amédée Caix de Saint-Aymour, *Histoire illustrée de la France* (1900): 26

Bridgeman Art Library / Lauros / Giraudon: 96 (Leon Joseph Florentin Bonnat,
    The Martyrdom of St. Denis); 97 (Jules Elie Delaunay, *St. Geneviéve
    Calming the Parisians on the Approach of Attila*)

Bridgeman-Giraudon / Art Resource, NY: 102

Clifford Boehmer / Harvard University Press: 1, 2, 4, 5, 6, 7, 8, 9, 10, 11, 12,
    13, 14, 15, 16, 17, 18, 19, 20, 22, 23, 24, 25, 27, 28, 29, 30, 31,
    32, 33, 34, 35, 38, 39, 40, 41, 42, 43, 44, 45, 49, 51, 52, 53, 64,
    65, 67, 70, 72, 74, 75, 76, 77, 79, 80, 84, 85, 86, 87, 89, 91, 98,
    104, 105, 107, 108, 109, 110, 113, 114, 115, 116, 117, 118, 119,
    120, 122, 129, 130, 131, 132, 133, 134, 135, pp. iii, 1, 301

Erich Lessing / Art Resource, NY: 48, 58, 61, 62, 81, 93, 123, 124, 126

Georges-Louis Le Rouge (1716): 88

Giraudon / Art Resource, NY: 103

Harvard Graduate School of Design, Loeb Library, Special Collections (Adam
    and Gabriel Perelle, *Vues de Paris et des Châteaux de L'Isle de France,*
    seventeenth century): 3, 36, 37, 46, 47, 50, 63, 69, 71, 78, 82, 90, 99

Harvard Map Collection, Harvard College Library: 66, 68, 73, 83, 94, pp.
    39, 69, 113, 155, 189, 213, Map 10 (Louis Bretez, *Plan de Paris:*

commencé l'année 1734, dessiné et gravé sous les ordres de Messire Michel Etienne Turgot, 1739); p. 9, Map 9 (Georg Braun and Franz Hogenberg, *Lvtetia vulgari nomine Paris,* 1572); p. 255 (Alexandre A. Vuillemin, *Plan de Paris*)

Isabelle Lewis: Maps 1, 2, 3, 4, 5, 6, 7, 8

James H. S. McGregor: 111

Jean Marot (ca. 1650): 100

The New York Public Library / Art Resource, NY: 128

Paul Joseph Victor Dargaud (1900): 121

Pierre Gabriel Berthault: 95 (*Transfert des mânes de Rousseau au Panthéon le 11 octobre 1794*)

Réunion des Musées Nationaux / Art Resource, NY: 54, 55, 56, 57, 59, 60, 101, 125, 127

Snark / Art Resource, NY: 21

INDEX

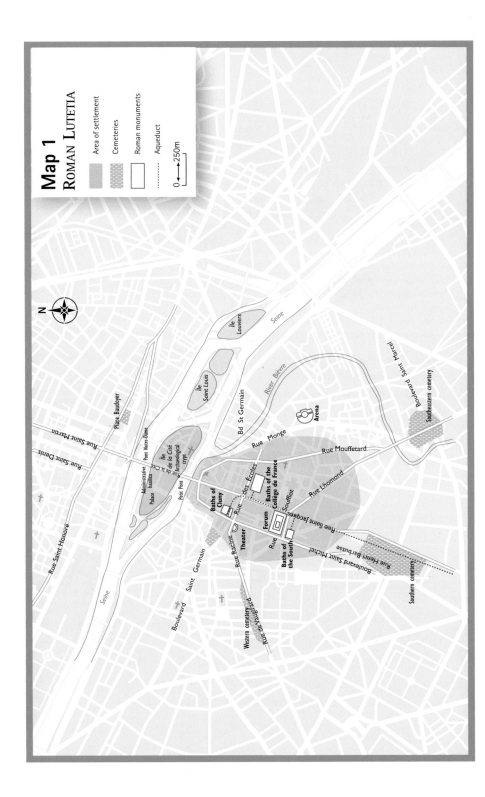

Map 1
ROMAN LUTETIA

- ▨ Area of settlement
- ▦ Cemeteries
- ▢ Roman monuments
- ⋯⋯ Aqueduct

0 ⊢—▶ 250m

N

Seine

Île Louviers

River Bièvre

Île Saint Louis

Bd St Germain

Arena

Rue Monge

Place Baudoyer

Rue Saint Martin

Rue Saint Denis

Pont Notre-Dame

Île de la Cité

Administrative Palace basilica

Pont Petit Pont

Archaeological crypt

Rue Mouffetard

Boulevard Saint Marcel

Southeastern cemetery

Rue des Écoles

Baths of the Collège de France

Rue Lhomond

Baths of Cluny

Rue Soufflot

Rue Saint-Jacques

Forum

Rue

Rue Racine

Theater

Baths of the South

Boulevard Saint Michel

Rue Henri Barbusse

Southern cemetery

Rue Saint Honoré

Seine

Boulevard Saint Germain

Western cemetery

Rue de Vaugirard

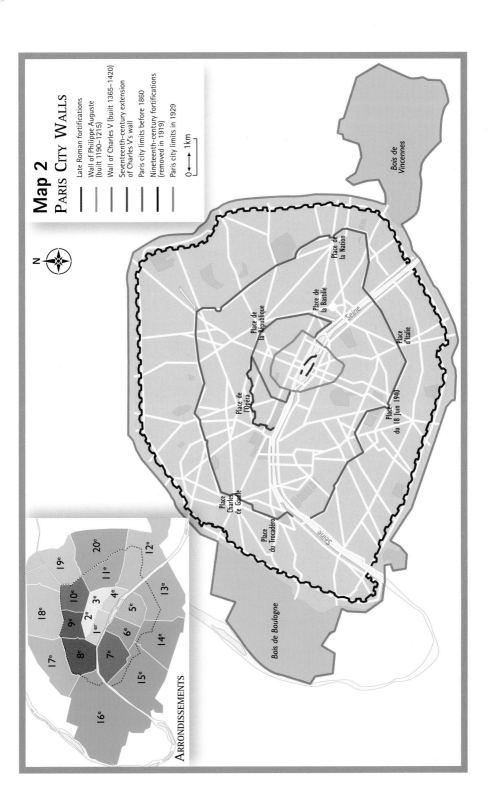

Map 2
PARIS CITY WALLS

Late Roman fortifications

Wall of Philippe Auguste
(built 1190–1215)

Wall of Charles V (built 1365–1420)

Seventeenth-century extension
of Charles V's wall

Paris city limits before 1860

Nineteenth-century fortifications
(removed in 1919)

Paris city limits in 1929

0 —— 1km

N

ARRONDISSEMENTS

17ᵉ
18ᵉ
19ᵉ
16ᵉ
8ᵉ
9ᵉ
10ᵉ
1ᵉʳ
2ᵉ
3ᵉ
11ᵉ
20ᵉ
7ᵉ
6ᵉ
4ᵉ
5ᵉ
12ᵉ
15ᵉ
14ᵉ
13ᵉ

Place de
la Nation

Place de
la République

Place de
la Bastille

Place de
l'Opéra

Place
d'Italie

Place
du 18 Juin 1940

Place
Charles
de Gaulle

Place
du Trocadéro

Seine

Seine

Bois de
Vincennes

Bois de Boulogne

Map 3

1. Wall of King Philippe Auguste
2. Sorbonne
3. Saint Germain des Prés
4. Saint Severin
5. Cluny Museum
6. Saint Julien le Pauvre
7. Saint Etienne du Mont
8. Collège de Beauvais
9. Hôtel de Ville
10. Medieval half-timbered houses
11. Hôtel de Sens
12. Saint Gervais and Saint Protais
13. Temple des Billettes
14. Museum of Arts and Occupations
15. Saint Nicolas des Champs
16. Saint Eustache
17. Saint Germain l'Auxerrois
18. Sainte Chapelle

0 ———— 300m

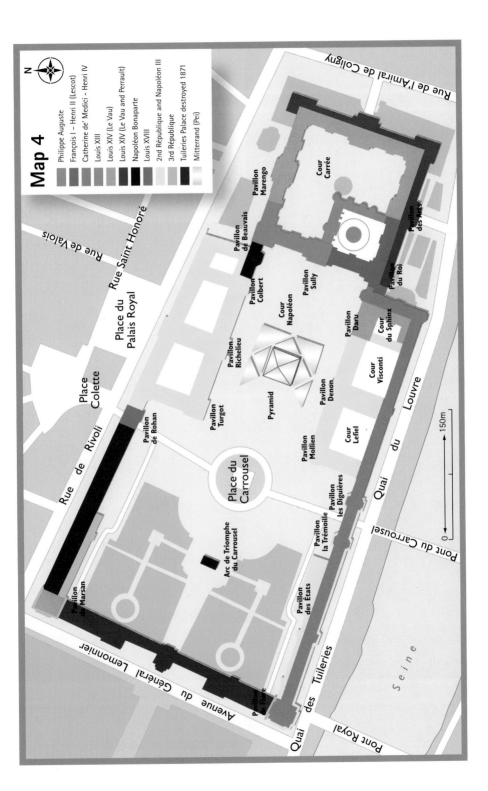

Map 4

- Philippe Auguste
- François I – Henri II (Lescot)
- Catherine de' Medici – Henri IV
- Louis XIII
- Louis XIV (Le Vau)
- Louis XIV (Le Vau and Perrault)
- Napoléon Bonaparte
- Louis XVIII
- 2nd République and Napoléon III
- 3rd République
- Tuileries Palace destroyed 1871
- Mitterrand (Pei)

Rue de l'Amiral de Coligny

Rue de Valois

Rue Saint Honoré

Place du Palais Royal

Place Colette

Rue de Rivoli

Pavillon de Rohan

Pavillon de Marsan

Avenue du Général Lemonnier

Pavillon de Flore

Quai des Tuileries

Pont Royal

Place du Carrousel

Arc de Triomphe du Carrousel

Pavillon des États

Pavillon la Trémoille

Pavillon les Diguières

Pavillon Mollien

Pavillon Turgot

Pyramid

Pavillon Richelieu

Pavillon Colbert

Pavillon de Beauvais

Pavillon Marengo

Cour Napoléon

Cour Carrée

Pavillon Sully

Pavillon Daru

Pavillon Denon

Cour du Sphinx

Cour Visconti

Cour Lefiel

Pavillon du Roi

Pavillon des Arts

Quai du Louvre

Pont du Carrousel

Seine

0   150m

Map 5

1. Place des Vosges
2. Hôtel de Sully
3. Saint Paul and Saint Louis
4. Pont Marie
5. Pont de la Tournelle
6. Pont au Change
7. Pont Neuf
8. Pont au Double
9. Place Dauphine
10. Square du Vert Galant
11. Grand Carré
12. Grand Couvert
13. Palais Royal
14. Bibliothèque Nationale
15. Institut de France

0   300m

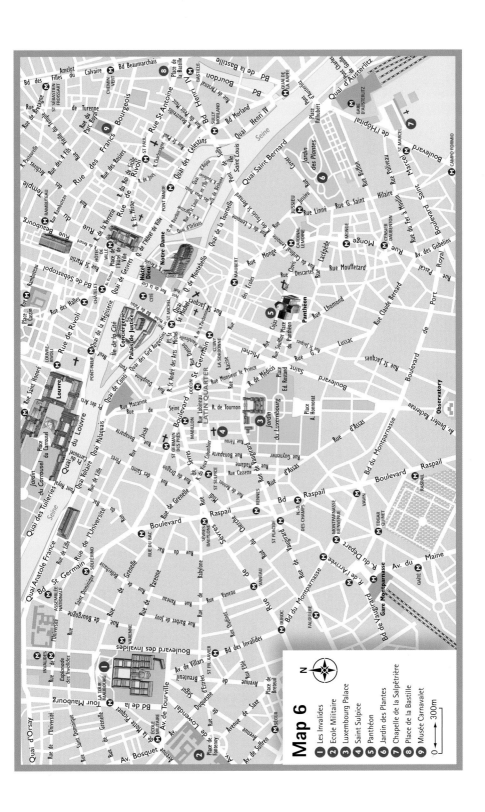

Map 6

- ❶ Les Invalides
- ❷ Ecole Militaire
- ❸ Luxembourg Palace
- ❹ Saint Sulpice
- ❺ Panthéon
- ❻ Jardin des Plantes
- ❼ Chapelle de la Salpêtrière
- ❽ Place de la Bastille
- ❾ Musée Carnavalet

N

0   300m

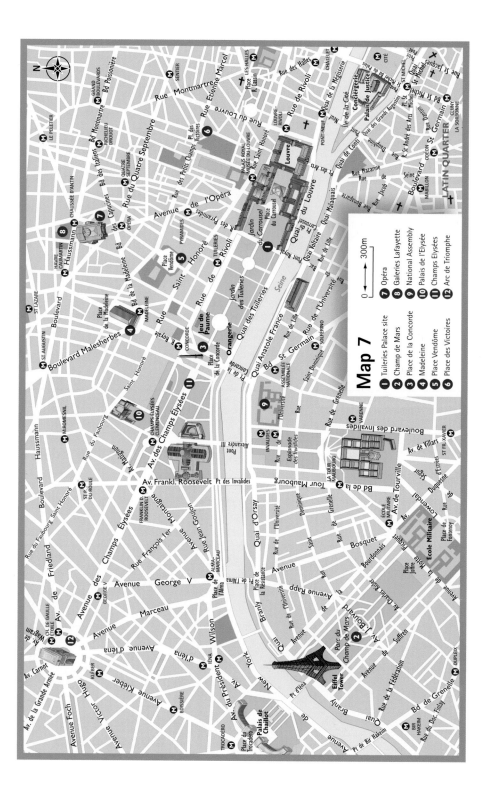

Map 7

- **1** Tuileries Palace site
- **2** Champ de Mars
- **3** Place de la Concorde
- **4** Madeleine
- **5** Place Vendôme
- **6** Place des Victoires
- **7** Opéra
- **8** Galeries Lafayette
- **9** National Assembly
- **10** Palais de l'Elysée
- **11** Champs Elysées
- **12** Arc de Triomphe

0 —— 300m

LATIN QUARTER

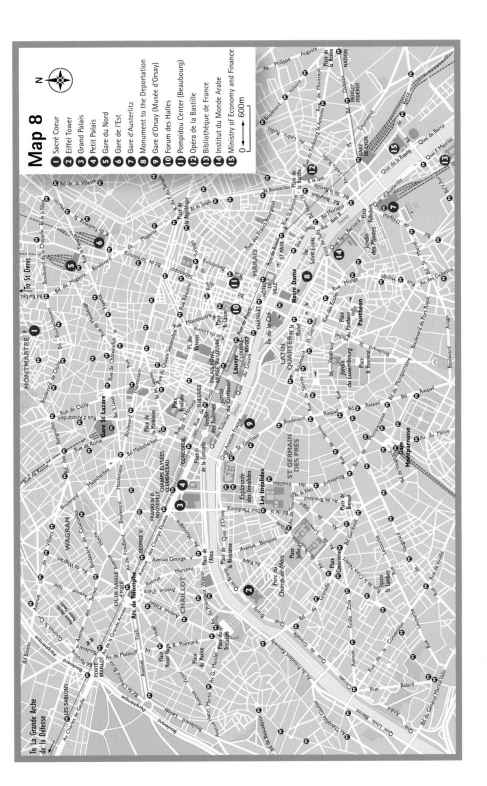

Map 8

1. Sacré Coeur
2. Eiffel Tower
3. Grand Palais
4. Petit Palais
5. Gare du Nord
6. Gare de l'Est
7. Gare d'Austerlitz
8. Monument to the Deportation
9. Gare d'Orsay (Musée d'Orsay)
10. Forum des Halles
11. Pompidou Center (Beaubourg)
12. Opéra de la Bastille
13. Bibliothèque de France
14. Institut du Monde Arabe
15. Ministry of Economy and Finance

0 —— 600m

N

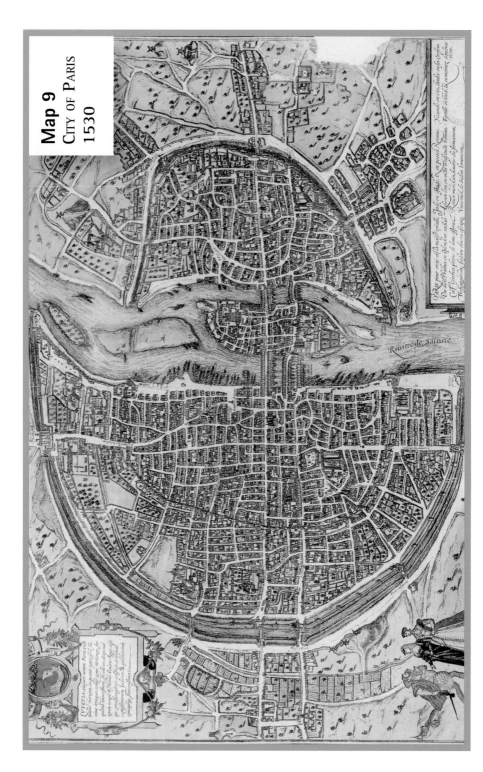

Map 9
CITY OF PARIS
1530

Riviere de Sainne

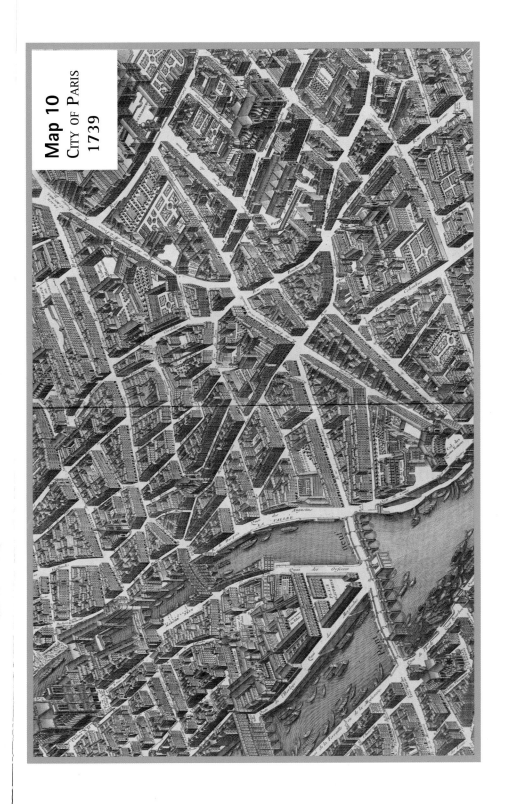

Map 10
CITY OF PARIS
1739